Recipes from Our All-Star Chefs

food network **favorites**

Meredith® Books
Des Moines, Iowa

A FOOD NETWORK THANK YOU TO:

First—to all of
the Food Network
chefs for their recipes.

EDITORS: Susan Stockton, Jill Novatt
WRITER: Rupa Bhattacharya
RECIPE TESTERS: Suki Hertz, Miriam Garron
RECIPE EDITOR: Miriam Garron
FOOD STYLISTS: Rob Bleifer, Krista Ruane,
Jay Brooks, Andrea Steinberg, Mory Thomas,
Bob Hoebee, Santos Loo
RESEARCHER: Jonathan Milder
FOOD PHOTOGRAPHERS: Mark Ferri,
Robert Jacobs, Craig Matthews
PROPS STYLIST: Francine Matalon-Degni
TALENT PHOTOGRAPHERS: Quentin Bacon,
Jean Claude Dhien, Steven Freeman,
Anders Krusberg

Meredith Books
1716 Locust St.
Des Moines, IA 50309-3023
www.meredithbooks.com

First Edition. Printed in the United States
of America
Library of Congress Control Number: 2005931460
ISBN-13: 978-0-696-23021-9
ISBN-10: 0-696-23021-6

FIRST THINGS FIRST.
THIS IS NO ORDINARY
STAR-CHEF COOKBOOK.

Food Network Kitchens has been the crossroads for some of the best and brightest chefs, home cooks, and cookbook authors in the world. There is a dynamic culinary team working behind the scenes with every one of them who passes through—learning, tasting, cooking, and styling the beautiful food you see on the air.

For the first time ever, we've gone through years of tapes and picked 10 of our favorite recipes from 11 of our most popular chefs, supplementing them with our own tips and tricks to help you taste a little bit of Food Network in your kitchen at home.

And we've been doing this for years—the FNK staff is made up of super-accomplished cooks, editors, and writers, who among them have written, developed, researched, edited, tested, and cooked thousands and thousands of recipes over the years, in every imaginable cuisine. We know food, and we know chefs—here's our first book featuring the best of both.

Over the more than 10 years we've been around, one thing has remained constant: the overwhelming demand from our fans for more. More recipes, more info, more background, more tips, more Alton, Bobby, Dave, Emeril, Giada, Mario, Michael, Paula, Rachael, Tyler, and Wolfgang.

So here it is. We're opening the studio doors and taking you with us behind the scenes. Step into our kitchen and let's go see what's cooking. These are the recipes that make us want to take our work home with us at night.

And that's not all. We've dug deep for never-before-seen Q&A with the chefs. Want to know what three ingredients Paula Deen can't live without? See page 147. Want to try Tyler's Ultimate Cheesecake or Emeril's famous Fried Oyster Salad? Turn to pages 204 and 76, respectively. Are you dying to know if Rachael really cooks dinner in half an hour, or Alton's guiltiest pleasure? We've got the answers to those too, on pages 167 and 11.

WELCOME TO OUR KITCHEN.
WE THINK YOU'LL LIKE IT HERE.

BEING A CHEF IS NOT FOR THE FAINT OF HEART.

It's rough, hot, frantic work, but none of these guys would rather be doing anything else. Most of them consider themselves the luckiest people in the world because they get to do what they love all day long: follow their passion for food. It's easy to feel fortunate when you're doing what you love, and when you feel fortunate, you want to share that with others. All of our chefs are deeply involved in their communities via charities, mentoring, or just giving back. So this book is meant to celebrate not only what they cook but also what they do for others. **FOOD NETWORK WILL BE DONATING A PORTION OF ITS RECEIPTS FROM THIS BOOK TO OUR CHEFS' FAVORITE CHARITIES.**

ALTON BROWN	BOBBY FLAY	DAVE LIEBERMAN	EMERIL LAGASSE	GIADA DE LAURENTIIS
HEIFER INTERNATIONAL	MEALS ON WHEELS	MEALS ON WHEELS	THE EMERIL LAGASSE FOUNDATION	SECOND HARVEST

HEIFER INTERNATIONAL
It has fought world hunger and poverty for almost 60 years by providing food- and income-producing animals, along with training in sustainable agriculture, to millions of impoverished families around the world.

SECOND HARVEST
The country's largest hunger relief organization distributes food to the hungry via more than 200 regional food banks and food-rescue organizations, feeding more than 23 million Americans every year.

THE EMERIL LAGASSE FOUNDATION
Established in 2002, seeks to inspire, mentor, and enable all young people, especially those from disadvantaged circumstances, to realize their full potential as productive and creative individuals, by supporting programs and educational opportunities for children within communities where Emeril's restaurants operate.

THE MEALS ON WHEELS ASSOCIATION OF AMERICA
Founded in 1974, it runs local meal-delivery programs around the country for the elderly and homebound, delivering a million meals a day around the country.

FOOD BANK FOR NEW YORK CITY
The nation's largest food bank collects and distributes food every day to provide more than 240,000 meals to more than 1,200 nonprofit community food programs throughout the city.

MARIO
BATALI
FOOD BANK
FOR NEW
YORK CITY

MICHAEL
CHIARELLO
MEALS ON
WHEELS

PAULA
DEEN
SECOND
HARVEST

RACHAEL
RAY
FOOD BANK
FOR NEW
YORK CITY

TYLER
FLORENCE
FOOD BANK
FOR NEW
YORK CITY

WOLFGANG
PUCK
MEALS ON
WHEELS

CONTENTS

IN FOOD NETWORK KITCHENS WE'RE ALL ON A FIRST NAME BASIS WITH OUR CHEFS—AND WE BET YOU ARE TOO.

ALTON 8

BOBBY 26

DAVE 46

EMERIL 66

GIADA 88

MARIO 106

MICHAEL 126

PAULA 144

RACHAEL 164

TYLER 186

WOLFGANG 206

food network KITCHENS 230

INDEX 249

alton
BROWN

He's our food-science guy. Between his quirky ideas and his incessant desire to find out how things work in and out of the kitchen, Alton keeps us constantly entertained, informed, amazed, and well fed.

Q+A

WITH ALTON BROWN

WHAT'S IN YOUR FRIDGE?

Right now? Watermelon, leftover barbecue, blueberries, some leftover tuna salad, my daughter's rice milk, yogurt, a jar of something I can't recognize, two jars of capers (wonder how that happened), my car keys (glad to find those), a pitcher of tea with mint sprigs in it, eggs, butter, ketchup, about seven different kinds of cheese, three different mustards, organic milk (we like milk), a lot more, but that's a start. Oh, and Jell-O®.

FAVORITE CUISINE?

American, which covers everything from Tibetan to Cuban.

ANY GUILTY PLEASURES?

I love nothing more than I love crunching ice. My mother always said I'd break a tooth, but I never have. It drives my family crazy. I also drink out of the carton when no one's looking . . . which is pretty bad for a guy who's really into food safety.

WHAT'S DIFFERENT ABOUT YOUR LIFE NOW THAT YOU'RE ON FOOD NETWORK?

It's like the old Joe Walsh song "… everybody's so different but I haven't changed."

WHAT DON'T WE KNOW ABOUT YOU THAT MIGHT BE SURPRISING?

I'm not funny in person.

Corn Dogs

1 gallon peanut oil

1 cup yellow cornmeal

1 cup all-purpose flour

2 teaspoons kosher salt

1 teaspoon baking powder

¼ teaspoon baking soda

½ teaspoon cayenne pepper

1 large jalapeño pepper, seeded and finely minced (about 2 tablespoons)

1 8.5-ounce can cream-style corn

⅓ cup grated onion

1½ cups buttermilk

4 tablespoons cornstarch, for dredging

8 beef hot dogs

Yield: 8 servings

Special equipment 8 sets wooden chopsticks from your local Chinese restaurant, not separated

1. Pour oil into a deep-fryer or large heavy pot and heat to 375°F.

2. In a medium mixing bowl, combine the cornmeal, flour, salt, baking powder, baking soda, and cayenne pepper. In a separate bowl, combine the jalapeño, corn, onion, and buttermilk. Add the dry ingredients to the wet ingredients all at once and stir only enough times to bring the batter together; there should be lumps. Set batter aside and allow to rest for 10 minutes.

3. Scatter the cornstarch in a dry pie pan. Roll each hot dog in the cornstarch and tap well to remove any excess.

4. Transfer enough batter to almost fill a large drinking glass. Refill the glass as needed. Skewer each hot dog on a pair of chopsticks and quickly dip in and out of the batter in the drinking glass. Immediately and carefully place each hot dog into the oil and cook until coating is golden brown, about 4 to 5 minutes. With tongs, remove to cooling rack and allow to drain for 3 to 5 minutes.

KITCHEN TIP Use as little cornstarch as possible, but coat each dog thinly to help the breading stay where you want it.

KITCHEN TIP Don't cook more than a few dogs at once; crowding the pan lowers the temperature of the oil, which makes for greasy dogs.

NOTE FROM THE KITCHENS

THE CORN DOG WAS INVENTED FOR THE TEXAS STATE FAIR IN 1942 AND BECAME AN IMMEDIATE FAVORITE AT STATE FAIRS, AMUSEMENT PARKS, AND PRETTY MUCH ANYWHERE PEOPLE WANTED THEIR FOOD SERVED BREADED, FRIED, AND ON A STICK.

French Onion Soup

5   sweet onions (such as Vidalias) or a combination of sweet and red onions (about 4 pounds)

3   tablespoons butter

    Kosher salt

2   cups white wine

10 ounces canned beef consommé (1¼ cup)

10 ounces chicken broth (1¼ cup)

10 ounces apple cider (1¼ cup) (unfiltered is best)

    Bouquet garni: thyme sprigs, bay leaf, and parsley tied together with kitchen string

1   loaf country-style bread

    Freshly ground black pepper

    Splash Cognac (optional)

1   cup grated fontina or Gruyère cheese

Yield: 8 servings

1. Trim the ends off each onion, then halve lengthwise. Remove peel and finely slice into half-moon shapes.

2. Set electric skillet to 300°F and add butter. Once butter has melted, add a layer of onions and sprinkle with a little salt. Repeat, layering onions and salt, until all onions are in the skillet. Don't stir until onions have sweated down for 15 to 20 minutes. After that, stir occasionally until onions are a dark mahogany color and reduced to approximately 2 cups. This should take an additional 45 minutes to 1 hour. Don't worry about burning the onions.

3. Add enough wine to cover the onions and turn heat to high, reducing the wine to a syrup consistency. Add consommé, chicken broth, apple cider, and bouquet garni. Reduce the heat and simmer 15 to 20 minutes.

4. Place oven rack in top third of oven and heat broiler. Cut country bread in rounds large enough to fit mouth of ovensafe soup crocks. Place the slices on a baking sheet and broil for 1 minute.

5. Season soup with salt and black pepper to taste and Cognac. Remove bouquet garni and ladle soup into crocks 1 inch below lip. Place bread, toasted sides down, on top of soup and top with cheese. Broil until cheese is bubbly and golden, 1 to 2 minutes.

KITCHEN TIP If you don't have an electric skillet, use a nonstick pan on low heat, stirring the onions occasionally.

Pressure Cooker Chili

3   pounds stew meat (beef, pork, and/or lamb)

2   teaspoons peanut oil

1½   teaspoons kosher salt

1   12-ounce bottle of beer, preferably a medium ale

1   16-ounce container salsa

30   tortilla chips

2   chipotle peppers canned in adobo sauce, chopped

1   tablespoon adobo sauce (from the chipotle peppers in adobo)

1   tablespoon tomato paste

1   tablespoon chili powder

1   teaspoon ground cumin

Yield: 4 servings

1. Place meat in a large mixing bowl and toss with the peanut oil and salt. Set aside.

2. Heat a 6-quart heavy-bottomed pressure cooker over high heat until hot. Add the meat in 3 or 4 batches and brown on all sides, approximately 2 minutes per batch. Once each batch is browned, place the meat in a clean large bowl.

3. Once all of the meat is browned, add the beer to the cooker to deglaze the pot. Scrape the browned bits from the bottom of the pot. Add the meat back to the pressure cooker along with the salsa, tortilla chips, chipotle peppers, adobo sauce, tomato paste, chili powder, and ground cumin and stir to combine. Lock the lid in place according to the manufacturer's instructions.

4. When the steam begins to hiss out of the cooker, reduce the heat to low, just enough to maintain a very weak whistle. Cook for 25 minutes. Remove from heat and carefully release the steam.

"WE RARELY HAVE MORE THAN HALF AN HOUR TO GET SOMETHING ON THE TABLE, and having a young child doesn't make timing any easier. I guess you could say we're guerilla cooks. We try to shop and plan ahead, but it never seems to work out. In other words, we're like every other American suburban family on the move."

Eggplant Pasta

2 medium-to-large eggplants

Salt

4 tablespoons olive oil

1 teaspoon minced garlic

½ teaspoon crushed red pepper flakes

4 small tomatoes, seeded and chopped

½ cup heavy cream

4 tablespoons basil chiffonade
(see Kitchen Tip, right)

¼ cup freshly grated Parmesan

Freshly ground black pepper

Yield: 4 servings

1. Peel each eggplant, leaving 1 inch of skin unpeeled at the top and bottom. Slice the eggplant thinly lengthwise, about ¼ inch thick. Evenly sprinkle each slice with salt and lay out for 30 minutes on a sheet pan fitted with a wire rack. Rinse with cold water and roll in paper towels. Slice the pieces into thin fettucine-like strips.

2. Heat the oil in a large sauté pan over medium heat. Add the garlic and crushed red pepper, and cook until garlic is lightly golden and aromatic. Add the eggplant "pasta" and toss to coat. Add the tomatoes and cook for 3 minutes. Add the cream and increase heat to thicken sauce.

3. Finally, add the basil and Parmesan and toss to combine. Season with black pepper to taste, but no salt, as the eggplant will already be salty.

KITCHEN TIP To chiffonade is to cut leafy vegetables or herbs into ribbons. Stack some leaves and roll them into a cylinder before slicing them thinly.

KITCHEN TIP This dish makes a great first course—it's hearty, rich, and satisfying.

ALTON SOMETIMES RETHINKS AN INGREDIENT TO MAKE THE MOST OF IT. Turning eggplant strips into noodles turns our notion of Eggplant Parmesan upside down, and the fact that it really does cook in a matter of minutes makes it taste even better.

City Ham

1 city-style (brined) ham, hock end (see Note, below)

¼ cup brown mustard

2 cups dark brown sugar

1 ounce bourbon, poured into a spritz bottle

2 cups crushed gingersnap cookies

Yield: 10 to 15 servings, depending on weight of ham

1. Heat oven to 250°F. Remove ham from bag, rinse, and drain thoroughly. Place a clean kitchen towel in the bottom of a roasting pan and then place ham, cut side down, on the towel. Using a small paring knife or clean utility knife set to the smallest blade setting, score the ham from bottom to top on a slight diagonal to the right. (If you're using a paring knife, be careful to only cut through the skin and first few layers of fat.) Rotate the ham after each cut so the scores are no more than 2 inches apart. Once you've made it all the way around, score the ham from bottom to top on a slight diagonal to the left to create a diamond pattern all over the ham. (Don't worry too much about precision here.) (See illustration.)

2. Remove the towel and tent the ham with heavy duty foil, insert a meat thermometer, and cook for 3 to 4 hours or until the internal temperature at the deepest part of the meat registers 130°F.

Remove the thermometer and use tongs to pull away diamonds of skin and any sheets of fat that come off with them.

3. Heat oven to 350°F. Dab the ham dry with paper towels, then brush on a liberal coat of mustard using either a basting brush or a clean paint brush (clean as in never touched paint). Sprinkle on brown sugar, packing loosely as you go, until the ham is coated. Spritz this layer lightly with bourbon, then loosely pack on as much of the crushed cookies as you can. Insert the meat thermometer (don't use the old hole) and return to the oven (uncovered). Cook until interior temperature reaches 140°F, approximately 1 hour.

4. Let the ham rest for 30 minutes before carving.

NOTE FROM ALTON A city ham is basically any brined ham that's packed in a plastic bag, held in a refrigerated case, and marked "ready to cook," "partially cooked," or "ready to serve." Better city hams are also labeled "ham in natural juices."

KITCHEN TIP We love the idea of using gingersnaps. All the flavors you want in the ham are already baked right into the cookie.

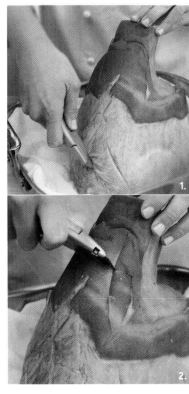

SCORING A HAM

1. HOLD THE HAM BY THE BONE AND MAKE SHALLOW DIAGONAL CUTS AT 2-INCH INTERVALS WITH YOUR KNIFE. CUTTING THROUGH THE SKIN AND TOP LAYER OF FAT WILL ALLOW THE MELTING FAT TO RUN OUT. ROTATE THE HAM AND CONTINUE ALL THE WAY AROUND. **2.** REPEAT THIS DIAGONAL SCORING PROCESS IN THE OTHER DIRECTION, MAKING DIAMOND SHAPES. DON'T WORRY TOO MUCH IF THE DIAMONDS AREN'T EXACT— EVENTUALLY YOU'LL BE PULLING OFF THE SKIN AND REMAINING FAT.

Red Snapper en Papillote

1 cup couscous

2 teaspoons salt, plus pinch for couscous

1 whole red snapper, cleaned, head on (about 2 pounds)

½ teaspoon freshly ground black pepper

1 small bunch fresh oregano

1 small bunch fresh parsley

1 whole lemon, thinly sliced

1 cup thinly sliced red onion

2 teaspoons minced garlic

1 cup halved grape tomatoes

1 cup drained and quartered artichoke hearts

¾ cup white wine

1 tablespoon butter

Yield: 4 servings

Special equipment Parchment paper; stapler (optional)

1. Preheat oven to 425°F. Place couscous in a bowl, cover with very hot water, and let sit for 10 minutes. Drain and season with a pinch of salt.

2. Cut parchment paper into a 15×48-inch sheet. Fold in half and lay on a baking or cookie sheet. Unfold the parchment and lay snapper diagonally on top of the bottom layer of parchment. Season fish inside and out with the 2 teaspoons salt and black pepper. Place herbs inside cavity of fish along with half of the lemon and half of the red onion slices.

3. Arrange couscous next to fish on all sides in a thin layer. Put garlic and remaining lemon and red onion slices on fish and lay tomatoes and artichoke hearts on the couscous. Pour wine over fish and dot with butter. Cover the fish with the other half of the parchment paper and fold over edges, stapling if necessary, to create an almost airtight seal.

4. Bake in oven for 30 minutes, rotating once. Cut open the parchment package carefully to avoid the hot steam and serve (be aware of bones in the fish).

KITCHEN TIP When buying a whole red snapper, look for a firm-fleshed fish with bright red skin, red gills, and clear eyes. Fish shouldn't smell fishy—it should smell like the ocean.

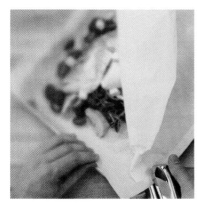

WRAP IT UP

THE WHITE WINE—ALONG WITH THE JUICES IN THE FISH AND VEGETABLES—TURNS TO STEAM IN THE OVEN, COOKING EVERYTHING THROUGH. THAT'S WHY YOU WANT TO MAKE THE PAPILLOTE AS AIRTIGHT AS POSSIBLE—SO THAT THE STEAM STAYS WHERE IT'S SUPPOSED TO.

English Muffins

½ cup nonfat powdered milk

1 tablespoon granulated sugar

1 teaspoon salt

1 tablespoon shortening

1 cup hot water

1 envelope dry yeast

⅛ teaspoon granulated sugar

⅓ cup warm water

2 cups all-purpose flour, sifted

Nonstick cooking spray

Yield: 8 to 10 servings

Special equipment: electric griddle; 3-inch metal rings (see Kitchen Tip, right)

1. In a bowl, combine the powdered milk, 1 tablespoon of sugar, ½ teaspoon of salt, shortening, and hot water; stir until the sugar and salt are dissolved. Let cool.

2. In a separate bowl, combine the yeast and ⅛ teaspoon of sugar in the warm water and set aside until yeast has dissolved, about 10 minutes. Add this to the powdered milk mixture. Add the sifted flour and beat thoroughly with a wooden spoon. Cover the bowl and let it rest in a warm spot for 30 minutes.

3. Preheat the griddle to 300°F. Add the remaining ½ teaspoon of salt to mixture and beat thoroughly. Place metal rings onto the griddle and coat lightly with cooking spray. Using a #20 ice cream scoop, place 2 scant scoops of the mixture into each ring and cover with a pot lid or cookie sheet and cook for 5 to 6 minutes. Remove the lid and flip rings using tongs. Cover with the lid and cook for another 5 to 6 minutes or until golden brown.

4. Place on a cooling rack, remove rings, and cool. Split with fork and serve.

KITCHEN TIP Take the tops and bottoms off tuna cans (look for the kind with flat, crimped tops and bottoms) for do-it-yourself metal rings.

KITCHEN TIP Ice cream scoops are numbered by how many scoops per quart they dish out, so a #20 scoop gives you 20 scoops per quart. The bowl is about 2¼ inches in diameter and contains a little more than an ounce.

WORKIN'

In Alton's world, anything goes. Garage tools are kitchen tools, heat's an ingredient, and there's never a reason not to try something new. He approaches cooking from the inside out, rethinking ingredients we've known (or thought we knew) for years and showing them to us in a whole new light. As far as he's concerned, food should be as much fun to make as it is to eat. He's all about getting to the conventional (the corn dog, chili, the English muffin, fish en papillote) via the unconventional (chopsticks, the pressure cooker, the tuna can, and the stapler, respectively), and he's always looking for reasons why, how, and why the heck not.

food network

NOTE
FROM THE
KITCHENS

YOU'D NEVER
THINK THIS PIE
WAS MADE
OUT OF THE
T-WORD.
ALTON SAYS
IT'S MADE
PEOPLE LOOK
HIM IN THE
EYE AND
CALL HIM
A LIAR WHEN
THEY TASTE
IT. BOTH OF
THESE DISHES
TAKE EVERYDAY
INGREDIENTS
AND RUN
WITH THEM
TO MAKE
LIGHT,
REFRESHING,
AND
REMARKABLY
HEALTHFUL
DESSERTS.

Moo-Less Chocolate Pie

2   cups semisweet chocolate chips

⅓   cup coffee liqueur

1   teaspoon vanilla extract

1   16-ounce block silken tofu (see Kitchen Tip, right)

1   tablespoon honey

1   9-inch prepared chocolate wafer crust

Yield: 8 servings

1. Place a small metal bowl over a saucepan filled with simmering water. Melt the chocolate chips and coffee liqueur in the bowl. Stir in vanilla.

2. Combine the tofu, chocolate mixture, and honey in a blender jar. Blend until smooth and liquefied.

3. Pour the filling into the crust and refrigerate for 2 hours, or until the filling is set.

KITCHEN TIP Silken tofu is soft and custardy. Look for it fresh in the refrigerated aisle or in a plastic tub in the international section of your grocery store.

Lemon-Ginger Frozen Yogurt

8   cups plain yogurt

½   cup light corn syrup

¾   cup granulated sugar

3   tablespoons fresh lemon juice

2   teaspoons finely grated lemon peel

1   tablespoon minced fresh ginger

¼   cup sliced crystallized ginger

Yield: 1½ quarts

1. Place yogurt in a cheesecloth-lined colander set over a bowl. Cover and refrigerate for 12 hours. At end of 12 hours, discard the liquid and cheesecloth.

2. In a bowl, combine the drained yogurt, corn syrup, sugar, lemon juice, lemon peel, and fresh ginger. Transfer mixture to ice cream maker and process per manufacturer's instructions, about 25 minutes. Transfer frozen yogurt to an airtight container, fold in crystallized ginger, and freeze for 2 hours.

KITCHEN TIP Draining the yogurt separates the curds from the whey and leaves you with a creamy-tasting yogurt cheese that becomes the base for your frozen yogurt.

"BY MELDING PINEAPPLE UPSIDE-DOWN CAKE (WHICH I'VE ALWAYS LOVED) WITH A PAN-BAKED CORNBREAD, we get something completely new, I think, yet something utterly nostalgic at the same time ... which doesn't make any sense at all." —ALTON

Pineapple Upside-Down Cornmeal Cake

¾ cup whole milk

1 cup coarse-ground cornmeal

4 ounces unsalted butter
(8 tablespoons)

1 cup packed dark brown sugar

6 slices canned pineapple in heavy
syrup

6 maraschino cherries

⅓ cup chopped pecans, toasted

3 tablespoons syrup from canned
pineapple

1 cup all-purpose flour

2 teaspoons baking powder

½ teaspoon salt

3 whole eggs

¾ cup granulated sugar

½ cup canola oil

Yield: one 10-inch cake

1. Preheat oven to 350°F. In a microwave-safe dish, bring the milk to a boil. Remove the milk from the microwave and add the cornmeal. Stir and let soak at room temperature for 30 minutes. Set aside.

2. Melt the butter in a 10-inch cast-iron skillet over medium heat. Once the butter has melted, add the brown sugar and stir until the sugar dissolves, about 2 minutes. Remove the skillet from the heat and carefully place 1 slice of pineapple in the center of the pan. Place the other 5 slices around the center slice in a circle. Place the cherries in the centers of the pineapple slices and sprinkle the nuts evenly over the fruit. Drizzle the reserved 3 tablespoons pineapple syrup over top.

3. Sift the flour, baking powder, and salt into a medium mixing bowl and whisk to combine. In a separate mixing bowl, whisk the eggs. Add the sugar to the eggs and whisk to combine. Add the canola oil and whisk. Add the cornmeal and milk mixture to the egg mixture and whisk to combine. Add this to the flour and stir just until combined. Pour the batter over the fruit in the skillet and bake for 35 to 45 minutes, until a cake tester comes out clean.

4. Remove from oven and let cool for about 30 minutes in the skillet. Set a platter on top of the skillet and carefully invert the cake.

bobby FLAY

He's all about big, bold grilled flavors. Behind the tough New York exterior, he's a humble, laid-back guy with a big heart.

Q+A

WITH BOBBY FLAY

WHY DID YOU BECOME A CHEF?
I didn't want to go to college, so my father insisted I get a job in the kitchen at a restaurant in New York City called Joe Allen—and I just fell in love with it.

WHAT'S YOUR FAVORITE THING TO COOK AT HOME?
Italian food, especially when *The Sopranos* is airing.

YOU TRAVEL A LOT FOR THE NETWORK. WHAT'S YOUR FAVORITE REGIONAL CUISINE?
I would say Southern cuisine is my favorite. I love grits, country ham, and biscuits.

YOU'RE REALLY INVOLVED WITH MENTORING. HOW DID YOU START?
When I was 17, someone gave me a scholarship to culinary school. Once my restaurants were doing well, I wanted to do the same for another New York City kid. So now, I work with a culinary class in a Queens high school and award an annual scholarship to the French Culinary Institute, where I went.

WHAT WOULD YOU SAY IF YOUR DAUGHTER DECIDED TO BECOME A CHEF?
I would say, "Great!" I love this profession, and it has been very good to me.

WHAT DON'T WE KNOW ABOUT YOU?
I am extremely loyal.

EVERYONE
LOVES
GUACAMOLE.
THIS IS A
WHOLE NEW
SPIN ON IT BOTH
TEXTURALLY
AND FLAVOR-
WISE; THE CORN
ADDS AN
ELEMENT OF
SWEETNESS
AND CRUNCH.
THIS RECIPE IS
A KEEPER THAT
WE'VE ALL MADE
AT HOME
FOR YEARS.

Charred Corn Guacamole with Chips

2 ears corn

2 tablespoons vegetable oil

2 ripe avocados, peeled, pitted, and diced

1 serrano chile, finely chopped

1 red onion, finely diced

Juice of 1 lime

¼ cup chopped fresh cilantro leaves

Salt and freshly ground black pepper

Blue, yellow, and white tortilla chips, as accompaniment

Yield: 8 servings

1. Preheat the grill. Remove the outer husk from the corn and loosen the silks without removing. Dunk ears into water and then place them directly onto a hot grill for 15 minutes, turning occasionally. Remove from grill. Remove remaining husks and silks and cut the kernels off of the cob.

2. In a bowl, combine corn, oil, avocado, serrano chile, onion, lime juice, and cilantro. Season with salt and black pepper to taste and serve with tortilla chips.

KITCHEN TIP Dunk the corn in water before putting it on the grill to make sure that the husk and silks don't burn while the corn steams. It's done when you start to see the outline of the kernels showing through the husk.

Grilled Potato Salad with Watercress, Green Onions & Blue Cheese Vinaigrette

12 small red new potatoes, skin on, parboiled, and sliced ¼ inch thick (see Kitchen Tip, right)

Olive oil to coat potatoes, plus ½ cup for vinaigrette

Salt and freshly ground black pepper

¼ cup aged sherry wine vinegar

1 small shallot, coarsely chopped

1 tablespoon Dijon mustard

½ pound watercress, coarsely chopped

2 green onions, coarsely sliced

½ cup crumbled blue cheese (recommended: Cabrales)

Yield: 4 servings

1. Preheat the grill to medium-high. Toss the potatoes with enough oil to coat them and season with salt and black pepper to taste. Grill until golden brown on both sides and just cooked through, about 5 to 7 minutes.

2. Combine the vinegar, shallot, mustard, and remaining ½ cup oil. Toss the potatoes in the vinaigrette. Using tongs, remove potatoes from the vinaigrette. Toss the watercress and green onions in the remaining vinaigrette. Place the potatoes onto a platter and top with blue cheese. Arrange the watercress and green onions on top.

KITCHEN TIP Parboiling means half-cooking. For this dish, cover the whole potatoes with cold water and bring the water to a boil. Once the water boils, take the potatoes off the heat, drain, and let them cool a bit before slicing and grilling.

KITCHEN TIP Cabrales cheese is a deeply complex and flavorful blue cheese from Spain that has a crumbly, dry texture. If you can't find it, use Roquefort.

BOBBY BUILT HIS NAME ON THE COMBINATION OF "HEAT AND SWEET," PAIRING COMPLEX chile flavors with bursts of bright, sweet tropical fruit. His influences span the globe, touching Asia, Spain, and the American South, but his culinary roots are in the Southwest. Not bad for a guy from New York City.

Grilled Oysters with Mango Pico de Gallo & Red Chile Horseradish

MANGO PICO DE GALLO

- 1 ripe mango, peeled, pitted, and cut into very small dice
- ½ red onion, peeled and cut into very small dice
- 1 small jalapeño, cut into very small dice

  Juice of 1 lime

- 2 tablespoons extra-virgin olive oil
- 2 teaspoons honey
- 2 tablespoons chopped fresh recao (see Kitchen Tip, right) or cilantro leaves

  Salt and freshly ground black pepper

RED CHILE HORSERADISH

- ½ cup prepared horseradish, drained
- 1½ tablespoons ancho chile powder (see Kitchen Tip, page 39)

  Salt

OYSTERS

- 20 oysters, scrubbed well

Yield: 4 servings

1. For the Mango Pico de Gallo: Mix together the mango, onion, jalapeño, lime juice, oil, honey, and recao or cilantro in a medium bowl. Season with salt and black pepper to taste and stir to combine. Let sit at room temperature for 30 minutes before using.

2. For the Red Chile Horseradish: Mix together the horseradish and ancho chile powder in a small bowl. Season with salt to taste.

3. For the oysters: Heat grill to high. Dip oysters in water, as the steam created will help them to open on the grill. Place oysters on the grill, close the cover, and grill until all have just barely opened, about 3 to 4 minutes. Discard any that do not open. Place ½ tablespoon of the Mango Pico de Gallo on top of each oyster and top that with a scant ½ teaspoon of the Red Chile Horseradish.

KITCHEN TIP Recao (sometimes called culantro or long coriander) is a tropical herb with long serrated leaves and a pungent flavor much like cilantro. It's widely used in the Caribbean, especially Puerto Rico, and also Southeast Asia.

MA
1. CUT A S
PIECE FROM
THE TOP AND
BOTTOM OF
THE MANGO.
2. STAND THE
MANGO ON END
AND CUT AWAY
THE SKIN FROM
TOP TO BOTTOM.
3. TURN THE
MANGO ON ITS
SIDE AND CUT
THE FLESH
FROM THE PIT,
FOLLOWING THE
CURVE OF THE
PIT. REPEAT
WITH THE OTHER
SIDES OF
THE MANGO.

GETS YOUR
GUESTS
INVOLVED WITH
THE FOOD—A
FANTASTIC WAY
TO GET THE ICE
BROKEN AND
PUT EVERYONE
AT EASE.

Grilled Shrimp in Lettuce Leaves with Serrano-Mint Sauce

SERRANO-MINT SAUCE

1   cup tightly packed mint leaves, plus additional for garnish

2   serrano chiles, chopped

4   cloves garlic, chopped

1   1-inch piece fresh ginger, peeled and chopped

2   teaspoons granulated sugar

¼   cup white wine vinegar

2   tablespoons fish sauce

Salt

SHRIMP

1½   pounds medium shrimp, peeled, deveined, and tails removed (about 36)

3   tablespoons canola oil

Salt and freshly ground black pepper

12   leaves green curly leaf lettuce

Chile oil, for drizzling (optional)

Fresh cilantro leaves for garnish

Yield: 4 servings

1. Preheat the grill to medium-high. Make the Serrano-Mint Sauce: Put all ingredients except salt in a blender. Pulse until smooth. Season with salt to taste.

2. Make the shrimp: In a large bowl, toss shrimp in oil and season with salt and black pepper to taste. Grill the shrimp for 1 to 2 minutes on each side, or until just cooked through. Be careful not to overcook the shrimp or they will be tough and rubbery. Remove from the grill.

3. Place about 3 shrimp in each lettuce leaf. Drizzle with the Serrano-Mint Sauce and a little chile oil, if desired. Sprinkle with a few cilantro leaves. Roll up the lettuce leaves and eat immediately.

KITCHEN TIP Chiles can seriously burn. When working with them, keep your hands away from your eyes and face and wash up well when you're done.

KITCHEN TIP To keep lettuce leaves whole for wrapping, flip the head of lettuce upside down on your cutting board and cut out the core with a paring knife. Gently peel back the leaves from the thick bottom part and they won't tear.

KITCHEN TIP You can find chile oil in the Asian aisle of your supermarket.

Tuna Burgers with Pineapple-Mustard Glaze & Green Chile-Pickle Relish

3 cups pineapple juice

½ cup white wine vinegar

1 tablespoon peeled and finely chopped fresh ginger

3 tablespoons soy sauce

¼ cup firmly packed light brown sugar

4 tablespoons Dijon mustard

3 tablespoons lime juice

1 teaspoon freshly ground white pepper

2 pounds fresh tuna steaks, very finely chopped

2 teaspoons pureed chipotle in adobo

1 tablespoon honey

2 tablespoons canola oil, plus additional to oil grill

2 green onions, thinly sliced

Salt and freshly ground black pepper

8 rolls

Watercress sprigs for garnish

Green Chile-Pickle Relish (see recipe, below)

GREEN CHILE-PICKLE RELISH

3 poblano chiles

3 dill pickles, finely diced

¼ cup finely chopped red onion

3 tablespoons fresh lime juice

2 tablespoons honey

3 tablespoons finely chopped cilantro leaves

3 tablespoons olive oil

Salt and freshly ground black pepper

Yield: 8 servings

1. Combine the pineapple juice, vinegar, ginger, soy sauce, and brown sugar in a small saucepan and bring it to a boil. Reduce the heat to low and simmer until the volume is reduced by half, about 30 minutes. Whisk in 2 tablespoons mustard, remove from the heat, and add the lime juice and white pepper. Let cool.

2. Combine the tuna, remaining 2 tablespoons mustard, pureed chipotle pepper , honey, oil, and green onions in a large bowl and season with salt and black pepper to taste. Shape the tuna mixture firmly into 8 round uniform patties about 1 inch thick. Refrigerate for 30 minutes; the burgers must be very cold to hold their shape when cooking.

3. Preheat the grill to medium-high. Lightly oil the grates of the grill. Grill burgers for 3 minutes on each side for medium doneness, basting often with the glaze. Serve the burgers on rolls with the watercress and Green Chile-Pickle Relish.

GREEN CHILE-PICKLE RELISH

1. Preheat a grill to medium-high. Place the poblano chiles on the grill and grill until the skin is blackened on all sides, about 5 minutes. Remove from the grill and place in a paper bag and let sit for 15 minutes. When the chiles are cool enough to handle, peel, seed, and finely chop them.

2. Combine poblano and remaining ingredients in a medium bowl and season with salt and black pepper to taste. Let sit at room temperature for 30 minutes before serving so that the flavors meld.

KITCHEN TIP Chop the tuna super-fine, form it, and chill it down for a nice, tight burger. If your knife skills aren't up to it, use a mezzaluna or pulse the tuna (carefully!) in the food processor.

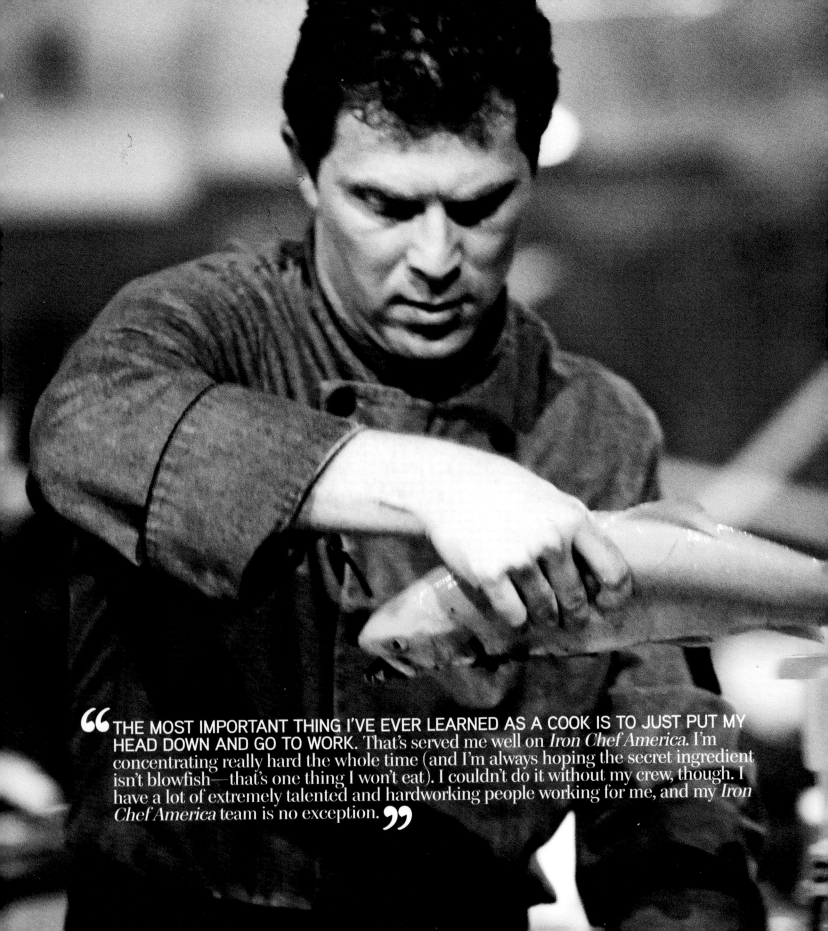

"THE MOST IMPORTANT THING I'VE EVER LEARNED AS A COOK IS TO JUST PUT MY HEAD DOWN AND GO TO WORK. That's served me well on *Iron Chef America*. I'm concentrating really hard the whole time (and I'm always hoping the secret ingredient isn't blowfish—that's one thing I won't eat). I couldn't do it without my crew, though. I have a lot of extremely talented and hardworking people working for me, and my *Iron Chef America* team is no exception."

Shredded Chicken & Tomatillo Tacos with Queso Fresco

6 tomatillos

1 serrano chile

Olive oil

½ small red onion, coarsely chopped

2 cloves garlic, coarsely chopped

1 cup chopped fresh cilantro leaves

Juice of 1 lime

2 tablespoons honey

1½ cups shredded rotisserie chicken

8 blue corn tortillas

1 cup crumbled queso fresco

Yield: 4 servings

1. Preheat the grill to medium. Husk and wash the tomatillos. Put the tomatillos and serrano chile on the grill and cook until blackened all over, about 2 to 3 minutes per side. Remove from the grill and roughly chop. Put them into a small sauté pan and briefly sauté in a little olive oil on the grates of the grill.

2. Put the tomatillos, serrano, onion, garlic, cilantro, lime juice, and honey in a blender and blend until smooth. Place the tomatillo mixture in a large sauté pan and place on the grates of the grill. Bring the mixture to a simmer, add the chicken, and heat through.

3. Place the tortillas on the grill and grill for 20 seconds on each side. Spoon the chicken mixture into the tortillas and top with a few tablespoons of queso fresco. Fold the tortillas in half and serve immediately.

KITCHEN TIP Tomatillos look like green-husked tomatoes. Store them loose in the vegetable drawer of your refrigerator; they'll keep for 3 weeks or more. After you take off the papery husk, use warm water to wash them and remove their sticky coating.

KITCHEN TIP Queso fresco—a fresh, white, mildly salty, and crumbly cow's milk cheese—can be found at Latino markets. If you can't find it, feta, ricotta, or mild goat cheese are all good substitutes.

BOBBY'S AS TIRELESS IN THE FIELD (TRAVELING NONSTOP, ALWAYS LOOKING FOR A NEW FOOD STORY) as he is at home (running three restaurants in New York and one in Las Vegas). He's got an admirable work ethic and incredible drive, but no matter how busy he is, he's never too busy to stop by our kitchen and say hi.

Spice-Rubbed Pork Tenderloin with Ancho Chile-Mustard Sauce

SPICE RUB

- 3 tablespoons ancho chile powder
- 1 teaspoon chile de arbol powder
- 1 tablespoon pasilla chile powder
- 1 tablespoon guajillo chile powder
- 1 teaspoon allspice
- 2 tablespoons brown sugar
- ½ teaspoon ground cinnamon

   Salt and freshly ground black pepper

ANCHO CHILE-MUSTARD SAUCE

- 4 cups chicken stock
- 1 cup apple juice concentrate
- 6 black peppercorns
- 1 teaspoon pureed canned chipotle in adobo
- 2 tablespoons ancho chile puree (see Kitchen Tip, right)
- 1 tablespoon Dijon mustard
- 2 tablespoons crème fraîche

   Salt and freshly ground black pepper

PORK TENDERLOIN

- 2 pork tenderloins, about 12 ounces each
- 2 tablespoons olive oil

Yield: 4 servings

1. Preheat the oven to 400°F. Make the Spice Rub: Combine all ingredients in a small bowl, including salt and black pepper to taste. Set aside.

2. Combine the chicken stock, apple juice, and peppercorns with the chipotle and ancho purees in a medium saucepan over high heat and reduce to a sauce-like consistency. Whisk in mustard and crème fraîche and cook for 1 minute. Season with salt and black pepper to taste.

3. Dredge the tenderloin in the spice rub mixture and pat off any excess. Heat the olive oil in a medium ovenproof skillet over medium-high heat until almost smoking. Add the pork tenderloin and sear well on all sides. Place the pan in the oven and continue cooking to medium-well, about 155°F on an instant-read thermometer, about 8 to 10 minutes. Let rest 10 minutes and slice into 1-inch pieces on the diagonal. Spoon sauce onto a platter and top with the slices of pork.

KITCHEN TIP If you can't find a large variety of chile powders in your supermarket, try online: Type the name of the chile powder you're looking for into a search engine and see if you can mail order it.

KITCHEN TIP To make chile puree, soak dried chiles in very hot water for at least an hour and whiz them through a food processor after they're plump.

ALL THESE CHILE POWDERS BRING SOMETHING DIFFERENT TO THE TABLE IN TERMS OF BOTH FLAVOR AND HEAT. THE SMALLER A CHILE IS, THE HOTTER ITS BURN. ANCHO CHILES ARE LARGE AND WIDE, WITH A MELLOW, FRUITY FLAVOR AND A SUBTLE AFTER-BURN. PASILLAS ARE THINNER THAN ANCHOS, SO THEY'RE A LITTLE BIT HOTTER, BUT THEY STILL HAVE A DEEP, NUTTY FLAVOR. GUAJILLO CHILES—YET SMALLER—UP THE FIERINESS ANTE. BUT THE TINIEST ONES— THE CHILES DE ARBOL—REALLY AREN'T MESSING AROUND WHEN IT COMES TO HEAT.

Grilled Steak & Papaya Salad

MARINADE AND TENDERLOIN

- 4 cloves garlic, chopped
- 1 Thai bird chile, chopped
- 2 tablespoons soy sauce
- 1 tablespoon fresh lime juice
- 2 to 3 tablespoons honey
- ¼ cup peanut oil
- 1½ pounds beef tenderloin

  Salt and freshly ground black pepper

PAPAYA SALAD

- 1 shallot, peeled and finely chopped
- 2 Thai bird chiles, finely chopped
- 1 tablespoon chopped fresh mint leaves
- ½ cup rice wine vinegar
- 2 teaspoons granulated sugar
- 2 tablespoons fish sauce
- 8 large red romaine lettuce leaves, cut into strips
- 1 bunch watercress

- 1 large green papaya, peeled and thinly shredded
- 2 carrots, peeled and thinly shredded
- ¼ cup chopped roasted peanuts, for garnish

  Chopped cilantro leaves, for garnish

Yield: 4 servings

1. Make the marinade: Put the garlic, chile, soy sauce, lime juice, honey, and oil in a mini food processor and process until smooth. Place beef in a small baking dish, pour the marinade over it, and turn to coat. Cover and marinate in the refrigerator for 1 hour.

2. Preheat the grill to medium-high. Remove the beef from the marinade and season it with salt and black pepper to taste. Grill the meat until charred and cooked medium-rare, 125°F to 130°F on an instant-read thermometer, about 10 to 12 minutes. Remove from the grill and let it rest 10 minutes before slicing into ¼-inch-thick slices.

3. Meanwhile, make the Papaya Salad: In a small bowl, whisk together the shallot, chiles, mint, vinegar, sugar, and fish sauce. Set aside. In another bowl, toss the lettuce leaves and watercress together and then arrange the mixture on a platter. Combine the papaya and carrots in a medium bowl. Evenly distribute the papaya mixture over the lettuce. Drizzle with a few tablespoons of the dressing.

4. Arrange the steak on top and drizzle with some more dressing. Garnish with chopped peanuts and cilantro.

KITCHEN TIP Beware, Thai bird chiles pack serious heat! Jalapeños, serranos, and even cayennes don't even come close. Though they're normally sold green, ripe red ones can occasionally be found during the summer months.

GREEN (THAT IS, UNRIPE) MEXICAN PAPAYAS ARE A CLASSIC INGREDIENT IN THAI COOKING, AND GREEN PAPAYA SALAD IS AN ICONIC THAI DISH. (IN THE UNITED STATES, MEXICAN PAPAYAS ARE BIGGER THAN THE MORE COMMON HAWAIIAN PAPAYA, WHICH SHOULD NOT BE EATEN UNRIPE.) THOUGH THEY'RE TRADITIONALLY SHREDDED WITH A CLEAVER, USE A MANDOLINE IF YOU'VE GOT ONE.

Fresh Fruit Batidos

1 cup mango sorbet

½ cup vanilla ice cream

½ cup chopped fresh mango, plus mango slices, for garnish

½ cup cold milk

1 to 2 tablespoons honey, or more to taste

Mint sprigs, for garnish

Yield: 1 serving

Put all the ingredients into a blender and blend until smooth. Pour into a 10-ounce glass and serve immediately. Garnish with a mango slice and mint sprig, if desired.

KITCHEN TIP See "How to Prep a Mango," page 33.

Rum Buttered-Glazed Grilled Pineapple with Vanilla-Scented Mascarpone

6 ounces unsalted butter (1½ sticks or ¾ cup)

2 tablespoons light brown sugar

¼ cup dark rum

1 ripe pineapple, peeled and sliced into ¼-inch-thick rounds

1 cup mascarpone

1 vanilla bean, split and seeds scraped (see Kitchen Tip, right)

½ cup fresh blueberries, for garnish

Yield: 4 servings

1. Preheat the grill to medium. Melt the butter, sugar, and rum in a small saucepan.

2. Grill pineapple on both sides until golden brown, about 2 to 3 minutes per side. Spoon the rum glaze over the grilled pineapple.

3. Whisk together mascarpone and vanilla seeds. Top each slice of pineapple with a dollop of vanilla mascarpone. Garnish with a few fresh blueberries.

KITCHEN TIP: Mascarpone is Italian triple-cream cheese made from cow's milk. If you can't find it, substitute whipped cream.

KITCHEN TIP To seed a vanilla bean, run a paring knife lengthwise down the middle and pull the bean apart. Use the back of the knife to scrape out the tiny, sticky black dots clustered on the inside—those are the seeds.

43

GRILLIN'

"**THERE'S NOTHING LIKE GRILLING IN THE CITY.** Here we're on a gorgeous roof garden in Queens (no, I don't live there; it's a set) with a spectacular view of the 59th Street Bridge. We've got three grills on at all times during production, and there are two full-time fire tenders whose job it is to make sure the fire is hot."

dave
LIEBERMAN

He's the boy next door—
if the boy next door was
a born entertainer. Dave's
a newcomer to TV (he
started a cooking show
in college), but having
a relaxed, good time with
friends is nothing new
to him.

Q+A WITH DAVE LIEBERMAN

WHO TAUGHT YOU HOW TO COOK?

My dad started me off, then I taught myself. I cooked in my campus apartment because the dining hall was inconvenient and the food wasn't great, so I decided I'd better cook for myself. It was part necessity, part pleasure, but mostly a device to get people to come over to my place.

WHAT WAS YOUR BIGGEST KITCHEN DISASTER?

There've been so many … spilling frying oil down the stove was probably the worst. I still avoid deep frying. My dad got me a fire extinguisher when I went to college.

WHAT DO YOU EAT ON YOUR DAYS OFF?

There's nothing wrong with takeout …

WHAT'S THE BEST MEAL YOU'VE EVER MADE?

When I was an exchange student in France, my host mother taught me how to make rabbit. When I got back, I found a whole rabbit in a market in Philadelphia and cooked it for my high school girlfriend's family. Let's just say they were pretty surprised.

ANY GUILTY PLEASURES?

Nutella.

Spicy Chinese Five-Spice-Rubbed Chicken Wings with Creamy Cilantro Dipping Sauce

40 chicken wing pieces or 20 whole chicken wings

2   tablespoons Chinese five-spice powder

1   tablespoon cayenne pepper

Kosher salt and freshly ground black pepper

Creamy Cilantro Dipping Sauce (see recipe, below)

Yield: 40 wings

CREAMY CILANTRO DIPPING SAUCE

⅓   cup chopped fresh cilantro leaves

¼   cup light sour cream

¼   cup mayonnaise

¼   cup plain yogurt

Juice of ½ lemon

Kosher salt and freshly ground black pepper

Yield: about 1 cup

1. Preheat oven to 500°F. If you have whole chicken wings, cut off wing tips and cut the wings in half at the joint. Discard wing tips or freeze to make stock. Place the wings in a large bowl. Sprinkle five-spice powder and cayenne on the wings; add generous pinches of salt, and about 15 grinds of black pepper. Rub the mixture into all the wings until no more loose rub remains.

2. Line the wing pieces up on a baking sheet so the side of the wing that has the most skin is facing up. Roast until cooked through, browned, and crispy, about 25 minutes. Serve hot with Creamy Cilantro Dipping Sauce.

CREAMY CILANTRO DIPPING SAUCE
Combine all sauce ingredients through the lemon juice in a mixing bowl. Whisk to incorporate fully and season with salt and black pepper to taste.

WE'RE ALWAYS KEEPING AN EYE OUT FOR NEW, COOL TAKES ON BUFFALO WINGS, AND DAVE TOTALLY NAILED THIS ONE. IT'S REALLY hard to get wings crispy when you're baking them, but this recipe does.

Black Bean Soup

10 slices bacon, finely chopped

2 medium onions, chopped (about 2½ cups)

6 cloves garlic, pressed

1 14.5-ounce can reduced-sodium chicken broth

1½ cups canned chopped tomatoes

2 tablespoons ketchup

2 teaspoons Worcestershire sauce

1 tablespoon chili powder

4 15.5-ounce cans black beans, drained but not rinsed

1 bunch cilantro, leaves picked and coarsely chopped

Kosher salt and freshly ground black pepper

Juice of ½ lime

Thinly sliced scallions, for garnish

Sour cream, for garnish

Grated cheddar cheese, for garnish

Yield: 8 to 10 servings

1. Put the bacon into a large heavy pot and place it over medium heat. Cook until it starts to give up its fat, about 4 minutes. Add the onions and cook, stirring, until they start to turn translucent, about 4 minutes. Stir in the garlic and cook until you can smell it, about 1 minute. Add the broth, tomatoes, ketchup, Worcestershire, and chili powder. Stir in the beans, turn the heat to high, and bring to a boil. Adjust the heat so the soup is bubbling gently and cook 10 minutes.

2. Stir the cilantro into the soup after it has been simmering 10 minutes. Cook until the soup is thickened, about 5 minutes. Add salt and black pepper to taste. Stir in the lime juice and serve with the garnishes.

KITCHEN TIP Garlic presses are convenient when you've got lots of garlic that needs to be crushed extra-fine. You don't even need to peel it, and you're saving yourself lots of knife work.

Curried Chicken Salad in Lettuce Cups

4 whole chicken thighs, bone in, skin on

1 lemon, quartered

½ bunch cilantro, roughly chopped

Kosher salt and freshly ground black pepper

¼ cup mayonnaise

1 teaspoon curry powder

1 teaspoon honey

1 teaspoon freshly squeezed lemon juice

3 scallions, thinly sliced

2 stalks celery, thinly sliced

¾ cup halved seedless red grapes

Butter lettuce leaves, for serving

Yield: 4 to 6 servings

1. Put the chicken thighs, lemon, and cilantro into a skillet or saucepan. Fill with water just to cover the chicken and season generously with salt and black pepper to taste. Bring to a boil over medium heat, then reduce the heat to maintain a very gentle simmer. Cook, uncovered, until the chicken is tender and falling from the bones, about 40 to 45 minutes. Remove the chicken from the poaching liquid and allow to cool. When cool, remove the skin and strip the meat from the bones, discarding the skin and bones. Reserve the meat.

2. In a bowl, mix together the mayonnaise, curry, honey, and lemon juice. Stir in the scallions, celery, and grapes until combined. Add the shredded chicken and toss to combine. Season with salt and black pepper to taste.

3. Serve heaping portions of the salad in butter lettuce leaves.

KITCHEN TIP Chicken thighs are inexpensive, and their rich meatiness makes them a good choice for this recipe. If you must have white meat, use breasts but reduce the poaching time to about 10 to 12 minutes.

ONE OF OUR FAVORITE THINGS ABOUT DAVE'S RECIPES IS THAT THEY PROVE THAT ANYONE CAN COOK SIMPLE, SOPHISTICATED DINNERS FOR FRIENDS WITHOUT BREAKING THE BANK. With Dave, it's almost always cheaper (and more fun) to stay in than go out.

Pan-Grilled Veggie Sandwiches with Ricotta, Arugula & Balsamic

Vegetable oil, for brushing

2 small zucchini, sliced lengthwise in ¼-inch-thick slices

2 small yellow squash, sliced lengthwise in ¼-inch-thick slices

2 red onions, sliced into ¼-inch rounds

Extra-virgin olive oil

1 tablespoon chopped garlic

Kosher salt and freshly ground black pepper

2 baguettes, about 24 inches long

1 16-ounce container ricotta cheese

1 bunch arugula, washed, dried, and stems discarded

Balsamic vinegar, to taste

1 small jar roasted red peppers, halved

1 small jar olive paste (optional)

Yield: 4 to 6 servings

1. Brush a large grill pan with vegetable oil and heat over medium-high heat. Before grilling, toss veggies with olive oil, garlic, and salt and black pepper to taste. Grill vegetables in batches until nicely colored and soft, about 6 to 12 minutes per batch. Wipe down the grill pan between batches to get rid of burnt-on bits.

2. Cut bread into 6-inch pieces. Cut pieces lengthwise but don't go all the way through. Spread a thick layer of ricotta on the bottom half of the bread. Sprinkle with some salt.

3. Toss arugula with olive oil, balsamic vinegar, and salt and black pepper to taste. Place dressed arugula on top of ricotta, then add generous amounts of the different grilled vegetables and the roasted red peppers. Spread a thin layer of olive paste on the top half of the bread, if desired.

THIS IS A GREAT
DO-AHEAD DISH
FOR A NOVICE
ENTERTAINER;
MAKE IT AHEAD
OF TIME SO
YOU CAN RELAX
AND TALK TO
YOUR GUESTS—
THE PASTA
TASTES EVEN
BETTER ONCE
THE FLAVORS
HAVE A CHANCE
TO MELD.

Bow Ties with Pesto, Feta & Cherry Tomatoes

1 pound bow tie pasta (farfalle)

¾ cup Pesto (see recipe, below)

½ pint cherry tomatoes, halved

1 cup crumbled feta cheese

Kosher salt and freshly ground black pepper

Olive oil, as needed

Yield: 4 to 6 servings

PESTO

5 big handfuls basil leaves
(about 2 hefty bunches)

½ cup pine nuts or ¾ cup walnuts

½ cup fresh grated Parmesan or pecorino cheese

Juice of 1 lemon

2 cloves garlic, peeled

Kosher salt

About 20 grinds freshly ground black pepper

¾ cup extra-virgin olive oil

Yield: about 1½ cups

1. Bring a large pot of salted water to boil. Stir in the pasta and cook, stirring occasionally, until al dente, about 10 minutes. Drain the pasta and run it under cold water just until it stops steaming. Bounce the pasta around to get rid of as much water as you can.

2. Dump the pasta into a large serving bowl. Stir in the Pesto until the pasta is coated. Toss in the cherry tomatoes and the crumbled feta. Season with salt and black pepper to taste. You can make the salad up to about 1 hour before you serve it. Check out the salt and black pepper just before you serve the salad. If it's looking a little dry, add some olive oil and stir it around.

PESTO

Place all ingredients with ½ cup of the oil in a blender and blend. With the motor running, gradually drizzle in the remaining ¼ cup of oil until pesto is thick and smooth.

KITCHEN TIP Leftover pesto? Great! Put it in an airtight freezer-safe container and pour a thin layer of olive oil over the top. Press a layer of plastic wrap right onto the oil, close the lid, and store in the freezer for up to 1 month. Toss with hot cooked pasta and serve as an entrée when you're pressed for time, or spread on crostini as an appetizer.

Spicy Coconut Shrimp with Mango-Basil Salsa & Lime Jasmine Rice

SALSA

- 1 mango, peeled, pitted, and finely diced (see page 33)
- 3 scallions, sliced
- 5 basil leaves, thinly sliced
- Juice of 1 lime
- Kosher salt and freshly ground black pepper

SHRIMP

- 1 or 2 fresh jalapeños, sliced
- 3 cloves garlic, thinly sliced
- 1 ½-inch piece fresh ginger, peeled and grated
- 2 tablespoons dark brown sugar
- 2 tablespoons soy sauce
- Zest from ½ lime
- ¼ cup coconut milk
- Small handful basil leaves, torn
- 2 tablespoons vegetable oil
- ½ teaspoon salt
- 15 grinds black pepper
- 1 pound peeled, deveined large shrimp (see Kitchen Tip, page 96)
- Lime Jasmine Rice (see recipe, below)

LIME JASMINE RICE

- 1 cup jasmine rice
- ¾ cup coconut milk
- ¾ cup water
- Pinch salt
- Zest from ½ lime

Yield: 2 to 4 servings

1. For the salsa: Combine all ingredients together in a mixing bowl. Make up to a day in advance. Keep tightly covered in the refrigerator.

2. For the shrimp: In a mixing bowl, combine jalapeños, garlic, ginger, brown sugar, soy sauce, lime zest, coconut milk, basil, vegetable oil, salt, and black pepper. Add the shrimp and marinate in the refrigerator for at least 30 minutes and up to 4 hours.

3. Heat a nonstick skillet over high heat. Use tongs or a fork to remove the shrimp from the marinade and place in an even layer in the pan, reserving marinade. Cook shrimp until well browned on each side, turning once, about 3 to 4 minutes total. Transfer cooked shrimp to a serving plate. Meanwhile, add reserved marinade to pan, bring to a boil, and cook until slightly thickened, about 5 minutes. Pour over the cooked shrimp and serve with Lime Jasmine Rice and Mango-Basil Salsa.

LIME JASMINE RICE

Put the rice, coconut milk, water, and salt in a saucepan and bring to a simmer. Cover and gently simmer until liquid is absorbed, about 12 to 15 minutes. Fluff with a fork and stir in the lime zest. Serve immediately.

KITCHEN TIP The zest of any citrus fruit is the brightly colored outside of the peel. Use a peeler or small hand grater to remove the zest, but leave the white part, called the pith, behind. It's bitter.

KITCHEN TIP Only cook shrimp until they just turn pink and are opaque throughout; overcooking will make them tough and chewy.

THE THING ABOUT DAVE IS THAT HE TOTALLY GETS IT. You have a tiny kitchen and roommates? So does he. You're busy with work but want to get a home-cooked meal on the table? Same with him. And he's friendly, approachable, and happy to share his secrets.

Roasted Salmon with Roasted Plum Tomatoes & Caramelized Lemons

4   plum tomatoes, quartered

    Olive oil

8   to 10 sprigs fresh thyme

    Kosher salt and freshly ground black pepper

2   7- to 8-ounce salmon fillets, about 1½ inches at their thickest point

    Handful fresh dill sprigs

1   lemon, cut in half

Yield: 2 servings

1. Preheat oven to 400°F. Place plum tomatoes in a shallow baking dish, drizzle with olive oil, and scatter thyme sprigs over all. Season with salt and black pepper to taste. Roast until tomatoes are softened but still have their shape, about 15 to 20 minutes. Cover loosely with foil and set aside.

2. Reduce oven temperature to 350°F. Lay the salmon fillets, skin sides down, with some space between them on a baking sheet or baking dish. Season with salt and black pepper to taste and cover with dill. Squeeze ½ of the lemon over all. Bake until firm, 15 to 20 minutes.

3. Meanwhile, slice the remaining lemon half into ¼-inch slices. Heat a skillet over high heat. Film the bottom of the pan with olive oil and add lemon slices. Sauté until brown on both sides, about 3 to 4 minutes total. Remove from heat and set aside.

4. Remove the aluminum foil from the tomatoes. Discard the herb sprigs. Place the tomatoes on a cutting board and roughly chop. Spoon chopped tomatoes into the center of each plate. Lay a piece of salmon over the tomatoes and lay the lemon slices to the side of the salmon. Serve immediately.

KITCHEN TIP Plum tomatoes contain less water than other tomatoes, making them ideal for roasting.

KITCHEN TIP Salmon's a great choice for the health-conscious; it's low in the bad fats and high in the good ones, and it's chock-full of omega-3 fatty acids, which are thought to prevent heart disease.

Red Wine Beef Stew with Potatoes & Green Beans

2 pounds beef chuck for stew, cut into 1-inch cubes

Kosher salt and freshly ground black pepper

3 tablespoons butter

4 medium carrots, peeled, halved lengthwise, and cut into 1-inch chunks

3 small onions, diced

2 tablespoons all-purpose flour

2 14.5-ounce cans reduced-sodium beef or chicken broth

2 cups dry red wine

1 cup canned crushed tomatoes

1 6-inch sprig fresh rosemary

2 medium russet or Yukon gold potatoes, peeled and cut into 1-inch chunks

2 handfuls green beans, ends trimmed

2 tablespoons chopped fresh parsley

Yield: about 10 servings

1. Season the beef cubes lightly with salt and black pepper. Heat 2 tablespoons of the butter in a heavy 6-quart pot over medium heat. As soon as the butter starts to turn brown, add half the beef and raise the heat to high. At first, the beef will give off some liquid, but once that evaporates, the beef will start to brown. Cook, turning the beef cubes on all sides until the pieces are as evenly browned as possible, about 5 or 6 minutes after the water has boiled off. If the pan starts to get too brown at any point, just turn down the heat a little. Scoop the browned beef into a bowl and brown the rest of the beef the same way using the remaining 1 tablespoon butter.

2. Scoop out the second batch of beef, then add the carrots and onions and adjust the heat to medium-high. Cook until the onion starts to turn translucent, about 5 minutes. Stir in the flour until it has been worked into the veggies and you can't see it any more. Pour in the beef or chicken broth, wine, and crushed tomatoes and toss in the rosemary. Slide the beef back into the pot and bring the liquid to a boil. Turn down the heat so the liquid is just breaking a gentle simmer. Partially cover the pot and cook 50 minutes. Stir the stew several times while simmering so it cooks evenly and nothing sticks to the bottom.

3. Stir the potatoes into the stew, cover the pot completely, and cook until the potatoes and beef are tender, stirring occasionally, about another 45 minutes. Add the green beans and cook for another 5 minutes until they turn bright green and are cooked through but still have a nice snap to them. Stir in the parsley.

KITCHEN TIP When you're making a stew, pick cuts of meat that'll do best with long, slow cooking. One of the best (and most affordable) cuts for stew is chuck. With time and low heat, the muscles in it turn tender and tasty.

KITCHEN TIP Brown the meat in small batches to get the best possible color (dark brown) and texture (crisp on the outside).

"COOKING TEACHES ME A LOT ABOUT PATIENCE. I always used to look for recipes that got everything done quickly, but now I enjoy techniques like braising and stewing that are really worth the wait."

THOUGH YOU DON'T SEE THEM LABELED AS SUCH OFTEN ANYMORE, CHICKEN CAN BE DIVIDED, BASED ON AGE, INTO COOKING METHODS. BROILERS AND FRYERS ARE THE YOUNGEST. THEY ARE USUALLY SMALLER AND MORE TENDER AND BENEFIT MOST FROM QUICK-COOKING METHODS LIKE, WELL, BROILING AND FRYING. ROASTERS ARE SLIGHTLY OLDER AND LARGER, WITH MORE FLAVORFUL BUT LESS TENDER MEAT THAT'S GREAT WHEN ROASTED. STEWING CHICKENS ARE THE LARGEST AND OLDEST, WITH DEEP FLAVOR THAT NEEDS LONG, SLOW SIMMERING.

Apricot-Glazed Chicken with Dried Plums & Sage

2 4- to 5-pound roasting chickens, cut into pieces

1 12-ounce jar apricot preserves

15 medium dried plums, pitted

⅓ cup olive oil

1 tablespoon white vinegar

1 tablespoon salt

1 tablespoon freshly ground black pepper

10 cloves garlic, peeled

20 to 30 sage leaves

Yield: about 8 servings

1. Preheat oven to 400°F. Trim any extra fat from the chicken pieces and transfer them to a foil-lined sheet pan or broiler pan. If you don't have a roasting pan that's large enough, use 2 shallow 13×9-inch baking pans. Toss all of the ingredients together with the chicken until the chicken is evenly coated with the sauce. Arrange the chicken pieces, skin sides up, in the pan, spaced evenly apart. If you're looking to prepare in advance, you can do everything up to this point and cover the roasting dishes and refrigerate until you're ready to roast the chicken.

2. Roast until the tops of the chicken pieces are browned and the chicken is cooked through, and the juices run clear, about 35 to 40 minutes.

WE'RE BIG FANS OF CONDIMENTS HERE IN FOOD NETWORK KITCHENS. We even have an ongoing discussion about which condiments we'd be if we were condiments (are you more mustard or marmalade?). It's great—when you're not sure what to make—to let yourself get inspired by the inside of your fridge door. This is just that kind of recipe.

NOTE FROM THE KITCHENS

WE COOK ALL DAY LONG IN OUR KITCHENS—THEN GO HOME AND COOK DINNER. A SIMPLE DESSERT LIKE THIS CRUMBLE IS A SWEET END TO A WEEKNIGHT DINNER.

Blueberry-Pecan Crumble

TOPPING

4 ounces pecan pieces (about 1 cup)

1 cup all-purpose flour

1¼ cups rolled (old-fashioned) oats

½ cup packed dark brown sugar

1 teaspoon ground cinnamon

A couple pinches salt

8 tablespoons butter, cut into small pieces

BERRIES

2 pints fresh blueberries

Juice of ½ lemon

3 tablespoons granulated sugar

2 tablespoons all-purpose flour

Yield: 6 to 8 servings

1. Preheat oven to 350°F. For the topping: Put all of the topping ingredients in a bowl and rub together with your hands until mixture sticks together in small clumps.

2. For the berries: Pour the blueberries into a 7×11-inch baking dish. Sprinkle the lemon juice over the berries, then the sugar and flour. Toss until the berries are coated with sugar.

3. Scatter the topping over the berries in an even layer. Bake until the topping is golden brown and the berry juice is bubbling up through the topping, about 45 to 50 minutes.

emeril
LAGASSE

He's truly larger-than-life.
In Emeril's world, food
is love, gaaahlic is king,
pork fat rules, and
kicking it up a notch
is an everyday affair.

Q+A WITH EMERIL LAGASSE

WHAT DO YOU COOK AT HOME?

I cook all the time. I can be in the studio all day, and I'll still go home and make dinner. I'm really inspired by the seasons, so my menus change constantly. My kids like chicken potpie, spaghetti Bolognese, red gravy and meatballs, Portuguese soup, roast chicken, smothered pork chops—and I have to make chicken soup at least once a week for my son.

WHAT ARE YOUR GUILTY PLEASURES?

I love frozen potato chips! (Emeril leaps up, runs to the freezer, and gets a bag of Zapps— a New Orleans brand of chips—for everyone at the interview.)

BIGGEST KITCHEN DISASTER?

Once I was in Aspen, making a pineapple upside-down cake, and I forgot about the effect altitude has on baking. So the whole thing blew up. I ran out and bought some bananas and ice cream for dessert instead. Who doesn't like Bananas Foster?

DID YOU HAVE A MENTOR?

Ella Brennan is one, for sure. But I've had lots and lots. Everyone needs mentors in this field to keep you learning and evolving as a cook.

WHAT DON'T WE KNOW ABOUT YOU THAT MIGHT BE SURPRISING?

When I'm not on camera, I'm actually a pretty mellow guy.

Mushroom Confit with Pasta Rags & Truffle Oil

2 pounds assorted wild and exotic mushrooms, such as shiitake, oyster, chanterelles, and creminis, cleaned and stemmed

Kosher salt and freshly ground black pepper

2 bay leaves

3 cloves garlic, smashed

2 sprigs fresh thyme

1 sprig fresh rosemary

2 tablespoons salt

2 quarts safflower oil or other light, non-flavored oil

1 pound fresh pasta sheets, torn into pieces

1 teaspoon truffle oil

½ cup shaved Parmigiano-Reggiano

2 tablespoons chopped chives

Kosher salt and freshly ground black pepper

Yield: 4 to 6 servings

1. Preheat oven to 275°F. In a large colander toss the mushrooms with salt and black pepper to taste. Set colander aside—over a bowl—for 1 hour, stirring occasionally. Allow the mushrooms to release as much liquid as possible. Drain the liquid from the mushrooms.

2. In a 1-gallon baking or roasting pan, combine the mushrooms, bay leaves, garlic, thyme, rosemary, 2 tablespoons salt, and vegetable oil. Stir well; make sure that the oil completely covers the mushrooms. Cover the pan with aluminum foil. Roast the mushrooms for 1 to 1½ hours, or until soft and tender. Remove from the oven and drain the mushrooms, reserving oil.

3. Bring a pot of salted water to a boil. Cook the pasta for 3 to 4 minutes and drain. In a mixing bowl, toss the pasta with the mushrooms, 2 to 3 tablespoons of reserved cooking oil, the truffle oil, cheese, chives, and salt and black pepper to taste. Serve immediately.

SHOWTIME

IF YOU'VE EVER BEEN IN THE AUDIENCE OF *EMERIL LIVE*, YOU KNOW WHAT IT'S LIKE TO GET SWEPT UP IN THE EXCITEMENT THAT IS EMERIL. Emeril's all about feeding the crowd—and between crew and audience, that crowd's usually about 200 people strong. People sample, share, and, as Emeril puts it, "make some friends."

WHEN WE
DECIDED TO DO
THIS BOOK, ONE
OF THE FIRST
RECIPES THAT
CAME TO MIND
WAS THIS ONE.
WE'VE BEEN
MAKING IT AT
HOME AND AT
OUR PARTIES
FOR YEARS. IT'S
NOT DIFFICULT
AND JUST
TAKES A LITTLE
BIT OF
PLANNING TO
BLOW YOUR
GUESTS' MINDS.

Duck Pastrami

1 tablespoon black peppercorns

1 tablespoon dried thyme

3 bay leaves, crumbled

1 teaspoon whole cloves

2 tablespoons minced garlic

1 teaspoon whole juniper berries, plus ⅓ cup crushed juniper berries

4 cups water

½ cup packed light brown sugar

½ cup kosher salt

1 whole boneless duck breast, split in half (2 to 2½ pounds)

¼ cup coarsely ground black pepper

Thinly sliced French bread, as an accompaniment

Creole mustard, as an accompaniment

Pickled onions, as an accompaniment

Yield: 4 to 6 servings

1. In a small mixing bowl, combine the peppercorns, thyme, bay leaves, cloves, garlic, and the 1 teaspoon whole juniper berries. In a saucepan combine the water, brown sugar, and salt. Bring to a boil and stir to dissolve the sugar and salt. Remove from the heat, add spice mixture, and steep for 1 hour.

2. Place the duck breast in a glass or plastic container. Pour the seasoned brine over the duck to cover completely. Cover with plastic wrap and refrigerate for 48 hours, turning the breasts several times. Remove the duck breasts from the brine, rinse thoroughly under running water, and pat dry.

3. Preheat the oven to 250°F. In a small bowl, combine the ⅓ cup crushed juniper berries and ground black pepper. Using the palm and heel of your hands, press ⅔ of the juniper mixture into the underside of the breasts. Press the remaining mixture onto the skin side. Place the breasts, skin sides down, on a rack in a roasting pan and roast for 1 to 1½ hours. Remove from the oven and let cool for 30 minutes.

4. Wrap breasts tightly in plastic wrap and place in an airtight container. Store in the refrigerator at least 1 week before using.

5. To serve, remove the meat from the plastic wrap and slice thinly. Serve with French bread and other accompaniments as appetizers or hors d'oeuvres.

Pork & Chorizo Burgers with Green Chile Mayonnaise

BURGERS

- ½ pound chorizo, outer casings removed, cut into 1-inch pieces
- 1½ pounds ground pork
- 1 tablespoon minced garlic
- 2 teaspoons Worcestershire sauce
- 1½ teaspoons Emeril's Essence (see page 81)
- ¾ teaspoon kosher salt
- ¼ teaspoon cayenne pepper
- 4 large hamburger buns, or 4 (6-inch) lengths French bread, split in half crosswise
- 1 cup coarsely grated pepper Jack cheese (optional)

  Green Chile Mayonnaise (see recipe, below)

Yield: 4 servings

GREEN CHILE MAYONNAISE

- 1 cup good-quality mayonnaise (homemade is best)
- 1 teaspoon minced garlic
- 1 poblano pepper, roasted and peeled
- 1 tablespoon fresh lime juice

  Kosher salt and freshly ground black pepper

Yield: about 1½ cups

1. Preheat the grill to medium-high. Place the chorizo in a food processor and process until finely chopped (sausage should appear crumbly). Transfer to a large bowl and add the ground pork, garlic, Worcestershire, Essence, salt, and cayenne pepper and mix gently but thoroughly, being careful not to overwork the mixture.

2. Form the mixture into four, 1-inch-thick patties and grill to desired doneness, about 5 minutes per side for medium. During the last 2 minutes of grilling, toast the buns and sprinkle the cheese over the tops of the burgers, if desired, and cook until melted.

3. Transfer the burgers to the bottom of the buns and place on plates. Generously top each burger with 2 tablespoons of the Green Chile Mayonnaise and place the tops of the buns over the sauce.

GREEN CHILE MAYONNAISE

In the bowl of a food processor, combine the mayonnaise, garlic, poblano, and lime juice and process until smooth. Season with salt and black pepper to taste.

Baby Arugula with Country Ham, Goat Cheese, Dried Cherries & Walnut Vinaigrette

3 to 4 ounces fully cooked, thinly sliced, boneless country ham

¾ cup walnut pieces

3 tablespoons rice wine vinegar

1 tablespoon honey

1 tablespoon minced shallots

½ cup walnut oil

Kosher salt and freshly cracked black pepper

8 cups fresh baby arugula, picked through and washed

⅓ cup dried cherries

2 to 4 ounces fresh goat cheese

Yield: 4 servings

1. Preheat the oven to 400°F. Heat a medium skillet over medium-high heat. Add the ham slices and cook until golden and crispy, 1 to 2 minutes per side. Remove from the skillet and julienne. Set aside.

2. Place the walnuts on a baking sheet and roast until golden, about 5 to 7 minutes. Remove from the oven and place in a medium mixing bowl. Add the vinegar, honey, and shallots to the warm nuts and let mixture sit 1 minute. Slowly whisk in the oil. Season with salt and black pepper to taste.

3. In a large mixing bowl, toss the greens with the cherries and the desired amount of the dressing. Mound some greens in the center of 4 plates. Arrange the crispy ham around the greens and crumble the cheese on top of the greens. Garnish the salad with additional cracked pepper.

KITCHEN TIP Country ham is made by salt-curing a pig's hind leg for 40 days, then hanging it to age for at least another 25 days (up to 180 days) in a hot, humid room. If you can't find country ham in your area, use prosciutto.

“ **I'VE ALWAYS BEEN INTERESTED IN THE FRESHEST INGREDIENTS,** which is why I'm so involved with farming—from hogs to greens. I have a strong connection to the soil: It's really important to me to know where my food comes from. ” —EMERIL

Fried Oyster Salad with Buttermilk Dressing & Corn-Jalapeño Relish

CORN-JALAPEÑO RELISH

1 tablespoon butter

2½ cups fresh corn kernels

⅔ cup chopped red bell pepper

⅔ cup chopped red onion

2 jalapeño peppers, seeded and minced

1 teaspoon kosher salt

2 tablespoons honey

2 teaspoons fresh lime juice

BUTTERMILK DRESSING

¾ cup buttermilk

¼ teaspoon minced garlic

3 tablespoons minced chives

1 jalapeño pepper, seeded and minced

½ teaspoon kosher salt

½ cup sour cream

OYSTERS

Vegetable oil, for frying

1 cup yellow cornmeal

½ cup all-purpose flour

1 tablespoon Emeril's Essence (see page 81)

⅔ cup buttermilk

1 tablespoon hot sauce

¼ teaspoon kosher salt, plus additional for seasoning

24 raw oysters, shucked, drained, and patted dry on paper towels

8 cups mixed baby greens, for serving

6 slices crisp-cooked bacon, crumbled, for garnishing

Yield: 4 servings

1. For the corn relish: Heat a heavy skillet over high heat. Add the butter and corn and cook until the corn begins to brown, stirring occasionally, about 3 minutes. Add the bell pepper, onion, jalapeños, and salt and cook until vegetables soften, about 3 minutes. Stir in the honey and lime juice and transfer to a mixing bowl. Set aside to cool to room temperature. (The relish may be made a day in advance and stored, covered, in the refrigerator.)

2. For the salad dressing: In the bowl of a blender, combine the buttermilk, garlic, chives, jalapeño, and salt and process until smooth. Transfer to a medium bowl and whisk in the sour cream. Dressing will be thin. Refrigerate for at least 1 hour to allow flavors to blend.

3. When ready to serve, prepare oysters for frying: Fill a large saucepan with high sides with at least 2 inches of oil and heat to 350°F. In a medium bowl, whisk the cornmeal with flour and Essence. In a second bowl, combine buttermilk, hot sauce, and salt, and stir to blend.

4. Working with 6 oysters at a time, dip the oysters first in the buttermilk mixture, then allow any excess to drip off before dredging the oysters in the cornmeal mixture. Repeat with the remaining oysters. Fry the oysters in the hot oil in batches, turning once, until golden brown and floating on the surface of the oil, about 1½ minutes. Transfer with a slotted spoon or tongs to a paper towel-lined plate to drain. Season immediately with salt to taste.

5. Divide the greens among 4 large salad bowls or plates and arrange spoonfuls of the Corn-Jalapeño Relish along the edge of the greens. Top with the oysters, then drizzle the dressing decoratively over all. Crumble the crispy bacon over each salad and serve immediately.

KITCHEN TIP This is the kind of recipe where it pays to think like a chef: Have the salad ready to go before you start frying—the oysters taste best when they're piping hot.

KITCHEN TIP To cut corn off the cob, snap the cob in half and stand each half, flat side down, in a bowl or roasting pan. Using a sharp paring knife, cut the kernels off the cob in straight lines downward, rotating the cob each time.

"I'M LUCKY, BECAUSE THERE IS A GREAT FISH STORE IN MY NEIGHBORHOOD WHERE I CAN GET UNBELIEVABLE OYSTERS. When I'm in New York, I love checking out all the little, 'old-school' markets and seeing what they have. I let the stores inspire me."

Emeril's Memory Stovetop Clam Boil

5 quarts water

3 cups clam juice

2 to 3 tablespoons liquid concentrated crab and shrimp boil (recommended: Zatarain's)

4 medium yellow onions, quartered

4 stalks celery, cut into thirds

3 heads garlic, halved

1 lemon, halved

2 tablespoons kosher salt

½ teaspoon freshly ground black pepper

4 ears fresh sweet corn, husked, cleaned, and cut into thirds

1½ pounds small red-skinned potatoes

2 pounds andouille or other smoked sausage, cut into 2-inch lengths

4 pounds steamer clams

8 ounces unsalted butter, melted (2 sticks or 1 cup)

1 loaf crusty French bread

Yield: 4 to 6 servings

1. Combine the water and clam juice in a 4-gallon stockpot fitted with a strainer insert. (This may also be done in a 3-quart stockpot without a strainer insert—simply remove clams, potatoes, corn, etc., using a large strainer or strain in a large colander placed in the sink.)

2. Add the crab boil, onions, celery, garlic, lemon, salt, and black pepper. Add the sweet corn and potatoes. Bring to a boil, reduce the heat to a simmer, and add the sausage. Cook, covered, until the potatoes are almost fork-tender, about 10 minutes.

3. While the boil is heating, clean the clams by scrubbing thoroughly and rinsing under cold running water. Fill the sink with cold water and swish clams back and forth to dislodge any sand and grit that may be caught in the necks. Rinse and repeat several times.

4. When the potatoes are almost fork-tender, add the clams, increase the heat to high, cover, and cook until the shells pop open, 6 to 8 minutes. Discard any clams that do not open.

5. Remove the strainer insert from the pot and drain the liquid. Serve the clam boil on paper bags or newspapers. Pass the melted butter and bread.

THIS IS ONE OF MY FAVORITE CHILDHOOD MEMORIES—my mom and dad would make this all the time. They didn't add a lot to it—it was all just simple, good ingredients. Now I like to add a few things, like fresh artichokes, asparagus, or whatever I have in the house. It's a great, fun thing to cook. —EMERIL

Stuffed Chicken Legs in Puff Pastry with Andouille Cream

4   boned (except for the knuckle or joint at the bottom of the drumstick) chicken legs, the thigh and the drumstick all in one piece (see Kitchen Tip, page 81)

2   teaspoons Emeril's Essence (see page 81)

Andouille Cornbread Stuffing (see recipe, below)

Kosher salt and freshly ground black pepper

2   tablespoons vegetable oil

2   17.3-ounce packages frozen puff pastry, thawed

1   large egg, lightly beaten with 1 teaspoon water

Andouille Cream (see recipe, right)

Yield: 4 servings

ANDOUILLE CORNBREAD STUFFING

1   teaspoon olive oil

4   ounces chopped andouille sausage

¼   cup chopped onions

¼   cup chopped green onions

2   tablespoons chopped celery

2   tablespoons chopped green bell peppers

1   tablespoon minced garlic

1   teaspoon Emeril's Essence (see page 81)

½   teaspoon kosher salt

3   turns freshly ground black pepper

1   cup coarsely crumbled cornbread

½   cup chicken stock

Yield: 1½ cups

ANDOUILLE CREAM

1   teaspoon olive oil

2   ounces chopped andouille sausage, casings removed

3   tablespoons peeled and chopped plum tomatoes

3   tablespoons chopped green onions

2   tablespoons chopped onions

1   tablespoon minced garlic

½   cup chicken stock

1½   cups heavy cream

2   teaspoons Emeril's Essence (see page 81)

½   teaspoon kosher salt

Yield: about 1½ cups

1. Preheat the oven to 375°F and line a baking sheet with parchment or waxed paper. Spread the meat of the chicken legs open and sprinkle the inside of each with ¼ teaspoon of the Essence. Sprinkle the outside of each leg with another ¼ teaspoon Essence and use your hands to coat thoroughly.

2. Divide the Andouille Cornbread Stuffing into 4 equal portions. Stuff the cavity of each leg with 1 portion of the stuffing and close the skin around it. Use kitchen twine to tie the tops of the legs closed. Season the chicken legs with salt and freshly ground black pepper to taste.

3. Heat oil in a large skillet over medium-high heat. Add chicken legs, in batches if needed, and sear until well browned on all sides, 2 to 3 minutes per side. (If searing chicken in batches, wipe skillet clean before searing the second batch.) Remove the chicken legs from the skillet, place on a baking sheet, remove string, and refrigerate until completely cooled.

4. Place each pastry sheet on a lightly floured surface and roll out to ⅛ inch thick. Cut each sheet into 2 equal-sided 9-inch triangles. Place 1 leg on each piece, seam side down, with the joint hanging over the edge. Brush the edges with the egg wash and fold the ends over to create a wrapper. Pinch the edges together to seal and place, seam side down, on the baking sheet. Bake for 40 minutes, remove from the oven, and brush with the remaining egg wash. Bake an additional 15 minutes, or until the crust is brown and the chicken is tender.

5. While the chicken is baking, prepare the Andouille Cream and cover and keep warm until ready to serve.

6. To serve, spoon ½ cup of the Andouille Cream onto each of 4 dinner plates and place a baked chicken leg on each.

ANDOUILLE CORNBREAD STUFFING

1. Heat the oil in a large skillet over high heat. Add the andouille and cook until rendered and brown, about 3 minutes. Add the onions and cook, stirring, for 3 minutes. Stir in the green onions, celery, and bell peppers and cook, stirring, for 2 minutes. Add the garlic and sauté for 1 minute.

2. Stir in the Essence, salt, black pepper, cornbread crumbles, and stock, and cook, stirring and shaking the skillet, for 2 minutes. Remove from the heat and set aside to cool.

ANDOUILLE CREAM

1. Heat the oil in a small saucepan over high heat. Add the andouille and sauté, breaking up the sausage with the side of a spoon, for 1 minute. Add the tomatoes, green onions, onions, and garlic and stir-fry for 1 minute.

2. Stir in the stock and deglaze the bottom of the pot. Add the cream, Essence, and salt and bring to a boil, stirring occasionally. Reduce the heat and simmer, stirring occasionally, until reduced and slightly thickened, about 30 to 35 minutes. Remove from the heat. Serve immediately or store, refrigerated, in an airtight container for up to 2 days. Reheat in a saucepan over low heat.

KITCHEN TIP Get to know a good butcher and have him bone the chicken legs for you. It's a bit complicated, and (we admit it) you've got plenty to keep you busy in this recipe.

EMERIL'S ESSENCE CREOLE SEASONING

2½   tablespoons paprika

2   tablespoons salt

2   tablespoons garlic powder

1   tablespoon freshly ground black pepper

1   tablespoon onion powder

1   tablespoon cayenne pepper

1   tablespoon dried oregano

1   tablespoon dried thyme

Yield: about ⅔ cup

Combine all ingredients thoroughly.

EMERIL PREFERS TO COOK ALL OF THE FOOD FOR HIS SHOWS 'LIVE.' BUT SOMETIMES, ONE OF EMERIL'S ALL-DAY DISHES (LIKE, SAY A BIG ROAST) WILL NEED MORE TIME THAN WE'VE GOT, SO THE KITCHEN GETS A FEW 'SWAP-OUTS' READY SO WE CAN SHOW WHAT THE FINISHED DISH LOOKS LIKE.

Asian-Style Braised Short Ribs

5   pounds beef short ribs, cut into
     4-ounce portions

1   cup soy sauce

¼   cup rice wine vinegar

3   cloves garlic, peeled and smashed

1   5-inch stalk lemongrass, halved and
     smashed

1   tablespoon peeled and minced
     fresh ginger

½   cup light brown sugar

4   cups water

½   cup sliced green onions, white parts
     only

¾   teaspoon crushed red pepper flakes

¼   cup fresh orange juice

¼   cup hoisin sauce

2   tablespoons fresh lemon juice

     Jasmine rice, for serving

2   teaspoons finely grated orange zest,
     for serving

     Sliced green onion tops, for garnish
     (optional)

Yield: 4 servings

1. Preheat the oven to 350°F. In a wide stockpot or Dutch oven, combine the short ribs, soy sauce, vinegar, garlic, lemongrass, ginger, brown sugar, water, green onion bottoms, crushed red pepper, and 2 tablespoons of the orange juice. Make sure that the stockpot is deep enough so that the short ribs are submerged in the liquid.

2. Bake the short ribs, covered, for about 3 hours, or until the meat is tender and falling off the bones. Remove the short ribs from the braising liquid and cover to keep warm. Increase the oven temperature to 425°F.

3. Skim the fat from the cooking liquid and discard. Add the hoisin sauce to the liquid and bring to a boil over medium-high heat. Reduce the liquid until only about 1¼ cups remain. Strain through a fine-meshed strainer, discarding the solids. Stir in the remaining 2 tablespoons orange juice and the lemon juice.

4. Return the short ribs and the reduced sauce to the stockpot or Dutch oven, coating the short ribs well with the sauce. Bake for 10 minutes, or until the short ribs are heated through and slightly glazed. Serve hot over jasmine rice. Season each portion with the grated orange rind and garnish with the green onions, if desired.

EMERIL'S AN AVID GOLFER WHO REALLY ENJOYS HITTING THE LINKS IN HAWAII. On his trips there, he soaks up all the Asian-inspired flavors and local ingredients and incorporates them into his own cooking back home.

NOTE FROM THE KITCHENS

THIS IS CLASSIC EMERIL. OF COURSE, THERE'S PORK FAT IN IT, BUT IT'S ALSO A TRIBUTE TO THE NEW ORLEANS FLAVORS CLOSE TO EMERIL'S HEART—AND THAT REALLY RESONATES WITH US.

Root Beer-Glazed Pork Chops with Bourbon-Mashed Sweet Potatoes & Caramelized Onions

CARAMELIZED ONIONS

- 8 tablespoons unsalted butter
- 2 pounds yellow onions, peeled and thinly sliced

PORK CHOPS & GLAZE

- 2 cups root beer
- 2 cups reduced veal stock
- 4 16-ounce double-cut bone-in pork chops
- 4 teaspoons Emeril's Essence (see page 81)
- 4 teaspoons olive oil
- 1 recipe Bourbon-Mashed Sweet Potatoes (see recipe, below)
-   Parsley leaves, for garnish

Yield: 4 servings

BOURBON-MASHED SWEET POTATOES

- 1¾ to 2 pounds sweet potatoes
- ½ cup heavy cream
- ¼ cup bourbon whiskey
- 3 tablespoons light brown sugar
- 2 tablespoons molasses
- 1 teaspoon kosher salt

1. For the caramelized onions: Melt the butter in a large skillet over medium-low heat. Add the onions and cook slowly, stirring occasionally, until golden brown and caramelized, 45 minutes to 1 hour. Remove from the heat and keep warm.

2. For the glaze: Combine the root beer and stock in a heavy medium saucepan. Bring to a boil over medium-high heat. Reduce the heat to medium-low and simmer until reduced to a thick syrup, about 1 cup, 50 minutes to 1 hour. Remove from the heat.

3. Preheat a grill to medium-high. Preheat the oven to 425°F. Season each chop on both sides with 1 teaspoon of the Essence. Grill for 3 minutes. Turn each chop ¼ turn to make grill marks and cook an additional 2 minutes. Turn and cook on the second side for 5 minutes.

4. Transfer to a baking sheet. Drizzle 1 teaspoon of the olive oil over each chop. Roast until cooked through and an instant-read thermometer inserted into the center reaches 150°F, 12 to 15 minutes.

5. Place the chops on 4 serving plates and drizzle with the glaze. Spoon the Bourbon-Mashed Sweet Potatoes and Caramelized Onions onto the plates, garnish with parsley leaves, and serve.

BOURBON-MASHED SWEET POTATOES

1. Preheat the oven to 350°F. Place the potatoes on a foil-lined baking sheet. Bake until tender and starting to ooze sugary syrup, about 1 hour and 15 minutes, depending on their size. Remove from the oven and let sit until cool enough to handle.

2. Cut a slit down each potato and scoop the flesh into a large bowl. Discard the skins. Add the cream, bourbon, brown sugar, molasses, and salt and beat on high speed with an electric mixer until smooth. Cover to keep warm, or gently reheat before serving.

KITCHEN TIP The root beer glaze works because it's got a great combination of flavors already built into the can. Depending on your preferred brand of root beer, you'll find anise, ginger, cinnamon, vanilla, and wintergreen flavors—all in one handy can.

Apple Tarte Tatin

6 to 8 Golden Delicious apples, peeled, cored, and halved

Juice of 1 lemon

6 tablespoons unsalted butter

1 cup granulated sugar

1 8-ounce sheet frozen puff pastry

Whipped cream or vanilla ice cream, for serving (optional)

Yield: 8 servings

1. Preheat the oven to 400°F. In a large bowl toss the apple halves with the lemon juice and set aside.

2. Melt the butter in a 9- or 10-inch skillet over high heat. Add the sugar and cook until the sugar melts and then caramelizes to an amber color, swirling the skillet, if necessary, for even browning. (Do not stir or sugar may crystallize.) Remove the skillet from the heat.

3. Place the apples, rounded sides down, in one layer in the caramel. Cut any remaining apple halves in half so that you now have apple quarters and place them in the caramel. Cover the skillet and return to the heat. Cook over medium-low heat until the apples are almost tender and have released their juices, 15 to 20 minutes. Remove the cover and carefully remove the apple pieces with a slotted spoon, leaving the juices behind. Increase the heat to medium and cook until the juices have reduced and are very thick and syrupy, about 15 minutes. Remove from the heat and let cool slightly, about 5 minutes. Carefully arrange the apples back in the pan, round sides down.

4. Let puff pastry dough sit at room temperature until slightly softened, about 5 minutes. On a lightly floured surface, roll dough to a 12-inch-diameter round about $3/16$ inch thick. Place the dough on top of the hot apples and tuck the edges into the skillet, carefully folding or pushing the overhang down tightly around the apples. Cut several slits in the dough to allow steam to escape while baking.

5. Bake until the puff pastry is golden, about 20 minutes. Remove tart from the oven and allow to cool for 5 minutes. Run a small knife around the edge of the skillet to loosen tart, then place a large plate or platter over the skillet. Using oven mitts, CAREFULLY grasp platter and skillet and invert, letting tart settle onto the platter and giving skillet a quick tap, if necessary. Carefully lift off the skillet and place any apples remaining in skillet on top of the tart. Cool slightly and serve warm, with whipped cream or ice cream, if desired.

ARRANGE THE APPLES

1. AFTER PEELING AND HALVING THE APPLES, USE A MELON BALLER TO CLEANLY REMOVE THE CORES. THEN TRIM OFF THE STEM AND BLOSSOM ENDS.
2. PLACE APPLE HALVES ROUNDED SIDE DOWN AND SNUG IN THE PAN OF HOT CARAMEL. CUT THE REMAINING HALVES INTO HALF AGAIN AND FILL ANY GAPS AS DECORATIVELY AS YOU CAN. WHEN IT'S TIME TO FLIP YOUR BAKED TART OUT OF THE PAN, YOUR APPLE PATTERN WILL APPEAR ON TOP.

THIS DISH IS AS CLASSIC AS EMERIL'S ROOTS ARE. Two French sisters, Carolina and Stéphanie Tatin, are credited with having invented it in the 1880s. It's a happy accident of a dish; Stéphanie put an apple tart in the oven upside down one day when the restaurant was busy, and the guests liked it so much, they wanted it all the time.

giada de LAURENTIIS

Famous for turning Italian food—once an all-day affair—into the kind of food you can make for a Tuesday after-work dinner, Giada's time-saving tweaks to favorite classics have made Italian truly *Everyday Italian.*

Q+A
WITH
GIADA
DE LAURENTIIS

HOW OFTEN DO YOU RETURN TO ITALY?
Once or twice a year.

WHAT DO YOU LOVE TO EAT WHEN YOU'RE THERE?
When I go, I have to have a plate of spaghetti with clams in Capri, *pizza bianca* in Rome, and gelato anywhere.

DID YOU EVER HAVE A HUGE KITCHEN DISASTER?
I was catering a Thanksgiving meal, so I roasted a turkey, carved it, and put it on a gorgeous platter. When I brought it out, I didn't see the client's dog—I tripped, the turkey hit the floor, and the dog got to it before I did. The client was understanding and, fortunately, had a few boxes of pasta in the pantry. So I just cooked a pasta dish and served the rest of the Thanksgiving trimmings with pasta.

Now I try not to cook with dogs around and always keep some pasta handy for emergencies.

ANY GUILTY PLEASURES?
I'm a chocoholic— I have to have a piece every day.

Spaghetti with Asparagus, Smoked Mozzarella & Prosciutto

2 pounds asparagus, trimmed

¾ pound spaghetti

4 tablespoons olive oil

4 garlic cloves, minced

Salt and freshly ground black pepper

6 ounces thinly sliced prosciutto, cut crosswise into strips

6 ounces smoked mozzarella cheese, diced (about 1 cup)

6 tablespoons thinly sliced fresh basil

Yield: 6 to 8 servings

1. Cook the asparagus in a large pot of boiling salted water until crisp-tender, about 2 to 3 minutes. With a spider or slotted spoon, remove the asparagus from the boiling water to a bowl of ice water to cool and stop the cooking. When cool, strain, cut asparagus into 1-inch pieces, and set aside.

2. Return the water in the pot to a boil, adding additional water, if necessary. Add the pasta and cook until al dente, tender but still firm to the bite, about 8 minutes. Drain the pasta, reserving 1 cup of the cooking liquid.

3. Heat the oil in a heavy large skillet over medium heat. Add the garlic and sauté until fragrant, about 20 seconds. Add the asparagus to the skillet and season with salt and black pepper to taste. Add the pasta and the reserved cooking liquid.

Toss to coat. Add the prosciutto, mozzarella, and basil and toss to combine. Turn off the heat, season with salt and pepper to taste, and serve.

KITCHEN TIP Prosciutto is Italian for ham —it's the salt-cured rear leg of a pig. Though it's made all over Italy, the best comes from Emilia-Romagna, in north central Italy, near Parma. Look for Prosciutto di Parma for that real Italian flavor.

KITCHEN TIP Cooking asparagus this way is called blanching; it keeps vegetables brightly colored and crisp. Plunging them in ice water is crucial to stop the cooking process at just the right time, so the vegetables keep their crunch and don't overcook.

WITH HER BACKGROUND IN CATERING AND HER EASYGOING, STREAMLINED RECIPES, Giada knows how to throw a great party and make it seem effortless. And Italian food is feasting food; there's something about these recipes that makes you want to call everyone you know to sit down to dinner.

Cinnamon-Pancetta Carbonara

8 slices pancetta (see Kitchen Tip, page 95) or bacon, chopped

¼ teaspoon ground cinnamon

2 cups whipping cream

1½ cups freshly grated Parmesan

6 large egg yolks

18 ounces fresh fettuccine

Salt and freshly ground black pepper

2 tablespoons chopped fresh chives

Yield: 6 servings

1. Bring a large pot of salted water to a boil over high heat. Sauté the bacon in a heavy large frying pan over medium-high heat until almost crisp, about 5 minutes. Sprinkle the cinnamon over the bacon and sauté until the bacon is crisp and golden, about 2 minutes longer. Remove from the heat and let cool slightly, about 2 minutes. Whisk in the cream and cheese. Whisk in the yolks to blend.

2. Add the fettuccine to the boiling water and cook until it is just tender but still firm to the bite, stirring occasionally, about 3 minutes. Drain. Add the fettuccine to the cream mixture and toss over medium-low heat until the sauce coats the pasta thickly, about 5 minutes (do not boil). Season the pasta with salt and black pepper to taste. Transfer the pasta to a large wide serving bowl. Sprinkle with chives and serve.

KITCHEN TIP Toss the sauce over low heat; you want the eggs to thicken but not scramble.

Stuffed Shells with Arrabbiata Sauce

2 tablespoons olive oil, plus extra for greasing baking sheet and dishes

1 12-ounce box jumbo pasta shells (approximately 36 shells)

6 ounces thinly sliced pancetta, diced

2 teaspoons crushed red pepper flakes

2 garlic cloves, minced

5 cups marinara sauce

2 15-ounce containers whole milk ricotta cheese

1⅓ cups grated Parmesan

4 large egg yolks

3 tablespoons chopped fresh Italian parsley leaves

3 tablespoons chopped fresh basil

1 teaspoon chopped fresh mint

1½ teaspoons salt

½ teaspoon freshly ground black pepper

1 cup shredded mozzarella cheese

Yield: 8 to 10 servings

1. Lightly oil a baking sheet and set aside. Lightly oil two 13×9×2-inch baking dishes and set aside. Bring a large pot of salted water to a boil over high heat. Partially cook the pasta shells until slightly tender but still quite firm to the bite, about 4 to 6 minutes. You will continue cooking the shells in the oven after they have been stuffed. Using a slotted spoon, drain the pasta shells and place them on the oiled baking sheet, spreading them out so that they don't stick together, and allow them to cool.

2. Heat the 2 tablespoons oil in a heavy medium saucepan over medium heat. Add the pancetta and sauté until golden brown, about 5 minutes. Add the red pepper flakes. Add the garlic and sauté until tender, about 1 minute. Add the marinara sauce and bring the sauce to a simmer, stirring often.

3. In a medium bowl, stir together ricotta, Parmesan, egg yolks, parsley, basil, mint, salt, and black pepper. Set aside.

4. Preheat the oven to 350°F. Spoon 1 cup of the sauce over the bottom of each of the baking dishes. Fill each cooked shell with about 1 to 2 tablespoons of the cheese mixture. Arrange the shells in the baking dishes. Spoon the remaining sauce over the shells, then sprinkle with the mozzarella. Bake in the lower third of your oven until the filling is heated through and the top is golden brown, about 25 to 30 minutes.

KITCHEN TIP Pancetta's not too different from bacon. They're both made out of pork belly, but bacon is smoked and pancetta is salt-cured.

DIRTY RICE IS A DISH FIRMLY ROOTED IN THE AMERICAN SOUTH, WHERE IT'S TRADITIONALLY MADE WITH CHICKEN LIVERS AND GIBLETS— MAKING THE RICE LOOK "DIRTY." WE LIKE GIADA'S VERSION BECAUSE— THOUGH HER WHOLE FAMILY IS ITALIAN— SHE'S AN ALL-AMERICAN GIRL, AND THIS DISH IS A GREAT BLEND OF BOTH TRADITIONS.

Dirty Risotto

5 cups reduced-sodium chicken broth

2 tablespoons butter

2 ounces pancetta, chopped

2 links (about 6 ounces) spicy Italian sausage, casing removed

¾ cup finely chopped onion

1 cup chopped red bell pepper

4 ounces button mushrooms, coarsely chopped

½ teaspoon salt

¼ teaspoon freshly ground black pepper

1½ cups Arborio rice or medium-grain white rice

¾ cup dry white wine

½ cup freshly grated Parmesan

1 tablespoon chopped fresh Italian parsley

Yield: 4 to 6 servings

1. In a medium saucepan, bring the broth to a simmer. Cover the broth and keep warm over low heat. In a large heavy saucepan, melt the butter over medium-high heat. Add the pancetta and sausage and sauté, breaking up with a spoon, until golden brown, about 5 minutes. Add the onion, bell pepper, and mushrooms and sauté until tender, scraping up the browned bits on the bottom of the pan, about 8 minutes. Season with salt and black pepper.

2. Add the rice and stir to coat. Add the wine and simmer until the wine has almost completely evaporated, about 1 minute. Add ½ cup of the simmering broth and stir until almost completely absorbed, about 2 minutes. Continue to add the broth ½ cup at a time, stirring constantly and allowing each addition of broth to be absorbed before adding the next, until the rice is tender but still firm to the bite and the mixture is creamy, about 25 to 30 minutes total.

3. Remove from the heat. Stir in three-quarters of the Parmesan. Transfer the risotto to a serving bowl. Sprinkle with the parsley and remaining Parmesan and serve immediately.

Shrimp Fra Diavolo

1 pound large shrimp, peeled and deveined

1 teaspoon salt, plus additional as needed

1 teaspoon dried crushed red pepper flakes

3 tablespoons olive oil, plus 1 to 2 tablespoons

1 medium onion, sliced

1 14.5-ounce can diced tomatoes

1 cup dry white wine

3 cloves garlic, chopped

¼ teaspoon dried oregano leaves

3 tablespoons chopped fresh Italian parsley

3 tablespoons chopped fresh basil

Yield: 4 servings

1. Toss the shrimp in a medium bowl with 1 teaspoon salt and the red pepper flakes. Heat 3 tablespoons oil in a heavy large skillet over medium-high heat. Add the shrimp and sauté for about a minute, toss, and continue cooking until just cooked through, about 1 to 2 minutes. Transfer the shrimp to a large plate; set aside.

2. Add the onion and 1 to 2 more teaspoons olive oil to the same skillet and sauté until translucent, about 5 minutes. Add the tomatoes with their juices, wine, garlic, and oregano. Simmer until the sauce thickens slightly, about 10 minutes.

3. Return the shrimp and any accumulated juices to the tomato mixture; toss to coat and cook for about 1 minute so the flavors meld together. Stir in the parsley and basil. Season with more salt to taste and serve.

KITCHEN TIP To prep shrimp: Peel back the shell starting at the head. When you reach the tail, gently pinch it off, taking care to leave the morsel of meat inside attached to the body. To devein, cut a shallow groove all along the back of the shrimp and rinse out the grayish-brown vein you see there.

GIADA'S ALL FOR THE BIG, CLASSIC ITALIAN FLAVORS THAT TASTE LIKE SOMEONE'S GRANDMOTHER SPENT ALL DAY in the kitchen. But for those of us who don't have Italian grandmothers or all day to spend in the kitchen, her recipes get us a no-fuss feast on the table on a day-to-day basis.

Tilapia with Lemon Vinaigrette

5 tablespoons extra-virgin olive oil

3 shallots, thinly sliced

1 large head radicchio (about
12 ounces), coarsely chopped

1 15-ounce can cannellini beans,
drained and rinsed

⅓ cup fish broth

Salt and freshly ground black pepper

6 5- to 6-ounce tilapia fillets

All-purpose flour, for dredging

Lemon Vinaigrette (see recipe, below)

Yield: 6 servings

LEMON VINAIGRETTE

2 teaspoons finely grated lemon zest

¼ cup fresh lemon juice
(about 2 lemons)

¼ cup lightly packed fresh Italian parsley

2 cloves garlic

½ teaspoon salt, plus additional
for seasoning

¼ teaspoon freshly ground black pepper,
plus additional for seasoning

⅓ cup extra-virgin olive oil

Yield: scant ⅔ cup

1. Heat 2 tablespoons of oil in a heavy large skillet over medium heat. Add the shallots and sauté until tender, about 2 minutes. Add the radicchio and sauté until wilted, about 5 minutes. Add the beans and broth and cook until the beans are heated through, stirring often, about 5 minutes. Season the radicchio mixture with salt and black pepper to taste.

2. Meanwhile, heat the remaining 3 tablespoons oil in a 14-inch nonstick frying pan over medium-high heat. Sprinkle the fillets with salt and black pepper to taste. Dredge the fillets in flour to coat completely. Shake off the excess flour and fry the fillets until they are golden brown on both sides and just cooked through, about 3 minutes per side.

3. Spoon the radicchio mixture over the center of the plates. Top with the fillets. Drizzle the vinaigrette over and serve immediately.

LEMON VINAIGRETTE

Blend the lemon zest, lemon juice, parsley, garlic, salt, and black pepper in a blender. With the machine running, gradually drizzle in the oil. Season the vinaigrette with additional salt and black pepper to taste.

THIS IS A VARIATION ON A TRADITIONAL DISH FROM NAPLES CALLED BISTECCA ALLA PIZZAIOLA, OR STEAK, PIZZA-MAN STYLE (WHY? BECAUSE IT WAS AN EASY LUNCH FOR THE PIZZA MAN; HE ALREADY HAD THE RED SAUCE). USING A PRE-MIXED SPICE BLEND FOR FLAVOR AND A PAN-SEARED PORK CHOP MAKES THIS DISH A GREAT QUICK DINNER, EVEN IF YOU'RE NOT THE PIZZA MAN.

Pork Chops alla Pizzaiola

2 tablespoons olive oil

2 1-inch-thick bone-in pork loin center-cut chops (about 12 ounces each)

Salt and freshly ground black pepper

1 small onion, thinly sliced

1 15-ounce can diced tomatoes in juice

1 teaspoon herbes de Provence

¼ teaspoon (or more) crushed red pepper flakes

1 tablespoon chopped fresh Italian parsley

Yield: 2 servings

1. Heat the oil in a heavy large skillet over medium-high heat. Sprinkle the pork chops with salt and pepper. Add the pork chops to the skillet and cook until they are well browned, about 3 to 4 minutes per side. Transfer the pork chops to a plate and tent with foil to keep them warm.

2. Add the onion to the same skillet and sauté over medium heat until crisp-tender, about 4 minutes. Add the tomatoes with their juices, herbes de Provence, and ¼ teaspoon of red pepper flakes. Cover and simmer until the flavors blend and the juices thicken slightly, stirring occasionally, about 15 minutes. Season the sauce with salt and more crushed red pepper to taste, if desired.

3. Return the pork chops and any accumulated juices from the plate to the skillet, turn the pork chops to coat with the sauce, and cook for another 3 minutes. Place 1 pork chop on each plate. Spoon the sauce over the pork chops. Sprinkle with the parsley and serve.

KITCHEN TIP A good spice blend is a great time-saver. Herbes de Provence is a blend of dried spices native to southern France, usually containing a blend of marjoram, thyme, rosemary, and lavender, sometimes with basil and fennel added.

Creamy Ricotta Tart with Pine Nuts

CRUST

1½ cups plus 2 tablespoons all-purpose flour

2 tablespoons granulated sugar

¾ cup pine nuts, toasted

    Pinch salt

4 ounces unsalted butter, melted and cooled slightly (½ cup)

FILLING

½ cup water

2 tablespoons granulated sugar

1 cup ricotta cheese

6 ounces cream cheese, at room temperature

2 large eggs

3 large egg yolks

¾ cups pine nuts, toasted

Yield: one 11-inch tart

1. Preheat the oven to 350°F. Make the crust: In the bowl of a food processor, pulse flour, sugar, pine nuts, and salt until finely ground. Add the butter. Pulse dough just until it comes together. Place the dough into an 11-inch-diameter tart pan with a removable bottom and press down to cover the bottom and sides of the pan. Refrigerate until the dough is firm, about 30 minutes.

2. Line the tart shell with aluminum foil and fill with pie weights or dried beans. Bake the tart shell in the lower third of the oven until just set, about 25 minutes. Carefully remove the foil and pie weights. Bake until the tart shell is lightly golden, about 10 minutes. Cool completely.

3. Make the filling: Stir the water with the sugar in a small saucepan over low heat just to dissolve the sugar; don't boil. Stir until the sugar dissolves and remove from the heat.

4. In the bowl of a food processor, pulse the ricotta cheese and cream cheese until smooth. Add the eggs and egg yolks, one at a time, and process until smooth. With the machine running, add the sugar syrup in a thin steady stream and process until smooth.

5. Pour the custard into the tart shell and bake until the filling is almost set, about 20 to 25 minutes. Scatter the toasted pine nuts over the top. Bake until the custard is set, about 10 minutes longer. Let the tart cool completely before serving. The tart can be wrapped in plastic wrap and refrigerated for up to 3 days. Bring the tart to room temperature before serving.

KITCHEN TIP Blind-baking—that is, baking an empty shell—is a key step here; you want the crust to be cooked before you add wet ingredients to it, or it'll get soggy.

“THESE ARE MY NONNA GIUSEPPENA'S BISCUITS. Nonna, my grandfather's mother, would make them as an afternoon treat on Sundays. I love them because they are so-oo flaky and light. They're a staple in my Sunday brunch basket.” —GIADA

Nonna's Lemon Ricotta Biscuits

2 cups all-purpose flour

½ teaspoon baking powder

½ teaspoon baking soda

½ teaspoon salt

1 cup granulated sugar, plus more for sprinkling

½ cup unsalted butter, at room temperature

1 tablespoon finely grated lemon zest (from 2 lemons)

1 cup whole-milk ricotta cheese

1 large egg

1 tablespoon fresh lemon juice

½ teaspoon almond extract

⅓ cup thinly sliced almonds

Yield: 12 biscuits

1. Line 12 muffin cups with paper liners. Preheat the oven to 350°F. Whisk the flour, baking powder, baking soda, and salt in a medium bowl to blend.

2. In a large bowl, using an electric mixer, beat 1 cup sugar, butter, and lemon zest in a large bowl until light and fluffy. Beat in the ricotta. Beat in the egg, lemon juice, and almond extract. Add the dry ingredients and stir just until blended (the batter will be thick and fluffy).

3. Divide the batter among the prepared muffin cups. Sprinkle the almonds and some sugar over the muffins. Bake until the muffins just become pale golden on top, about 20 minutes. Cool slightly. Serve warm or at room temperature.

KITCHEN TIP One of the easiest ways to get grated lemon zest is to use a rasp grater. If you don't have one, use the small holes of a box grater.

RIC... "RECOO... ITALIAN. W... CHEESEMAKE... IN ROME NEEDED TO FIGURE OUT WHAT TO DO WITH THE WHEY LEFT OVER FROM MAKING ROMANO CHEESE, AND THEY REALIZED THAT WHEN THE WHEY WAS HEATED UP (THAT IS, RECOOKED), IT TURNED INTO THE MILD WHITE CHEESE WE NOW KNOW AS RICOTTA. WHOLE-MILK RICOTTA GIVES THESE BISCUITS A CREAMY TEXTURE, AND THOUGH EITHER AMERICAN OR ITALIAN RICOTTA WILL WORK FOR THIS RECIPE, IF YOU SEE ITALIAN-MADE RICOTTA IN YOUR SUPERMARKET OR CHEESE STORE, TRY IT. IT'S DELICIOUS.

Chocolate Amaretti Cake

Butter-flavored nonstick cooking spray

¾ cup chopped bittersweet chocolate or semisweet chocolate chips

1 cup slivered almonds

1 cup baby amaretti cookies (about 2 ounces)

½ cup unsalted butter, room temperature

⅔ cup granulated sugar

2 teaspoons orange zest, about 1 orange

4 large eggs

Unsweetened cocoa powder, for garnish

Yield: 8 servings

1. Preheat the oven to 350°F. Spray a 9-inch springform pan with the nonstick spray. Refrigerate. Microwave the chocolate until melted and smooth, stirring every 20 seconds, for about 1 minute.

2. In the bowl of a food processor pulse the almonds and cookies until finely ground. Transfer the nut mixture to a medium bowl. Add the butter and sugar to the processor and blend until creamy and smooth. Add the grated orange zest and pulse briefly, until incorporated. Add the eggs, one at a time, and blend until incorporated. With a rubber spatula, scrape down the sides of the mixing bowl and blend again. Add the nut mixture and melted chocolate. Pulse until blended. Clean the sides of the bowl. Blend again.

3. Pour the batter into the prepared pan. Bake until the center puffs and a tester inserted into the center of the cake comes out clean, about 35 to 40 minutes. Cool the cake in the pan for 15 minutes. Transfer the cake to a platter. Sift the cocoa powder over the top and serve.

HERE AT THE FOOD NETWORK, WE THROW A LOT OF PARTIES, AND THIS CAKE (which we make in a mini-muffin tin, baking for 8 to 10 minutes, or until the centers puff) is always a hit. We put the minis out, turn around, and they're gone the next time we check.

mario BATALI

He's a brilliant guy who puts his soul into his food. Mario's encyclopedic knowledge of Italian food and tradition makes his flavors so authentic, his recipes need subtitles.

Q+A
WITH MARIO BATALI

WHO TAUGHT YOU HOW TO COOK?
My family taught me. My Grandma Batali is my biggest inspiration. Her Sunday dinners were as epic as they were simple, and hours of joyous family celebration were spent at her table.

WHAT'S WITH THE CLOGS AND SHORTS?
Comfort is the main thing when I'm at work.

FAVORITE NEW YORK CITY STREET FOOD?
Gray's Papaya® (hot dogs and papaya juice).

WHAT'S IT LIKE BEING AN IRON CHEF?
It's intensely nervous-making. I love to cook and the competition is always tough, but it's a great way to keep my edge.

WHAT WAS YOUR BIGGEST KITCHEN DISASTER?
There is no disaster that can't be fixed— or at least given a new title!

WHAT DON'T WE KNOW ABOUT YOU THAT MIGHT BE SURPRISING?
I love punk rock.

109

2-Minute Calamari, Sicilian Lifeguard-Style:
Calamari al Bagnino Siciliano

ISRAELI
COUSCOUS HAS
AN INTERESTING
HISTORY: IN THE
1950S, ISRAEL'S
FIRST PRIME
MINISTER
COMMISSIONED
RICE AND
COUSCOUS-LIKE
PASTAS FOR
THE WAVES OF
NEW
IMMIGRANTS TO
ISRAEL USED TO
THOSE FOODS.
THESE QUICK-
COOKING PASTA
PEARLS ARE A
FAVORITE OF
THEIRS, OURS,
AND—WE'RE
ASSUMING—OF
SICILIAN
LIFEGUARDS
TOO.

Kosher salt

1 cup Israeli couscous

¼ cup extra-virgin olive oil, plus extra for drizzling

2 tablespoons pine nuts

4 cloves garlic, thinly sliced

2 tablespoons currants

¼ cup capers

1 tablespoon crushed red pepper flakes

¼ to ½ cup white wine

2 cups Mario's Basic Tomato Sauce (see recipe, right)

1½ pounds cleaned calamari, tubes cut into ¼-inch rounds, tentacles halved

5 scallions, thinly sliced, reserve some for garnish

Freshly ground black pepper

Yield: 4 servings

1. Bring 3 quarts of water to a boil and add 1 tablespoon of salt. Set up an ice bath nearby. Cook the couscous in the boiling water for 2 minutes, then drain and immediately cool it in the ice bath. Once cooled, drain it again and set aside to dry on a plate.

2. In a 12- to 14-inch sauté pan, heat the oil until just smoking. Add the pine nuts, garlic, currants, capers, and crushed red pepper and sauté until the pine nuts are golden brown, about 2 minutes. Add the white wine and tomato sauce and bring to a simmer.

3. Add the couscous and bring to a boil. Add the calamari, stir to mix, and simmer for 2 or 3 minutes, or until the calamari is just cooked and completely opaque. Toss in the scallions. Season with salt and black pepper to taste, pour into a large warm bowl, sprinkle with the reserved scallions, drizzle with olive oil, and serve immediately.

MARIO'S BASIC TOMATO SAUCE

¼ cup extra-virgin olive oil

1 Spanish onion, cut into ¼-inch dice

4 garlic cloves, thinly sliced

3 tablespoons chopped fresh thyme or 1 tablespoon dried

½ medium carrot, finely grated

2 28-ounce cans peeled whole tomatoes, crushed by hand and juices reserved

Salt

1. In a 3-quart saucepan, heat the olive oil over medium heat. Add the onion and garlic and cook until soft and light golden brown, about 8 to 10 minutes.

2. Add the thyme and carrot and cook 5 minutes more, until the carrot is quite soft. Add the tomatoes and juice and bring to a boil, stirring often. Lower the heat and simmer for 30 minutes, or until as thick as hot cereal. Season with salt to taste.
Yield: 4 cups

KITCHEN TIP Mario's restaurants make tons of this sauce every day. If you can't use all that one recipe makes, it'll hold 1 week in the refrigerator or up to 6 months in the freezer.

Arancine with Ragu: *Arancine con Ragu*

SAFFRON RISOTTO

5 to 6 cups chicken or beef stock

⅛ teaspoon ground saffron

4 tablespoons unsalted butter

1½ cups Arborio rice

Salt and freshly ground black pepper

1 large egg yolk, at room temperature

RAGU

½ cup olive oil

2½ pounds ground veal

1 medium onion, finely chopped

1 cup tomato paste

1 6-ounce piece Parmesan rind

2 carrots, peeled and quartered

1 teaspoon granulated sugar

3 cups chicken stock

Salt and freshly ground black pepper

ARANCINE

2 egg whites, beaten

2 cups fine dry bread crumbs

Cooking oil

Yield: 6 servings

1. To make the risotto: In a medium-sized saucepan, heat the stock until almost boiling. Turn the heat to very low and stir in the saffron. In a 10- to 12-inch saucepan, melt 3 tablespoons of the butter over medium-high heat. Add the rice and cook, stirring continuously with a wooden spoon, until the rice is coated in the butter and begins to turn translucent, about 2 minutes. Be careful not to let the rice burn. Keeping the heat at medium-high, begin ladling the hot broth into the rice, about 2 ladlefuls at a time. Constantly stir with the wooden spoon until the rice has absorbed almost all of the broth. Continue adding the broth bit by bit, until the rice is al dente or tender, about 20 minutes. Once the rice is cooked, season with salt and black pepper to taste.

2. Remove from the heat and immediately add the egg yolk and the remaining tablespoon of butter. Stir to thoroughly combine and set aside to cool.

3. To make the ragu: In a large, heavy-bottomed saucepan, cook the olive oil, veal, and onion over high heat. Stir often and continue cooking until the veal loses its pink color.

4. Add the remaining ingredients through the 3 cups of chicken stock. Turn the heat to medium-low and allow the ragu to simmer for about 1 to 1½ hours, until quite thickened. Season with salt and black pepper to taste, stir well to combine, and remove the ragu from the heat. Let the ragu cool, about 45 minutes.

5. When the ragu is cool to the touch, wet hands with a little water and place a scant cup of rice into the palm of one hand and use the fingers of your other hand to form a cup-like well in the center. Tuck a generous tablespoon of the ragu in the center, then gently fold the outer edges of the rice around the ragu to enclose completely. You should have a ball of stuffed rice, and there should not be any ragu leaking out. You may need to add a little more rice to keep the ball closed. Set the arancine aside and use the remaining rice and the remaining ragu to make about 5 more balls.

6. Roll each finished ball carefully in the beaten egg whites, then dredge in the bread crumbs. Place the arancine on a tray and refrigerate for 30 minutes. In the meantime, heat 4 inches of cooking oil in a fryer or deep frying pan to 360°F. Carefully place 3 balls at a time into pan and fry until golden brown, about 3 to 4 minutes, stirring with tongs or a kitchen spoon to keep them moving. Drain cooked balls on paper towels and place on a large platter. Serve immediately.

KITCHEN TIP Save and freeze your Parmesan rinds to add great nutty flavor to anything you simmer them in. Ask your cheesemonger for some if you don't have any on hand.

KITCHEN TIP This recipe makes lots and lots of ragu—freeze the leftovers for *arancine* (or just a quick pasta dinner) anytime.

ON FIRE!

MARIO STUDIED THEATER IN COLLEGE, AND HIS COOKING ON *IRON CHEF* IS DRAMATIC EVERY STEP OF THE WAY. Expect to see flambéing, rapid-fire mezzaluna chopping, and any and every kitchen gadget imaginable. And he takes it all super-seriously—he loves the competition and the chance to create both spectacle and spectacular food.

NOTE FROM THE KITCHENS

THIS IS A CLASSIC MARIO RECIPE. AS MARIO LIKES TO SAY, "DON'T GILD THE LILY." THAT IS, DON'T GO OVERBOARD WHEN YOU'VE GOT SOMETHING THAT'S BEAUTIFUL ALREADY. SO HERE, HE'S TAKING SIMPLE, HIGH-QUALITY INGREDIENTS AND NOT DOING A LOT TO THEM TO MAKE THEM SHINE. THIS DISH IS ALL ABOUT THE SUM OF ITS PARTS, SO THE QUALITY OF THE INGREDIENTS IS PARAMOUNT. MARIO'S LOOKING FOR THE PERFECT EXPRESSION OF THE CLAM HERE, SO USE THE BEST ONES YOU CAN FIND.

Clam Sauté: *Sote di Vongole*

  3 tablespoons extra-virgin olive oil

  2 cloves garlic, thinly sliced

2¼ pounds fresh clams, scrubbed and rinsed (New Zealand cockles or Manila clams)

  1 cup dry white wine (see Kitchen Tip, right)

  2 tablespoons chopped fresh parsley

Yield: 4 servings

1. In a 12- to 14-inch saucepan with a lid, heat the oil over medium-high heat until hot but not smoking. Add the garlic and cook until soft and light golden brown, about 5 minutes.

2. Add the clams. Pour in the wine and cover the pan. Steam the clams until they open, about 8 minutes. Remove from the heat and discard any clams that did not open. Serve immediately, garnished with parsley.

KITCHEN TIP To clean clams, scrub with a bristle brush under cold running water.

KITCHEN TIP When you're cooking with wine, it's best to use something that you'd want to drink with the finished dish. Bottles labeled "cooking wine" are generally salted and overall pretty unappealing (historically, that was to prevent cooks from drinking on the job).

Penne with Cauliflower:
Penne con Cavolofiore

½ cup extra-virgin olive oil

1 clove garlic, crushed

2 pounds tomatoes, peeled, seeded, and chopped, or 4 cups canned plum tomatoes, drained and chopped

1 head cauliflower, broken into florets

½ cup very hot water, plus 6 quarts cold water

2 tablespoons salt, plus more for seasoning

1 pound dry penne

2 bunches Italian parsley, finely chopped to yield ½ cup

Freshly ground black pepper

½ cup freshly grated caciocavallo, Parmigiano-Reggiano, or pecorino

Yield: 6 servings

1. In a 12- to 14-inch sauté pan, heat the olive oil over medium-high heat and add the garlic. Cook gently until softened and very light golden brown. Add the tomatoes and cook, stirring, until they begin to break down. Add the cauliflower and stir well. Add ½ cup very hot water, lower the heat to medium, and cook about 15 to 20 minutes, or until the cauliflower is tender.

2. Bring 6 quarts of cold water to a boil and add 2 tablespoons salt. Add the penne and cook according to package directions, until tender but al dente, and drain.

3. Add the drained pasta to the pan with the cauliflower. Stir in parsley. Season with salt and black pepper to taste and toss for 1 minute over high heat. Divide evenly among 6 warmed pasta bowls, top with grated cheese, and serve immediately.

KITCHEN TIP Caciocavallo (which means "cheese on horseback") is a pulled-curd cow's milk cheese, made like provolone and hung out to age. The flavor is somewhere between Parmigiano-Reggiano, provolone, and mozzarella. If you have a hard time finding it, Parmigiano-Reggiano is a good choice for this dish.

IN THE SUMMERTIME, USE FRESH TOMATOES FOR THIS DISH. MAKE PEELING EASIER BY CUTTING A SMALL "X" INTO THE BOTTOM OF EACH TOMATO, THEN DROPPING THE TOMATOES FIRST INTO SIMMERING WATER FOR A FEW SECONDS AND THEN INTO AN ICE BATH TO COOL; THE SKIN'LL SLIP RIGHT OFF. IN THE WINTER, CANNED TOMATOES ARE YOUR BEST BET FOR FLAVOR—MARIO'S FAVORITE ARE FROM SAN MARZANO, A REGION NEAR NAPLES.

MARIO'S PASSIONATE ABOUT FINDING THE MOST AUTHENTIC INGREDIENTS, AND WHEN WE FIRST STARTED taping his shows, we had the hardest time locating a lot of the cheeses, sausages, and even vegetables he called for. For example, we'd never even heard of cardoons until he asked for them. Now, thanks to his show, these ingredients are becoming *molto* widespread.

Linguine with Crab, Radicchio & Garlic:
Linguine al Granchio

IS BEⅭ
TO SOUPS AⁿD
MEAT-BASED
SAUCES, DRY
PASTA'S
DISTINCTIVE
BITE WORKS
WELL WITH
SEAFOOD- AND
VEGETABLE-
BASED SAUCES.
AND WHEN WE
ASKED MARIO
HIS THREE
DESERT-ISLAND
INGREDIENTS,
DRY PASTA WAS
ONE OF THEM.
(THE OTHER
TWO WERE
EXTRA-VIRGIN
OLIVE OIL AND
SEA SALT.)

2 tablespoons salt

1 pound linguine

¼ cup extra-virgin olive oil

3 shallots, finely chopped

4 cloves garlic, thinly sliced

1 teaspoon crushed red
   pepper flakes

1 cup dry white wine

2 tablespoons unsalted butter

½ pound fresh crabmeat

½ head radicchio, shredded

2 scallions, thinly sliced

Yield: 4 servings

1. Bring 6 quarts water to a boil and add salt. Cook the pasta according to the package instructions, until just al dente, and drain, reserving a little pasta water.

2. Meanwhile, in a 12- to 14-inch sauté pan, heat the oil until smoking. Add the shallots, garlic, and crushed red pepper and sauté until golden brown, about 4 to 5 minutes. Add the wine, bring to a boil, then add the butter, and remove from heat.

3. Add the drained pasta to the pan with the wine mixture and return pan to heat. Add crab, radicchio, and scallions and toss until radicchio is wilted, about 1 minute. Add a little reserved pasta water, if necessary, to thin the sauce. Pour into a warm serving bowl and serve.

Osso Buco with Toasted Pine Nut Gremolata:
Osso Buco ai Pignoli

4 3-inch-thick veal shanks (about 3½ to 4 pounds)

   Salt and freshly ground black pepper

6 tablespoons extra-virgin olive oil

1 medium carrot, sliced into ¼-inch rounds

1 small Spanish onion, chopped into ½-inch dice

1 celery stalk, sliced ¼ inch thick

2 tablespoons chopped fresh thyme leaves

2 cups Mario's Basic Tomato Sauce (see page 111)

2 cups chicken stock, additional stock if necessary

2 cups dry white wine

   Gremolata (see recipe, below)

Yield: 4 servings

GREMOLATA

¼ cup finely chopped Italian parsley

¼ cup pine nuts, toasted under the broiler until dark brown

   Zest of 1 lemon

Yield: ½ cup

1. Preheat the oven to 375°F. Season the shanks all over with salt and black pepper to taste. In a heavy-bottomed 6- to 8-quart oven safe pan, heat the olive oil until smoking. Place the shanks in the pan and brown all over, turning to get every surface, 12 to 15 minutes. Remove the shanks and set aside.

2. Reduce the heat to medium, add the carrot, onion, celery, and thyme leaves and cook, stirring regularly, until golden brown and slightly softened, 8 to 10 minutes. Add the tomato sauce, chicken stock, and wine and bring to a boil.

3. Return the shanks back to the pan; if sauce doesn't come halfway up shanks, add more stock. Cover the pan with a tight-fitting lid (if it doesn't have a lid, cover it tightly with aluminum foil). Cook in the oven until the meat is nearly falling off the bone, about 2 to 2½ hours. Remove the pan from the oven and let stand for 10 minutes before serving with Gremolata.

GREMOLATA

Mix the parsley, pine nuts, and lemon zest loosely in a small bowl. Set aside until ready to serve.

ROLL IT UP

THIS RECIPE MAKES TWO RATHER LARGE STUFFED MEATBALLS—ACTUALLY, MORE LIKE JELLY ROLLS—THAT PRESENT BEAUTIFULLY WHEN SLICED THIN AND GLAZED.

Stuffed Meatballs: *Polpettone Ripieni*

½ pound finely ground lean veal

½ pound finely ground lean beef

1 cup plus 3 tablespoons freshly grated bread crumbs

1 cup freshly grated pecorino

3 large eggs

Salt and freshly ground black pepper

20 to 30 leaves flat-leaf spinach, stems removed

1 carrot, peeled and cut into 6 slices lengthwise

3 tablespoons all-purpose flour, plus additonal for dusting rolls

6 slices prosciutto

6 slices caciocavallo (see Kitchen Tip, page 115)

6 tablespoons extra-virgin olive oil

2 sprigs rosemary

1 cup chicken stock

½ cup dry red wine

Yield: 4 to 8 servings

1. In a large bowl, combine the veal, beef, 1 cup bread crumbs, grated cheese, eggs, and salt and black pepper to taste and mix thoroughly with hands.

2. Bring 6 quarts of water to a boil and add 1 tablespoon salt. Dip the spinach leaves in the water to just wilt and immediately remove. Add the carrot slices to the boiling water and cook for 4 to 5 minutes, then drain and set aside.

3. Combine the 3 tablespoons flour with the remaining 3 tablespoons bread crumbs and heavily dust a wooden work board with the mixture. Pat the veal mixture into a rectangle that is 16 inches long by 5 inches wide and about ½ inch thick. Lay the spinach leaves over the meat, leaving a 1-inch border on the short sides. Lay the carrot slices over the spinach in the same fashion, then layer the prosciutto and the caciocavallo. Carefully roll the meat into a jelly roll, making it as firm as possible. Cut the roll in half crosswise, sealing the ends thoroughly with the meat to keep the cheese from oozing out during cooking. Dust the outsides with flour.

4. In a frying pan large enough to hold both rolls, heat olive oil over medium-low. Add rosemary and rolls and brown meat on all sides, turning carefully with a wooden spoon or 2 spatulas. When meat is brown, remove and discard as much oil as possible. Return meat to pan. Pour half the chicken stock and half the wine over rolls, turn heat to medium-low, cover, and cook 15 minutes. (If liquid evaporates, add a little water to pan.) Remove cover, turn meat over, and pour remaining chicken stock and wine over them. Cover again and cook an additional 15 minutes.

5. Transfer meat rolls to a cutting board. Return skillet to medium-high heat and add ½ cup water to pan. Cook down, scraping up any brown bits, until you have 2 to 3 tablespoons glaze. Strain to remove rosemary. Let rolls cool to room temperature, then slice as thinly as possible; serve with glaze drizzled over.

KITCHEN TIP To taste the meatballs for seasoning in Step 1, fry up a small patty.

KITCHEN TIP If you can't find caciocavallo, use half provolone and half mozzarella for this recipe.

MARIO'S ORIGINALLY FROM SEATTLE, WHERE HE GREW UP IN A BIG, FOOD-LOVING FAMILY. His grandfather opened Seattle's first Italian-food specialty shop in 1903, and his dad recently opened Salumi, a small restaurant/meat counter two blocks from the original Batali store.

FENNEL IS AN HERB (THOUGH WE TREAT IT LIKE A VEGETABLE) WITH AN ANISE-LIKE FLAVOR, A CELERY-LIKE TEXTURE, AND A LONG HISTORY GOING BACK TO THE ANCIENT ROMANS. LOOK FOR LARGE WHITE BULBS WITH A PEARLY SHEEN AND HEALTHY-LOOKING GREEN FRONDS.

Pork with Sweet Garlic & Fennel:
Arista con Aglio e Finocchio

2 tablespoons extra-virgin olive oil

1 bulb fennel, thinly sliced, fronds removed and reserved for garnish

6 1-inch-thick center-cut pork chops

Salt and freshly ground black pepper

Flour, for dredging

2 teaspoons fennel seeds

1 cup high-quality white wine

Sweet Garlic (see recipe, below)

SWEET GARLIC

2 tablespoons extra-virgin olive oil

1 head garlic (about 12 cloves), cloves peeled and separated

2 cups Cinzano or other sweet white wine

Yield: 6 servings

1. Preheat the oven to 300°F. In a 10- to 12-inch skillet, heat the oil until almost smoking. Add the fennel slices and cook over high heat until tender and browned, about 5 minutes.

2. Season the pork chops with salt and black pepper to taste and dredge them in flour. Add the pork chops to the pan and cook 1 minute on each side, until evenly browned. Remove the skillet from heat and sprinkle 1 teaspoon fennel seeds on 1 side of the chops. Turn and sprinkle the remaining teaspoon on the other sides.

3. Add the wine and Sweet Garlic and place the skillet in the oven to cook for 15 minutes, until just cooked through. Garnish with four fennel fronds and serve immediately.

SWEET GARLIC
Combine oil and garlic in a 12- to 14-inch sauté pan and cook over high heat until the cloves are browned. Add the Cinzano and reduce the liquid until syrupy.

KITCHEN TIP Cinzano is also known as sweet vermouth. It's a traditional drink from Turin, made out of white wine infused with sugar, alcohol, and herbs until it takes on a deep amber color and a rich, fruity flavor.

Lamb with Olives: *Agnello alle Olive*

2 pounds boneless leg of lamb, cut into 2-inch chunks

1 tablespoon all-purpose flour

¾ cup extra-virgin olive oil

Salt and freshly ground black pepper

Juice of 1 lemon

1 cup Brown Chicken Stock (see recipe, below)

¾ cup small black olives, pitted, plus ¾ cup left whole

1 bunch fresh oregano

1 tablespoon crushed red pepper flakes

Yield: 4 to 6 servings

BROWN CHICKEN STOCK

2 tablespoons extra-virgin olive oil

3½ pounds chicken wings, backs, and bones

3 carrots, coarsely chopped

2 onions, coarsely chopped

4 ribs celery, coarsely chopped

3 quarts water

2 tablespoons tomato paste

1 tablespoon black peppercorns

1 bunch parsley stems

Yield: about 1½ quarts

1. Dust the meat with the flour. Heat the olive oil over high heat in a Dutch oven and add the meat to sear on all sides. Season the meat with salt and black pepper to taste and moisten with the lemon juice and ½ cup stock. Cover and simmer 30 minutes.

2. Add the pitted olives, half the oregano, red pepper flakes, and the remaining ½ cup stock. Cover and simmer until the meat is fork-tender, about 1½ hours. Serve sliced, with the pan juices drizzled over and the remaining whole olives on the side. Sprinkle the remaining oregano over each slice.

BROWN CHICKEN STOCK

1. In a large, heavy-bottomed saucepan, heat the oil over high heat until smoking. Add all the chicken parts and brown all over, stirring to avoid burning. Remove the chicken and reserve. Add the carrots, onions, and celery to the pot and cook until soft and browned.

2. Return the chicken to the pot and add 3 quarts of water, tomato paste, peppercorns, and parsley. Stir with a wooden spoon to dislodge the browned chicken and vegetable bits from the bottom of the pan. Bring almost to a boil, then reduce heat and cook at a low simmer until reduced by half, about 2 hours, occasionally skimming excess fat.

3. Remove from heat, strain, and press on the solids with the bottom of a ladle to extract out all liquids. Stir the stock and set aside. Refrigerate stock in small containers for up to a week or freeze for up to a month.

KITCHEN TIP Squish a few olives at a time with the flat side of your chef's knife to pop the pits out easily.

KITCHEN TIP We love having homemade stock in the freezer. We make a big batch once a month and freeze it in plastic bags for whenever we need it.

"I LOVE COOKING IN EXTRA-VIRGIN OLIVE OIL . . . it adds such a delicious flavor to everything the oil anoints." —MARIO

Rum & Ricotta Fritters:
Fritelle di Ricotta e Rhum

Extra-virgin olive oil

20 ounces fresh whole-milk ricotta

5 large eggs, separated, yolks lightly beaten

¼ cup dark rum

2 tablespoons granulated sugar

1⅓ cups all-purpose flour

1 tablespoon baking powder

Confectioners' sugar

Yield: 3½ dozen fritters

1. In a large, heavy-bottomed pan over medium heat, slowly heat at least 4 inches of extra-virgin olive oil to 350°F to 355°F.

2. In the bowl of a food processor, pulse the ricotta until it is smooth and creamy. Turn the ricotta out into a large bowl and add the lightly beaten yolks, rum, and sugar, beating well.

3. Sift together the flour and baking powder and add to the ricotta mixture.

4. Beat the whites to stiff but not dry peaks and fold them gently into the ricotta mixture.

5. Drop scant tablespoons of the batter into the oil. Cook the fritters until golden, then turn and cook the other side. Remove with a slotted spoon and drain on paper towels. Dust with confectioners' sugar. Serve immediately.

KITCHEN TIP Don't worry if the batter looks too wet; that's the secret to these delicious fritters.

michael CHIARELLO

To us, he embodies California country living. He's all about relaxed style, inviting warmth, and using simple, healthy ingredients with knock-your-socks-off flavor.

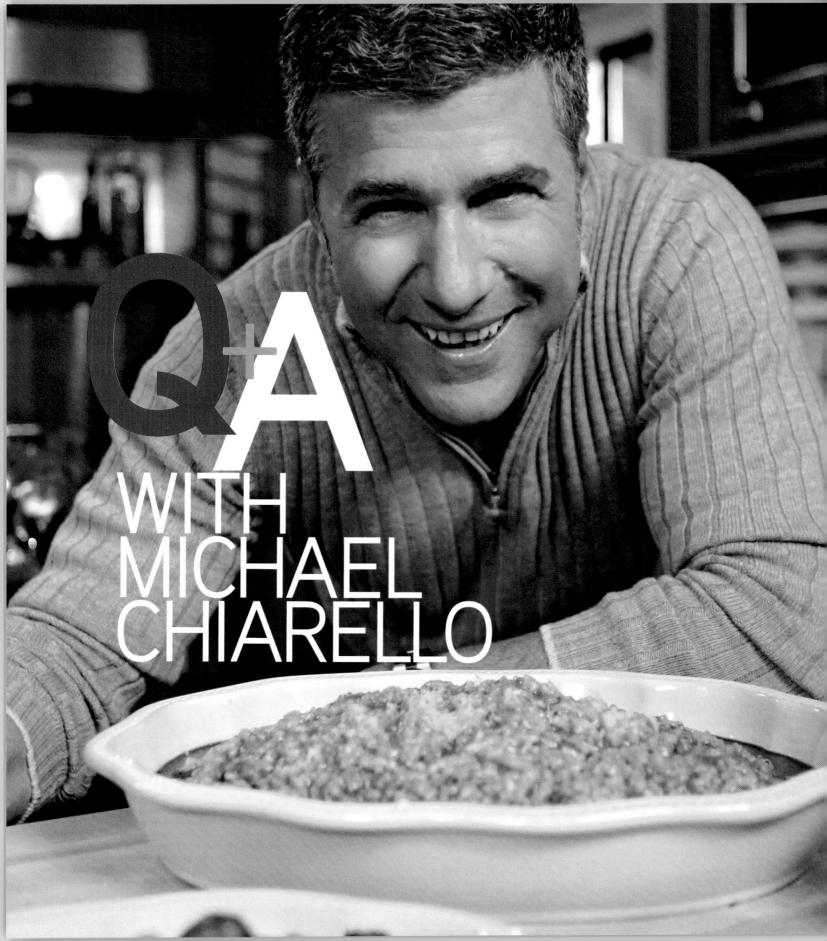

Q+A
WITH MICHAEL CHIARELLO

WHY DID YOU BECOME A CHEF?
My mother taught me how to love those close to you by cooking what they cherish. And besides, great food always makes you feel good.

WHAT WAS THE MOST IMPORTANT THING YOU LEARNED WHILE IN TRAINING?
A cook emulates someone else's food, but a chef has his or her own style.

NAME THE THREE INGREDIENTS YOU MUST ALWAYS HAVE IN YOUR KITCHEN.
Gray salt (salt is the new olive oil . . .), extra-virgin olive oil, Parmigiano-Reggiano.

SO WHY DO YOU LOVE GRAY SALT SO MUCH?
It's simple: FLAVOR. Almost anything you cook will taste 10% better with it. It's like changing from vegetable oil to extra-virgin olive oil.

WHAT'S DIFFERENT ABOUT YOUR LIFE NOW THAT YOU'RE ON THE FOOD NETWORK?
If you think someone is smiling at you because they think you're cute ... it's actually because they watch you on TV. And everyone always checks out what's in your cart at the grocery store.

"I WAS FIRST TURNED ON TO THESE OLIVES (THE PERFECT COCKTAIL SNACK) WHILE AT HARRY'S BAR IN VENICE. The perfect snack can make a good cocktail great." —MICHAEL

Crispy Olives Stuffed with Sausage

¼ pound (1 link) fresh Italian sausage

1 teaspoon minced garlic

Salt

½ teaspoon crushed red pepper flakes
(optional)

1 8-ounce jar large pitted green olives

4 to 6 cups peanut oil, for deep-frying

½ cup all-purpose flour

2 large eggs

½ cup fine bread crumbs

Freshly ground black pepper

2 teaspoons extra-virgin olive oil

Yield: 6 to 8 servings

1. Remove the sausage meat from the casing and place in a medium bowl. Add the garlic, a pinch of salt, and crushed red pepper, if using. Mix to evenly distribute the ingredients.

2. Drain the olives and rinse under cold water. Remove the pimientos, if necessary. Stuff each of the olives with ¼ to ½ teaspoon of the sausage mixture.

3. Heat the oil in a deep fryer or stockpot to 375°F. Spread the flour on a dinner plate. Break the eggs into a shallow bowl and beat lightly. Spread the bread crumbs on another dinner plate and sprinkle them with salt and black pepper to taste. Toss the olives with the olive oil to coat evenly. Roll the olives in the flour, coating them all over and shaking off the excess. Then dip them in the egg, letting any excess drip back into the bowl. Finally, coat the olives all over with the bread crumbs. As each olive is coated, place it on a tray. Cover the olives and refrigerate until you are ready to fry them.

4. Fry the olives until golden brown and the sausage in the middle is cooked through, about 3 minutes. The olives will bubble vigorously until they are nearly done, so watch for splatters. Drain on paper towels to absorb any excess oil. Serve warm or at room temperature.

Bruschetta with White Bean Puree

¾ cup white marrow beans (or other white beans), cooked and cooled, 1 cup cooking liquid reserved

2 tablespoons olive paste

2 tablespoons minced fresh thyme leaves, plus 6 sprigs, for garnish (garnish optional)

¼ cup extra-virgin olive oil, plus additional for drizzling

¼ teaspoon gray salt, plus additional for seasoning

Freshly ground black pepper

1 loaf thick Italian bread

2 cloves garlic, peeled

Yield: 8 to 10 servings

1. Make the white bean puree: Puree the beans in a food processor until smooth, adding the reserved liquid, as necessary, for a finished consistency that is spreadable but not too thin. Add the olive paste and minced thyme and puree again. While pureeing, add ¼ cup olive oil and season with ¼ teaspoon salt and black pepper to taste. Transfer puree to a serving dish and garnish with sprigs of thyme, if desired.

2. Make the bruschetta: Cut Italian bread into thick slices. Toast and/or grill until light brown and crispy. Then swipe the bread once with a clove of fresh garlic and drizzle with olive oil. Spread with the white bean puree. Finish with a pinch of gray salt and freshly ground black pepper to taste.

KITCHEN TIP You can also use canned white beans for this recipe; drain and rinse them before processing. Add a little vegetable or chicken stock to the food processor if you need to smooth out the consistency.

KITCHEN TIP Jarred olive paste is a great pantry item. Pick some up in the grocery store to save time on making your own.

Homemade Tomato Soup

1 14-ounce can chopped tomatoes

  Salt and freshly ground black pepper

¾ cup extra-virgin olive oil

1 stalk celery, diced

1 small carrot, diced

1 yellow onion, diced

2 cloves garlic, minced

1 cup chicken broth

1 bay leaf

2 tablespoons butter

¼ cup chopped fresh basil

½ cup heavy cream (optional)

Yield: 4 servings

1. Preheat the oven to 450°F. Strain the tomatoes, reserving the juices, and spread on a baking sheet. Season with salt and black pepper to taste, drizzle with ¼ cup of the olive oil and roast until caramelized, about 15 minutes.

2. Meanwhile, in a saucepan, heat the remaining olive oil over medium heat. Add the celery, carrot, onion, and garlic and cook until softened, about 10 minutes. Add the roasted tomatoes, reserved tomato juices, chicken broth, bay leaf, and butter. Simmer until vegetables are very tender, about 15 to 20 minutes.

3. Add basil and cream, if using. Remove bay leaf. Puree with a handheld immersion blender until smooth.

KITCHEN TIP If you don't have an immersion blender, cool the liquid for at least 5 minutes and transfer to a regular blender, filling no more than halfway. Don't seal the top—lift one corner up a little to let the steam escape, put a kitchen towel on top, pulse a few times, then blend on high until smooth.

HOW TO TRIM AN ARTICHOKE
1. TRIM OFF THE END OF THE STEM, THEN PULL OFF TOUGH OUTER LEAVES
2. USE A KNIFE

TOMATOES THEY'RE ROASTED TO BRING OUT A LITTLE EXTRA FLAVOR AND SWEETNESS. MICHAEL SERVES THIS WITH LITTLE CHEESE SANDWICHES ON THE SIDE—FOR SOPHISTICATED COMFORT FOOD, YOU CAN'T GO WRONG.

Salami Salad with Tomatoes & Mozzarella

1 pound salami, cut into ¼-inch pieces

6 tomatoes, diced

½ cup fresh basil leaves

½ pound mozzarella, cut into ½-inch pieces

  Salt and freshly ground black pepper

  Extra-virgin olive oil, for drizzling

  Vinegar, for drizzling

Yield: 8 to 10 servings

In a large bowl, combine salami, tomatoes, basil, and mozzarella. Season with salt and black pepper to taste. Drizzle with olive oil and vinegar and toss well.

KITCHEN TIP Try different kinds of salami in this salad: spicy sopressata or Calabrese, fennely *finocchiona*, or garlicky Genoa.

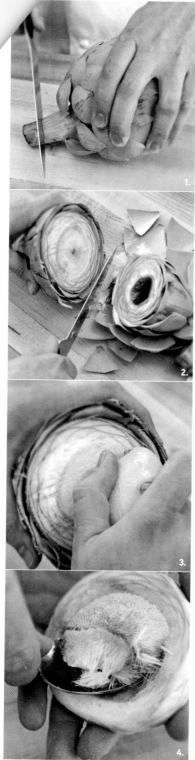

TEM,
OFF
TER

A CHEF'S
E TO CUT OFF
HE TOP HALF
AND DISCARD.
3. RUB ARTICHOKE
WITH THE LEMON
HALF AS YOU GO
TO PREVENT
DISCOLORATION.
4. SCRAPE OUT
THE CHOKE (THE
FUZZY CENTER)
WITH A SPOON.

1.

2.

3.

4.

Lemon-Braised Artichokes over Pasta

ARTICHOKES

½	cup extra-virgin olive oil
½	cup freshly squeezed lemon juice
1½	teaspoons finely chopped fresh thyme
1½	teaspoons minced garlic
1½	teaspoons kosher salt
	Small pinch freshly ground black pepper
4	medium-to-large artichokes
½	lemon

PASTA

1	pound fettuccine
¼	cup olive oil
4	cloves garlic, sliced
2	teaspoons fresh oregano leaves
½	cup chicken broth or stock
4	cups spinach, stemmed and washed
¼	cup chopped fresh Italian parsley leaves
1	tablespoon butter
	Kosher salt
	Freshly ground black pepper
	Grated Parmesan, for serving

Yield: 6 servings

1. Prepare the artichokes: Preheat the oven to 375°F. Combine the olive oil, lemon juice, thyme, garlic, salt, and black pepper in a medium nonreactive saucepan. Mix well and set aside while preparing the artichokes.

2. Clean the artichokes down to the hearts (see instructions at left). Cut the hearts into quarters and immediately place in the marinade.

3. When all the artichokes are trimmed, put the pan over high heat and bring to a boil. Pour the artichokes and marinade into a baking dish (or cook them in the saucepan if it is ovenproof), cover with foil, and cook in the oven until the artichokes are tender when pierced with a fork, about 45 minutes. Remove from the oven and let cool in the cooking liquid.

4. Make the pasta: Cook fettuccine according to package directions. While pasta is cooking, heat olive oil in a large skillet over medium heat. Add garlic and cook, stirring, until garlic is golden. Add the oregano and broth. Bring to a simmer and stir in the spinach to wilt.

5. Add the artichokes. Drain the pasta, reserving some of the cooking water, and place in a serving bowl. Pour the artichoke mixture over the pasta and toss with the parsley and butter and season with salt and black pepper to taste. Thin with reserved pasta water, if necessary. Sprinkle with Parmesan and serve.

MICHAEL
SOMETIMES
SERVES THIS
SALAD AS A
MAIN COURSE
ALONGSIDE A
GRILLED
CHICKEN
BREAST. HE
TOLD US NOT TO
LEAVE OUT THE
DRIED FRUIT—IT
ADDS SERIOUS
RICHNESS. IN
THE FALL AND
WINTER YOU
CAN USE FIGS,
APPLES, PEARS,
OR PERSIMMONS
IN PLACE OF
THE GRAPES,
WHILE IN
SUMMER YOU
CAN USE PLUMS,
APRICOTS, AND
PEACHES.

Sicilian Harvest Salad

½   cup raisins

    Boiling water

1   cup halved large seedless grapes

1   tablespoon diced dried apricots
(¼-inch dice)

1½ tablespoons Fried Rosemary (see
recipe, below)

¼   large red onion, cut into small slivers

    Juice of 1 large lemon

5   tablespoons extra-virgin olive oil

    Salt and freshly ground black pepper

1   large head radicchio (about ¾ pound)

2   cups loosely packed baby spinach

12 thin slices prosciutto or ¼ pound
sausage, grilled and cubed (optional)

1   tablespoon pine nuts, toasted

Yield: 4 servings

FRIED ROSEMARY

    Rosemary sprigs

    Oil for deep-frying

1. Put the raisins in a small bowl and pour boiling water over them to cover. Let stand until plump and soft, about 10 minutes. Drain.

2. Put the raisins, grapes, apricots, rosemary, and onion in a large bowl. Add the lemon juice and stir in the olive oil. Season with salt and black pepper to taste.

3. Separate the radicchio into leaves, saving the heart for another use. Tear into bite size pieces and add to the dried fruit mixture along with the spinach. Toss well. Divide among 4 plates and top with the prosciutto, if using. Scatter the pine nuts over the top.

FRIED ROSEMARY

1. Heat 1 inch of oil in a deep sauté pan to 350°F. Deep-fry the rosemary for 30 seconds and drain on paper towels.

2. Strip the leaves off the stems and crush the leaves in the paper towels to remove any excess oil. Mince and store in a clean, tightly sealed container.

KITCHEN TIP Stand back after you add the rosemary to the oil— the resin in it makes it likely to spatter a little.

136

Seared Pork Tenderloin with Cocoa-Spice Rub

1 tablespoon whole white peppercorns

1 tablespoon whole coriander seeds

4½ tablespoons ground cinnamon

2 teaspoons ground nutmeg

1 teaspoon ground cloves

3½ tablespoons unsweetened cocoa

4 tablespoons sea salt, preferably gray

2 12- to 16-ounce pork tenderloins

2 tablespoons extra-virgin olive oil

Yield: 4 servings

1. Preheat the oven to 400°F. In a medium saucepan over medium heat, toast white peppercorns and coriander seeds until they begin to pop. Remove from heat and grind to a fine powder in a spice mill or coffee grinder. Mix the ground pepper and coriander with remaining spices, cocoa, and salt.

2. Trim the pork tenderloins of fat and silver skin. Rub with a generous amount of the cocoa-spice rub. Heat the olive oil in a large sauté pan over medium-high heat until hot but not smoking. Sear each tenderloin on all sides until it's a rich brown color, about 2 minutes on each side. Remove tenderloins from heat, place in the oven, and roast until an instant-read thermometer registers 155°F, about 12 to 15 minutes.

3. Let the tenderloins rest out of the oven for at least 10 minutes before carving.

NOTE FROM MICHAEL Extra cocoa-spice rub will keep in an airtight container for up to 3 months.

KITCHEN TIP If you don't want to clean out your coffee grinder, a mortar and pestle works just fine too.

COCOA IN SAVORY FOOD? IT SEEMS A LITTLE STRANGE, BUT COCOA ACTUALLY HAS A LONG HISTORY AS A SAVORY INGREDIENT, GOING BACK ALL THE WAY TO THE FIRST MILLENNIUM B.C. MICHAEL LOVES CALIFORNIA COCOA, BUT ANY GOOD UNSWEETENED COCOA, COMBINED WITH THE REST OF THE SPICE RUB, GIVES THE MEAT A RICH, DARK AROMATIC COMPLEXITY THAT MAKES THE WHOLE HOUSE SMELL GOOD.

"THESE RIBS ARE KILLER.
I could be a vegetarian if it wasn't for pork." —MICHAEL

Baby Back Ribs
with Espresso Barbecue Sauce

2 racks baby back ribs (about 4 to
    6 ribs per person)

    Gray salt and freshly ground
    black pepper

    Espresso Barbecue Sauce
    (see recipe, below)

Yield: 4 to 6 servings

ESPRESSO BARBECUE SAUCE

4 tablespoons extra-virgin olive oil

4 tablespoons mashed and minced
    garlic

1 cup cider vinegar

½ cup soy sauce

2 cups ketchup

2 cups honey

    Gray salt

2 demitasse cups espresso (or about
    ½ cup strong coffee or instant
    espresso)

    Freshly ground black pepper

Yield: 5 to 6 cups

1. Preheat the oven to 325°F. Cut each rack of ribs in half along the bone so they can be easily stacked. Lay them out on parchment paper for easy cleanup.

2. Sprinkle liberally with salt and black pepper on both sides and pat into the meat. (Make sure to over-season the ribs because part of the salt and pepper will inevitably come off in the pan.) On a cookie sheet lined with aluminum foil, shingle the ribs close together. Put in the oven, rotating the layers every 30 minutes, until they are tender and almost falling off the bone, about 2 hours.

3. Half an hour before serving, transfer ribs to a preheated grill on low heat (if using coals, make sure they have burnt down to the embers). Brush ribs with Espresso Barbecue Sauce and close grill. Grill the ribs, turning and brushing with sauce every 10 minutes, until the ribs are well glazed, about 30 minutes.

ESPRESSO BARBECUE SAUCE
In a sauté pan over medium-high heat, add the olive oil and heat. Add the garlic and sauté until it gets light brown, about 1 minute. Add cider vinegar, soy sauce, ketchup, and honey and stir well. Add a pinch of gray salt, then whisk in the coffee. Add freshly ground black pepper to taste. Bring to a simmer and cook for 10 minutes. Let cool and store in refrigerator for up to 2 weeks.

KITCHEN TIP A demitasse cup is a small cup used for serving espresso—usually 3 to 4 ounces.

KITCHEN TIP For mashed and minced garlic, crush each garlic clove with the flat side of your knife, then chop it finely.

"THESE SHRIMP MAY BE ANGRY, BUT YOU WILL LOVE THEM WITH THE REFRESHING CITRUS SALAD. Try cooking the shrimp ahead of time and serving them at room temperature for easy entertaining." —MICHAEL

Angry Shrimp with Citrus-Spinach Salad

FLOUR MIXTURE

1 cup all-purpose flour

1½ tablespoons Anaheim chile powder

1 tablespoon gray salt

1 teaspoon freshly ground black pepper

SALAD

2 blood oranges

2 tangelos

2 grapefruit

Gray salt and freshly ground black pepper

Extra-virgin olive oil

2 pounds (16- to 20-count shrimp), peeled but with the tail on (about 4 per person)

6 large cloves garlic, thinly sliced

2 serrano or jalapeño peppers, thinly sliced

1½ cups fresh basil leaves, stemmed and cleaned

1 tablespoon julienned orange zest

3 cups prewashed spinach, stems removed

Yield: 8 servings

1. For the flour mixture: Combine the ingredients and set aside in a container. This step can be done the day before.

2. For the salad: Peel and cut the citrus fruit into sections over a large serving plate, making sure to remove the pith. Reserve the fruit sections on the plate. Drain the juice from the plate into a bowl. Season liberally with gray salt and black pepper to taste. Whisk in olive oil to form a vinaigrette (it should be about 2 parts juice to 1 part oil). Season citrus sections with salt and black pepper to taste. Drizzle a little of the vinaigrette on them to marinate.

3. Preheat a sauté pan over high heat. Dredge the shrimp in the flour mixture. This will create a nice crust and allow them to stay crispy at room temperature. Add a few tablespoons olive oil to the pan and put in one layer of shrimp. You want them to brown, so don't toss or move them. Add a little more oil if the flour absorbs what is already in the pan. When golden brown, turn the shrimp over. Let them brown on the other side, toss, and turn out onto a cookie sheet.

4. Add about ¼ cup more olive oil to the hot sauté pan. Drain pan juices from the cookie sheet into the sauté pan. Add sliced garlic and cook, stirring often, until light brown. Add chiles and cook until soft. Add the basil and stand back—there's a lot of water in basil and it will pop. Let it get crispy, less than a minute. While this is happening, arrange shrimp over the marinating citrus. Add the orange zest to the basil/garlic/chile mixture in the sauté pan. Season with salt and black pepper to taste, then spoon basil/garlic/chile mixture over the shrimp.

5. Toss spinach with the citrus vinaigrette and mound on top of the shrimp.

KITCHEN TIP Blood oranges and tangelos look amazing in this salad, but they aren't always in season. Any type of orange or tangerine can be substituted.

SEGMENTING CITRUS

1. SLICE OFF THE TOP AND BOTTOM OF THE FRUIT.

2. STAND IT UP ON ONE FLAT END AND SLICE DOWN FOLLOWING THE CURVE OF THE FRUIT, REMOVING PEELS OF SKIN AND ALL WHITE PITH.

3. USE A PARING KNIFE TO CUT BETWEEN MEMBRANES, RELEASING ONE SEGMENT.

4. FREE THE SEGMENT AND MOVE TO THE NEXT ONE, TURNING EMPTY MEMBRANES LIKE LEAVES OF A BOOK.

Mango Dos Leches

6 large eggs, at room temperature

1 cup granulated sugar

⅛ teaspoon salt

1 cup all-purpose flour

1 14-ounce can sweetened condensed milk

2 cups whole milk, scalded

1¼ cups mango puree

1 teaspoon almond extract

1 teaspoon vanilla extract

1 mango, diced

2 tablespoons dark rum

2 to 3 tablespoons brown sugar

Yield: 8 servings

1. Preheat the oven to 350°F. Line a 9×11-inch baking pan with parchment paper. With an electric mixer, whip the eggs, sugar, and salt until tripled in volume. Fold in the flour. Pour the mixture into the prepared baking pan and bake until puffed and golden and a cake tester comes out clean, about 25 to 30 minutes. Set aside to cool.

2. Turn the cake out of the pan, remove the parchment paper, and return the cake to the pan. With a fork, poke holes all over the top of the cake.

3. Combine the condensed milk with the scalded milk, mango puree, almond and vanilla extracts and pour over the cake. Allow the cake to soak in the liquid for 2 hours.

4. Combine the mango, rum, and brown sugar, toss well, and marinate while the cake soaks. Serve the cake with the marinated mango.

KITCHEN TIP To scald milk, heat it in a heavy-bottomed pot over medium heat just until small bubbles begin to form around the edges—don't let it boil.

paula
DEEN

Our voice of Southern comfort food, Paula's got a school-of-hard-knocks background that inspires us all and a distinctly down-South style we can only call home cookin'.

Q+A
WITH PAULA DEEN

WHAT THREE INGREDIENTS CAN'T YOU LIVE WITHOUT?
Butter, mayo, and cream cheese.

WHAT'S YOUR FAVORITE THING TO COOK?
Southern food, of course!

HOW'D YOU LEARN TO COOK?
My grandmother and my Aunt Peggy taught me. My oldest food memory is being 3 years old and being spoon-fed vanilla flavoring by my Aunt Trina.

WHAT'S DIFFERENT ABOUT YOUR FOOD FROM WHEN YOU STARTED?
My original bag-lunch delivery business, the Bag Lady, was limited to what I could make in my own kitchen—with my restaurant, the Lady and Sons, the sky is the limit!

HOW ARE YOU ALWAYS IN SUCH A GOOD MOOD—WHAT'S YOUR SECRET?
I learned early in life that life is short and every new day is a gift from God.

WHAT'S COOL ABOUT BEING A CHEF?
I get instant gratification. People tell me what they think about my work right after eating it!

WHAT'S THE MOST IMPORTANT THING YOU LEARNED ABOUT FOOD?
I learned not to be afraid to experiment. Food brings people together no matter what.

Tomato Pie

4 tomatoes, peeled and sliced

Salt

10 fresh basil leaves, chopped

½ cup chopped green onions

Black pepper

1 9-inch prebaked deep-dish pie shell

1 cup grated mozzarella

1 cup grated Cheddar

1 cup mayonnaise

Yield: 6 servings

1. Preheat oven to 350°F. Place the tomatoes in a colander in the sink in a single layer. Sprinkle with salt and allow them to drain for 10 minutes.

2. Pat the tomatoes dry with paper towels. Layer the tomato slices, basil, and onions in the pie shell. Season with salt and black pepper to taste. Combine the grated cheeses and mayonnaise. Spread the mixture on top of the tomatoes and bake until the cheese is melted and the top is lightly browned, about 30 minutes. Cut into slices and serve warm.

KITCHEN TIP Salting and draining the tomatoes not only makes them taste better but also keeps your crust from getting soggy with tomato water. This dish is best in the summertime, when tomatoes are full of flavor.

STUFFING THE SHRIMP

1. PLACE THE SHRIMP "BELLY UP" (THAT'S THE CONCAVE SIDE) AND MAKE A SHALLOW CUT FROM TAIL TO HEAD; BE CAREFUL NOT TO CUT ALL THE WAY THROUGH. OPEN UP THE SHRIMP A BIT AND TOP WITH A SMALL MOUND OF FILLING, PRESSING LIGHTLY.

2. WRAP WITH BACON SO THE ENDS MEET ACROSS THE FILLING AND PUSH A TOOTHPICK THROUGH THE BACON, SHRIMP, AND FILLING TO CLOSE.

Lady & Sons Crab-Stuffed Shrimp

2 tablespoons butter

3 green onions, finely chopped

½ cup finely chopped green bell pepper

¼ teaspoon garlic powder

2 tablespoons heavy cream

1 tablespoon Dijon mustard

Dash cayenne pepper

½ cup saltine cracker crumbs

¼ cup mayonnaise

1 large egg

2 tablespoons fresh parsley, finely chopped

Juice of ½ lemon

1 pound crabmeat, picked over

1½ pounds jumbo shrimp (about 24 shrimp), peeled, deveined, tails on

12 slices bacon, halved crosswise

Steamed white rice, for serving (optional)

Basil Cream Sauce (see recipe, below)

Yield: 4 servings

BASIL CREAM SAUCE

2 tablespoons butter

1 tablespoon olive oil

1 teaspoon minced garlic

½ cup diced onions

¼ cup white wine

2 cups heavy cream

1 teaspoon chicken base

3 tablespoons Pesto (see recipe, below)

PESTO

2 cups fresh basil leaves

1 cup walnut pieces

1 cup grated Parmesan

1 teaspoon minced garlic

1 cup olive oil

Yield: about 1½ cups

1. Preheat the oven to 425°F. Melt butter in a skillet over medium heat and cook the green onions, green pepper, and garlic powder until the peppers are limp. Place in a bowl and add the cream, mustard, and cayenne pepper and mix well. Add cracker crumbs, mayonnaise, egg, parsley, and lemon juice; mix well. Gently fold in crabmeat. Form into small patties small enough to stuff into the shrimp; set aside.

2. Split shrimp down the belly to the tail, being careful not to cut through. Stuff each shrimp with crabmeat mixture. Wrap shrimp in bacon and secure with a toothpick. Place on a baking pan and cook in the oven until bacon is crisp and shrimp are pink, about 15 to 20 minutes.

3. To serve, arrange 6 shrimp on each plate on a bed of rice, if desired. Drizzle with Basil Cream Sauce.

BASIL CREAM SAUCE

Heat the butter and olive oil in a skillet over medium heat. Add garlic and onion and cook until lightly browned, about 5 minutes. Add the white wine and reduce by half. Add the heavy cream and chicken base and reduce by half again. Add the Pesto, bring to a simmer, and heat until slightly thickened, about 2 to 3 minutes.

PESTO

In a food processor, blend all the ingredients until a coarse paste is formed. Place in an airtight container and refrigerate until ready to use. See page 57 for tips on using leftover Pesto.

SUPPER'S ON

FOR PAULA, COOKIN'S ABOUT FAMILY AS MUCH AS IT'S ABOUT FOOD.
Her shows are packed full of crowd-pleasers for any group, whether it's a picnic lunch, a romantic dinner for two, or a tailgate with friends. And you can always bet dessert'll be a part of it. Paula's sweet tooth is almost as legendary as her desserts are.

Seared Diver Scallops with Bacon & Whole-Grain Mustard Rub & Crème Fraîche-Mashed Potatoes

CRÈME FRAÎCHE

- 1 cup plus 2 tablespoons heavy cream
- ¾ cup sour cream

POTATOES

- 2 pounds small red potatoes
- 1 teaspoon salt
- 1 8-ounce package cream cheese, at room temperature
- 2 teaspoons roasted garlic (see Kitchen Tip, right)
- 1 teaspoon Paula's House Seasoning (see recipe, right)
- 1 teaspoon seasoned salt
- 4 tablespoons unsalted butter, plus more for greasing
- ¼ cup sliced green onions
- 1 tablespoon chopped chives

SCALLOPS

- 4 slices smoked bacon, quartered
- 3 tablespoons whole-grain mustard
- 16 scallops, U-10 dry pack preferred (see Note from the Kitchens, right)

  Vegetable oil

Yield: 4 servings

1. Prepare the crème fraîche ahead of time: Combine 1 cup of the heavy cream with ½ cup of the sour cream, cover with plastic wrap, and let stand at room temperature for 12 to 24 hours. Stir well and refrigerate for 4 hours.

2. Preheat the oven to 350°F. Make the Crème Fraiche-Mashed Potatoes: Place the potatoes in a pot, cover with cold water, and add the salt. Bring to a boil, cook potatoes for 20 to 25 minutes, and drain. With an electric mixer, beat the potatoes with the cream cheese, the remaining ¼ cup sour cream, remaining 2 tablespoons heavy cream, garlic, House Seasoning, and seasoned salt. Stir in the butter and onions. Place the mashed potatoes in a lightly greased 2-quart round casserole, spoon the crème fraiche on top, and sprinkle with chives. Bake until potatoes are hot, 20 to 30 minutes.

3. For the scallops: In a food processor, puree bacon and mustard to a smooth paste consistency. Coat the scallops with the puree. Chill for 30 minutes.

4. Heat a couple tablespoons oil in an ovenproof skillet over medium-high heat and sear the scallops on both sides. Some of the topping will come off in the pan. Remove the scallops to a baking sheet

and spoon any topping from the pan on top of them. Place in the oven and bake for 8 to 10 minutes. Remove the scallops and allow them to rest for 2 minutes before serving. Place some Crème Fraiche-Mashed Potatoes on each of 4 plates and top each with 4 scallops.

KITCHEN TIP To save time, you can buy prepared crème fraîche at the grocery store.

KITCHEN TIP To roast garlic, preheat the oven to 350°F. Cut the top off a head of garlic and rub it with a tablespoon of oil. Wrap it in aluminum foil and bake for about 20 to 30 minutes, then take it out and unwrap it slightly. When it's cool enough to handle, squeeze the cloves out of the skin.

PAULA'S HOUSE SEASONING

- 1 cup salt
- ¼ cup black pepper
- ¼ cup garlic powder

Yield: 1½ cups

Mix ingredients together and store in an airtight container for up to 6 months.

NOTE
FROM THE
KITCHENS

THIS TERRINE
MAKES THE
PERFECT LIGHT
LUNCH FOR
ENTERTAINING;
IT'S A PRETTY,
SUMMERY
CENTERPIECE
THAT TASTES
BEST MADE
IN ADVANCE.

Mosaic Chicken Terrine

2 large eggs

½ teaspoon lemon pepper

½ teaspoon seasoned salt

4 6- to 8-ounce skinless, boneless
   chicken breast halves

2 cups grated Parmesan

2 14.5-ounce cans artichoke hearts,
   drained and cut in half

6 slices mortadella, salami, or
   prosciutto

12 to 16 fresh basil leaves or 8 spinach
   leaves

1 cup mayonnaise

½ clove garlic, minced

1 teaspoon fresh dill or
   ½ teaspoon dried

1 teaspoon chopped parsley leaves

   Buttery crackers, for serving

Yield: 12 to 14 servings

1. Preheat the oven to 350°F. Line a
9×4-inch loaf pan with parchment paper.
In a small bowl, beat the eggs and add the
lemon pepper and salt. Dip the chicken
breasts into the egg mixture and then in
the Parmesan. Dip the artichoke hearts
into the egg and then the Parmesan.

2. Layer two chicken breasts on the
bottom of the pan. Cover the chicken with
3 slices mortadella, salami, or prosciutto.
Cover the sausage with half of the
artichoke hearts, then with basil leaves,
using all of the leaves. Repeat the layers of
chicken, sausage, and artichoke hearts.
Cover with parchment paper or foil. Place
a heavy weight on top of the terrine while
baking to compress the layers. Place the
loaf pan into a larger pan and pour hot
water into the larger pan to come half way
up the sides of the loaf pan. Bake for
1 hour 20 minutes.

3. Let the terrine cool completely,
then refrigerate it for several hours
or overnight.

4. In a bowl, combine the mayonnaise,
garlic, dill, and parsley. Chill the
mayonnaise mixture.

5. To serve, carefully turn the terrine out of
the pan onto a platter and slice into
¾-inch slices. Serve with chilled
mayonnaise mixture and buttery crackers.

KITCHEN TIP A brick wrapped in a few
layers of aluminum foil makes a good
ovenproof weight to compress this terrine
while baking.

155

Bubba's Country-Fried Steak & Gravy

1½ cups plus ¼ cup all-purpose flour

½ teaspoon freshly ground black pepper

8 4-ounce tenderized beef round steaks (have butcher run them through cubing machine)

1¼ teaspoons Paula's House Seasoning (see page 153)

1 teaspoon seasoned salt

¾ cup vegetable oil

1½ teaspoons salt

4 cups hot water

½ teaspoon monosodium glutamate (recommended: Ac'cent™) (optional)

1 bunch green onions or 1 medium yellow onion, sliced

Yield: 4 servings

1. Combine 1½ cups flour and ¼ teaspoon black pepper in a small bowl. Sprinkle one side of the meat with the House Seasoning and the other side with the seasoned salt and then dredge the meat in the flour mixture.

2. Heat ½ cup oil in a large heavy skillet over medium-high heat. Fry the steaks in batches, adding more oil as needed, until browned, about 5 to 6 minutes per side. Remove each steak to a paper towel-lined plate to drain.

3. Make the gravy by adding the remaining ¼ cup flour to the pan drippings, scraping the bottom with a wooden spoon. Stir in the remaining ¼ teaspoon black pepper and the salt. Reduce the heat to medium and cook, stirring frequently, until the flour is medium brown and the mixture is bubbly. Slowly add the water and the monosodium glutamate, if using, stirring constantly. Return the steaks to the skillet and bring to a boil over medium-high heat. Reduce the heat to low and place the onions on top of the steaks. Cover the pan and let simmer for 30 minutes. Serve.

KITCHEN TIP Beef round steaks come from the upper leg of the cow, with lean, dense meat that definitely benefits from a quick run through the butcher's cubing machine—or a pounding with the rough side of your meat mallet.

FOOD REALLY IS PAULA'S FAMILY BUSINESS. Her sons have been helping her out since the very beginning, and Bubba, her little brother, has his own restaurant a stone's throw away from Paula's. When Bubba was doing a lot of hunting, he called Paula up to ask her what he should do with all the meat he had. Paula taught him how to make this steak and named it after him for good measure.

Stuffed Pork Chops with Grits

CUTTING A POCKET

WITH A SMALL, SHARP KNIFE, MAKE A 2- TO 2½-INCH-LONG CUT ALL THE WAY TO THE BONE. KEEPING THE BLADE PARALLEL TO YOUR WORK SURFACE, WORK THE BLADE BACK AND FORTH A BIT TO ENLARGE THE INSIDE POCKET.

PORK

4 1½- to 2-inch-thick pork chops, bone in, split to bone

1 pound bulk sausage, split into 4 equal portions

   Paula's House Seasoning, as needed (see page 153)

   Olive oil, for brushing

GRITS

2 cups water

1¼ cups milk

1 teaspoon salt

1 cup quick-cooking grits (not instant)

½ cup butter (1 stick)

Yield: 4 servings

1. For the pork: Preheat the grill. Meanwhile, stuff each pork chop with the sausage and rub the chops liberally with House Seasoning to taste. Secure each pork chop with a wooden skewer or toothpicks (Remember to remove before serving!).

2. Brush some oil on the grill grate to prevent sticking. Grill the chops over direct heat until nicely browned, about 5 to 6 minutes on each side. Move the chops to indirect heat. Cover the grill and cook, until an instant-read thermometer reads 160°F, about 20 to 30 minutes.

3. For the grits: In a small pot, bring the water, milk, and salt to a boil. Slowly stir the grits into the boiling mixture. Stir continuously and thoroughly, until the grits are well mixed. Lower the temperature and simmer for 3 to 4 minutes, stirring occasionally. Add more water, if necessary. Grits are done when they have the consistency of smooth cream of wheat. Stir in half the butter and serve with remaining butter divided equally on top of each portion.

Piggy Pudding

16 links pork breakfast sausages

Butter, for greasing

4 to 5 tart apples, peeled, cored, and cut into ¼-inch slices

1 7.5-ounce package yellow cornbread mix, batter prepared according to package directions

1 cup maple syrup, for serving

Fresh sage, for garnish

Yield: 4 servings

1. Preheat the oven to 450°F. Cook the sausages in a skillet over medium heat until done, piercing with a fork to let out the fat. Drain and arrange them in a greased 9-inch square baking dish. Layer the sliced apples on top. Pour the cornbread batter over all and bake until the cornbread is done, about 30 minutes. Serve with warm maple syrup and garnish with sage.

KITCHEN TIP This is a great make-ahead brunch dish. You can either prepare it the night before, refrigerate overnight, and pop it in the oven in the morning, or bake it at night and reheat it in the morning.

KITCHEN TIP Use tart apples—such as Granny Smiths—in this pudding; they make a great contrast to the cornbread and sausage.

NOTE
FROM THE
KITCHENS

THIS IS A GREAT
PANTRY-ITEM
CASSEROLE
(WE'D BET YOU
HAVE MOST
OF THESE
INGREDIENTS IN
YOUR PANTRY
RIGHT NOW) AND
AS COMFORTING
AS SOUTHERN
COMFORT FOOD
GETS.

Corn Casserole

1   15.25-ounce can whole kernel corn,
    drained

1   14.75-ounce can cream-style corn

1   8-ounce package corn muffin mix
    (recommended: Jiffy™)

1   cup sour cream

½   cup butter, melted, plus more for
    greasing

1   to 1½ cups shredded Cheddar cheese

Yield: 6 to 8 servings

1. Preheat the oven to 350°F. In a large bowl, stir together both cans of corn, corn muffin mix, sour cream, and melted butter. Pour into a greased 1½-quart casserole dish. Bake until golden brown, about 45 to 50 minutes.

2. Remove from the oven and top with the cheese. Return the casserole to the oven for 5 to 10 minutes, or until the cheese is melted. Let stand for at least 5 minutes and then serve warm.

KITCHEN TIP Letting this casserole sit for a few minutes makes it easier to serve. If you'd rather dive in right away, well, we don't blame you.

PAULA'S FOOD IS AS DOWN-HOME AS IT GETS. It's the food her grandmothers used to make, and it's the food their grandmothers made too—classic, homegrown, and not afraid of flavor.

Tennessee Banana-Black Walnut Cake with Caramel Frosting

CAKE

- 2 cups all-purpose flour, plus more for pan
- ½ teaspoon baking soda
- ½ cup solid vegetable shortening
- 1½ cups granulated sugar
- 2 large eggs
- 2 ripe bananas, mashed
- ¼ cup buttermilk
- 1 teaspoon pure vanilla extract
- 1 cup chopped black walnuts (see Note and Kitchen Tip, right)

FROSTING

- ½ cup butter, softened
- 1 cup packed dark brown sugar
- ⅓ cup heavy cream, plus more as necessary
- 1 tablespoon pure vanilla extract
- 1 16-ounce box confectioners' sugar
- 2 cups finely chopped black walnuts, for garnish (optional)

Yield: 12 servings

1. Preheat the oven to 350°F. Grease and flour two 9-inch round cake pans. For the cake: In a medium bowl, stir together the flour and baking soda; set aside.

2. In a large bowl, using an electric mixer, cream together the shortening and sugar, about 2 to 3 minutes. Add the eggs one at a time, mixing well after each addition. Mix in the mashed bananas, buttermilk, and vanilla. Add the flour mixture; mix until just combined. Stir in the black walnuts.

3. Pour into the prepared pans and bake until a toothpick inserted in the centers of the cakes comes out clean, about 30 to 35 minutes. Cool in the pans on a cooling rack for 10 minutes. Remove the cakes from the pans and cool completely.

4. For the frosting: Melt the butter in a small saucepan. Add the brown sugar and cream. Cook over medium-low heat until the sugar is dissolved, about 2 minutes.

Remove from the heat and add vanilla. Transfer to a large bowl. Using a handheld electric mixer, beat in the confectioners' sugar a little at a time until smooth. If frosting is too thick, add 1 tablespoon heavy cream at a time until the consistency is right.

5. Sandwich the two layers together with the frosting. Frost the outside of the cake. Press the chopped black walnuts on the sides of the cake, if desired.

NOTE FROM PAULA DO NOT substitute English walnuts for black walnuts.

KITCHEN TIP The two most common types of walnuts are black walnuts and English walnuts. Black walnuts are stronger tasting than English walnuts—they're rich and smoky with a hint of wine. Look for them online or by mail order if you can't find them near you.

Is It Really Better Than Sex? Cake

1   18.25-ounce box yellow cake mix, plus ingredients to prepare

1   20-ounce can crushed pineapple

1⅓   cups granulated sugar

1   3.4-ounce box French vanilla pudding, plus ingredients to prepare

1½   cups heavy cream

1   cup flaked, sweetened coconut, toasted

Yield: 16 to 20 servings

1. Preheat the oven to 350°F. Prepare the yellow cake mix as directed using a greased 13×9×2-inch pan and bake for 30 to 35 minutes.

2. While the cake is baking, combine the pineapple and 1 cup sugar in a saucepan and bring it to a boil over medium heat, stirring constantly. Remove from the heat and allow it to cool slightly. Remove the cake from the oven and, using a fork, pierce holes into the cake. Pour the pineapple mixture over the hot cake and set aside.

3. Prepare the pudding according to package directions. Spread the pudding over the cake and refrigerate until it is thoroughly chilled. Whip the heavy cream and remaining sugar until stiff. Cover the top of cake with whipped cream and sprinkle the toasted coconut on top.

KITCHEN TIP Make sure to buy sweetened flaked coconut for this cake. Toast coconut on a baking sheet lined with parchment or waxed paper in a 350°F oven for 10 to 15 minutes or until golden brown and start checking after 8 minutes and every 2 minutes thereafter, stirring occasionally.

DON'T EVER EXPECT PAULA TO BE ON TIME. Wherever she goes, people stop her to tell her their stories, and no matter how busy she is or where she has to be, Paula's always got time to listen. Paula can make a total stranger feel like family, just by saying that magic word "y'all."

rachael RAY

Whether she's zipping around the kitchen or scouting out eats on the road, Rachael's always on the lookout for food and fun.

Q+A WITH
RACHAEL RAY

DO YOU REALLY COOK 30-MINUTE MEALS AT HOME?
Yes, but sometimes a glass of wine or two turns it into a 45-minute meal.

WHAT'S YOUR FAVORITE ROAD FOOD BETWEEN NEW YORK CITY AND HOME IN ALBANY?
Turkey jerky in pouches or Sbarro's® stuffed pizza with broccoli and spinach and lots of red pepper flakes on top.

WHERE DO YOU GET ALL YOUR ENERGY?
Starbucks.® Black coffee with a little ground cinnamon on top.

WHAT'S THE BEST MEAL YOU EVER HAD?
The last meal my mom made me—until I eat the next meal she'll make for me.

HOW HAS FAME CHANGED YOUR LIFE?
Huh? I work as hard as ever. My family treats me the same—they may even pick on me more. And people do come up to me to say they love the food on the show, but no one treats me like a celebrity; they treat me like a friend or relative. I guess all that's changed are my shoes (they are much cuter these days) and I get more hugs.

USING
COMPLETE
(THAT IS, JUST-
ADD-WATER)
PANCAKE MIX
HERE IS
BRILLIANT.
WHAT'S IN
THE MIX?
ESSENTIALLY,
EGGS, MILK,
AND FLOUR—
EVERYTHING
YOU NEED FOR
BREADING,
IN ONE
HANDY BOX.

Buffalo Popcorn Chicken Bites

Vegetable oil, for frying

2½ cups complete pancake mix, any brand

1¼ cups water

8 teaspoons hot sauce

1¼ pounds chicken tenders or chicken breast, cut into small bite-size pieces

Salt

2 scallions, finely chopped

1 teaspoon coarse black pepper, ⅓ palm-full

1 cup store-bought, good-quality refrigerated blue cheese dressing (recommended: Marie's™)

Cut celery sticks, store-bought

Yield: 4 servings

1. In a deep-sided skillet, heat 1½ inches of vegetable oil over medium heat. If you wish to test the oil, add a 1-inch cube of bread to the hot oil. If it turns deep golden brown in 40 seconds, the oil is ready.

2. While the oil is heating, make the batter. In a wide mixing bowl, combine 2 cups of the pancake mix, 1¼ cups water, and about 6 teaspoons hot sauce. (Use a regular teaspoon you would stir coffee with—that's what I did. I don't, technically, have a set of actual measuring spoons.)

3. Place the remaining ½ cup pancake mix in another wide mixing bowl. Arrange the batter and the bowl of dry pancake mix near the cooktop and the heating oil. Line a plate with a few sheets of paper towels and keep within reach.

4. Once the oil is heated and ready, toss the chicken pieces in the remaining 2 teaspoons hot sauce, then toss them in the dry pancake mix, coating evenly and shaking off any excess. The plain dry pancake mix will help the batter stick to the chicken pieces. Add some of chicken to the batter. You are going to want to work in three to four batches coating and frying. Using a fork, toss the bites in the batter. Remove the first batch from the batter, shaking off the excess batter as you carefully add them to the hot oil. Fry for 2 minutes on the first side, or until it's a deep golden brown. Flip and continue to fry for another 2 minutes, or until deep golden brown all over. Remove from the oil and drain on the paper towel-lined plate; season with salt to taste. Repeat until all the popcorn chicken bites are fried.

5. Stir the scallions and black pepper into the blue cheese dressing. Serve the chicken bites immediately with the dipping sauce. Garnish the platter with celery sticks.

KITCHEN TIP Get the celery sticks from your grocery store's salad bar to spare yourself the chopping.

WE DON'T KNOW WHERE SHE GETS HER ENERGY OR HER IDEAS, BUT IT ALL JUST KEEPS COMING. She's incredibly hardworking, generating recipes left and right, and though she's totally focused on the clock when she's working, she's still full of laughs. Rachael's always described herself as "beer out of the bottle," so it should come as no surprise that the wrap party after each round of taping is bowling. The good, the bad, and the downright embarrassing of bowling abilities are divided into teams with names like the "ray-ders" and the "40-dollar-niners."

THOUGH OUR
TIP CALLS THIS
AN AFTER-
SCHOOL SNACK,
IT'S NOT JUST
FOR KIDS. OUR
KITCHENS STAFF
GOBBLED THESE
NACHOS DOWN
IN ABOUT FIVE
MINUTES.

Chili Dog Nachos

1 tablespoon vegetable oil, 1 turn of the pan (see page 174)

1 pound ground sirloin

  Salt and freshly ground black pepper

2 hot dogs, sliced into ½-inch pieces

1 small onion, chopped

2 teaspoons Worcestershire sauce

2 tablespoons chili powder

2 teaspoons ground cumin

1 8-ounce can tomato sauce

1 sack yellow corn tortilla chips

1 10-ounce bag shredded yellow Cheddar

  Sour cream, for garnish

  Salsa, for garnish

2 chopped scallions, for garnish

Yield: 4 servings

1. Heat a medium skillet over high heat. Add the oil, then the beef and begin to brown and crumble with a wooden spoon, about 2 minutes. Season with salt and black pepper to taste, then add the sliced hot dogs and continue browning, another 3 minutes. Add onion, Worcestershire, chili powder, and cumin. Cook another 3 to 5 minutes. Add tomato sauce and simmer 5 minutes more.

2. Preheat the broiler. Arrange the corn chips on a platter or in a casserole dish. Top the chips with the cooked chili dog topping. Cover the chili dog sauce with cheese. Melt the cheese under the hot broiler 2 minutes, until melted and bubbly. Garnish with sour cream, salsa, and chopped scallions.

KITCHEN TIP Make the chili dog topping the day before so when you're ready to serve it, all you have to do is throw it together and cook. Or make a big batch and freeze in small containers for an after-school snack anytime.

Shrimp Dean Martinis

1½ pounds super-size jumbo shrimp, peeled, deveined, tail on, or buy them precooked

2 ribs celery, finely chopped

2 rounded spoonfuls prepared horseradish

Juice of ½ lemon

1 teaspoon hot sauce

½ cup chili sauce

½ cup ketchup

½ cup vegetable juice (recommended: V8™)

Salt and freshly ground black pepper

1 lemon, wedged

Yield: 4 servings

1. If you bought raw shrimp, steam them until pink, about 5 minutes, then run them under cold water to stop the cooking. Chill until ready to serve.

2. Mix the celery, horseradish, lemon juice, hot sauce, chili sauce, ketchup, and vegetable juice together and season with salt and black pepper to taste. Pour the sauce into four martini glasses and surround the rims with chilled shrimp. Serve lemon wedges on cocktail forks alongside the glasses.

KITCHEN TIP Not only is this dish fast and easy, it's elegant too. To really make it special, decorate the glasses with a swirl of lemon peel or frost them in the freezer beforehand. And keep a bowl nearby for the tails so your guests don't feel like they have to eat them.

Grilled Mushroom Salad Subs

NOTE FROM THE KITCHENS

SHERRY VINEGAR IS MADE JUST LIKE SHERRY WINE IS AND AGED IN WOODEN BARRELS FOR AT LEAST TWO YEARS AND SOMETIMES UP TO 30 YEARS. JUST A SPLASH OF IT ADDS COMPLEXITY TO A DISH.

2   baguettes, halved lengthwise, split, and some of the soft insides removed

¼   cup sherry vinegar

2   rounded tablespoons spicy mustard

1   tablespoon Worcestershire sauce

½   cup EVOO (extra-virgin olive oil)—eyeball it

6   cloves garlic, finely chopped

8   portobello mushrooms, stems removed and wiped clean with damp cloth

    Coarse salt and coarse black pepper

¼   cup parsley, a generous handful, finely chopped

6   cups deveined triple-washed spinach, coarsely chopped

¾   pound Manchego cheese (common sharp Spanish table cheese, available in the specialty cheese case), thinly sliced; sharp Cheddar may be substituted

4   piquillo peppers, pimientos, or roasted red peppers, patted dry and cut into strips

Yield: 4 servings

1. Preheat a grill pan to medium-high heat or prepare an outdoor grill. Preheat the oven to 300°F. Place the hollowed bread in oven to crisp for 5 minutes.

2. In a small bowl, whisk together the sherry vinegar, mustard, Worcestershire sauce, EVOO, and garlic. Put the mushrooms into a shallow dish and pour the marinade over the caps. Turn the caps in the marinade and season with salt and black pepper to taste. Let stand 10 minutes.

3. Grill the mushrooms 4 to 5 minutes on each side and remove to a cutting board a few at a time. Thinly slice the mushrooms and transfer them back to the dish you marinated them in, adding the parsley and spinach as you go, layering hot mushrooms with the herb and greens. Once all the hot sliced mushrooms are mixed with the spinach, the greens will wilt a bit. Toss the salad and adjust the salt and black pepper to taste.

4. Pile the salad into the crispy bread and top with Manchego and red peppers of choice, then set bread tops in place and serve immediately.

KITCHEN TIP Piquillo peppers are tangy, spicy-sweet Spanish peppers that come already roasted in a jar. They're delicious.

RACHAEL LIBERATES COOKING FROM MEASUREMENTS, ONE "PALM-FULL" AT A TIME. See that spice in her hand? That's a palm-full, or about a tablespoon. She doesn't own proper measuring spoons, and oil's always calibrated in "turns around the pan." How much "EVOO" (extra-virgin olive oil) is one turn around the pan? It's a tablespoon—or about as much as you get when you drizzle a circle in the pan. Rachael puts the home cook in control. You want less oil? Love spices, but have small palms? It's your dinner; you get to choose.

Cod with Burst Grape Tomatoes, Parsley-Mint Pesto Broth & Roast Fingerling Potato Crisps with Herbs

POTATO CRISPS

4 large fingerling potatoes

2 tablespoons extra-virgin olive oil

Salt and freshly ground black pepper

2 tablespoons chopped fresh tarragon leaves or 2 teaspoons dried

2 tablespoons chopped fresh chives or 1 teaspoon dried

2 tablespoons chopped fresh flat-leaf parsley

FISH

1 1¾- to 2-pound cod fillet, cut into 4 portions (buy thick center cuts for this dish rather than pieces that include thin ends)

Juice of ½ lemon

Salt

Extra-virgin olive oil, for drizzling

½ pint whole grape tomatoes

BROTH

½ cup flat-leaf parsley, a couple of handfuls

¼ cup mint leaves, a handful

1 cup chicken broth

1 small shallot or ½ large shallot, coarsely chopped

Salt and freshly ground black pepper

4 tablespoons light olive oil or vegetable oil, for frying

4 cloves garlic, peeled and very thinly sliced

Yield: 4 servings

1. Preheat the oven to 400°F. Preheat an oven-safe skillet over high heat or wrap rubber handles in double layers of foil to protect them in the oven. Prick the potatoes 3 or 4 times each with a fork and cook them in the microwave on high for 5 minutes. When the potatoes are cool enough to handle, slice them into ¼-inch pieces lengthwise. Coat them with the olive oil and salt and black pepper to taste. Arrange them on a cookie sheet in a single layer and roast for 20 minutes. Do not move them or turn them as they cook.

2. Pat the cod dry, squeeze a little lemon juice over it, and season it with salt to taste. Drizzle the fish with olive oil. Add the cod, seasoned sides down, to the very hot skillet and sear for 2 minutes. Drizzle the tomatoes with olive oil, season them with salt and black pepper to taste, and add them to the fish. Sear the tomatoes for 1 minute, then transfer the pan to the oven and roast the fish and tomatoes until the fish is firm and opaque and the tomatoes have all burst, about 8 minutes.

3. Put the parsley, mint, chicken broth, and shallot in a food processor or blender and puree. Transfer to a small sauce pot and bring to a simmer. Season the broth with salt and black pepper to taste.

4. Heat the light frying oil in a small skillet over medium heat. Add the sliced garlic to the hot oil and let it fry until crisp and golden brown, 3 to 5 minutes. Drain the garlic chips on a paper towel and reserve.

5. When the potatoes are very brown and crisp on the bottom side and tender on the top side, remove them from the oven. Coat them liberally with the fresh chopped herbs.

6. Pour warm parsley-mint broth onto each dinner plate. Remove the fish from the oven. Place the fish in the pools of parsley-mint broth. Arrange the potato slices and tomatoes decoratively around the fish. Top the dish off with a scattering of garlic crisps and serve.

KITCHEN TIP Fingerling potatoes are small, thin-skinned, and finger-shaped (that's where the name comes from), with yellow, tender, buttery insides and thin skin that doesn't need peeling.

Cream of Mushroom Egg Noodle Fake-Bake, Hold the Canned Soup

MUSHROOM SAUCE

- 1 tablespoon EVOO (extra-virgin olive oil), 1 turn of the pan (see page 174)
- 2 tablespoons unsalted butter
- 12 button mushrooms, brushed off with damp towel and chopped
- 2 tablespoons all-purpose flour
- 1 cup chicken broth
- 1 cup whole milk or heavy cream
- ⅛ teaspoon ground nutmeg (preferably freshly grated)

  Salt and freshly ground black pepper

MUSHROOM SAUTÉ

- 2 tablespoons EVOO (extra-virgin olive oil) (see page 174)
- 1 shallot, thinly sliced
- 2 portobello mushroom caps, halved and thinly sliced
- ½ pound fresh mixed wild mushrooms, shiitakes, oyster, woodear, your pick, stems trimmed and caps thinly sliced
- 1 tablespoon fresh thyme, from 4 sprigs, finely chopped

  Salt and freshly ground black pepper

- ⅓ cup dry white wine—eyeball it—or more broth

CASSEROLE

- 1 pound extra-wide egg noodles

  Softened butter

- ¾ pound Gruyère or Swiss Emmentaler cheese, shredded
- 3 tablespoons chives (12 to 15 blades), chopped

Yield: 4 servings

1. Bring a large pot of water to a boil for the egg noodles. For the mushroom sauce: Heat a medium sauce pot over medium heat. Add EVOO (1 turn of the pan, about a tablespoon), then add butter. When the butter melts, add the chopped button mushrooms and cook until just tender, about 5 minutes. Sprinkle with the flour and cook 1 minute. Whisk in the chicken broth and bring to a bubble, then stir in milk or cream. Reduce the heat to low and gently simmer. Season sauce with nutmeg and salt and black pepper to taste.

2. For the mushroom sauté: Heat a nonstick skillet over medium-high heat. Add the EVOO (2 turns of the pan, about 2 tablespoons), then add the shallot and mushrooms. Cook the mushrooms until tender, about 8 minutes. Season with thyme and salt and black pepper to taste. Deglaze the pan with ⅓ cup dry white wine or a little broth. Reduce the heat to medium-low and let the liquid cook off.

3. Preheat the broiler to high. While the mushrooms cook, drop the egg noodles into the boiling water, add some salt, and cook the noodles to al dente so they still have a bite to them. Drain the noodles and return them to the hot pot. Add the mushroom sauce to the pot and toss noodles to coat in sauce.

4. To assemble casserole: Lightly grease a casserole dish with softened butter, then transfer the cream of mushroom noodles to the dish. Top with the mushroom sauté and the shredded cheese. Put the casserole under the broiler and melt the cheese until it bubbles and is brown at the edges. Garnish with chives.

KITCHEN TIP Emmentaler is what you think of when you think of Swiss cheese. It's got big holes, it's sweet and fruity, and it's made with part-skim milk, so it's lower fat than most cheeses, but it's all flavor. Gruyère is nuttier tasting, softer, and creamier than Emmentaler, and though the combination of both is classic, it never gets old.

QUICK!

ON SET, RACHAEL'S JUGGLING FOOD FROM THE CABINET TO THE COUNTERTOP STRAIGHT TO THE PAN—AND IT REALLY DOES ALL HAPPEN IN 30 MINUTES OR LESS. She streamlines the whole process of cooking, and between her countertop garbage bowl (for fewer trips to the trash can) to the cutting board next to the pan (for rapid chop-and-drop), she's skimming minutes off dinner every night.

"BACON, LEEK, TOMATO? YEAH!
It's like a BLT, but better." —RACHAEL

Marinated Grilled Flank Steak with BLT-Smashed Potatoes

3 cloves garlic, finely chopped

1 tablespoon grill seasoning blend (recommended: Montreal Steak Seasoning™)

1 teaspoon smoked paprika, ground chipotle chile powder, or ground cumin

2 teaspoons hot sauce—eyeball it

1 tablespoon Worcestershire sauce

2 tablespoons red wine vinegar, 2 splashes

⅓ cup extra-virgin olive oil, plus additional for drizzling

2 pounds flank steak

2½ pounds small, red skin new potatoes

1 leek, trimmed of tough top

4 slices thick-cut smoky bacon (recommended: applewood-smoked bacon), chopped

1¾ cup chicken broth or stock, heated

1 vine-ripe tomato, seeded and chopped

Salt and freshly ground black pepper

1 cup sour cream, to pass at table

Yield: 4 servings

1. Mix the garlic, steak seasoning, smoked paprika, chipotle powder, or cumin, hot sauce, Worcestershire sauce, and vinegar. Whisk in the ⅓ cup oil. Place the meat in a shallow dish and coat it evenly in the marinade. Let stand 15 minutes.

2. Cut larger potatoes in half, leaving very small potatoes whole. Place the potatoes in a pot and cover with water. Bring to a boil and cook potatoes 12 to 15 minutes, until tender.

3. Heat a grill pan or outdoor grill to high heat. Cut the leek in half lengthwise and chop it into ½-inch pieces. Put leeks in a big bowl of water and release all the dirt from them with a good swish, separating all the layers. Lift the leeks out and drain them in a colander.

4. Grill flank steak 6 to 7 minutes on each side.

5. Put a drizzle of extra-virgin olive oil into a hot nonstick skillet over medium-high heat. Cook the bacon 3 to 5 minutes, until it begins to crisp and has rendered most of its fat. Add the leeks to the skillet and cook 3 to 5 minutes more, until the leeks are tender.

6. Drain the potatoes and return them to the hot pot. Smash the potatoes with the chicken broth. Add the BLT: bacon, leeks, and tomato to the potatoes and continue to smash. Season the potatoes with salt and black pepper to taste. Remove the steak from the grill and let the juices redistribute before slicing, about 10 minutes. Thinly slice the meat on an angle, cutting the meat against the grain. Top BLT potatoes with a dollop of sour cream and serve with flank steak.

KITCHEN TIP Flank steak is a boneless, super-flavorful cut that's best cooked no more than medium-rare. Slicing it against the grain makes it a little less chewy.

Make-Your-Own-Tacos Bar

CHIPOTLE TURKEY FILLING

1 tablespoon EVOO (extra-virgin olive oil), 1 turn of the pan (see page 174)

1⅓ pounds ground turkey breast, the average weight of 1 package

1 small onion, chopped

2 cloves garlic, chopped

2 chipotles in adobo sauce, chopped

1 rounded tablespoon chili powder, a rounded palm-full (see page 174)

1 cup tomato sauce

½ cup water

Salt

PORK & BELL PEPPER FILLING

1 tablespoon EVOO (extra-virgin olive oil), 1 turn of the pan (see page 174)

1⅓ pounds ground pork

½ red bell pepper, chopped

½ yellow bell pepper, chopped

1 small green bell pepper, chopped

1 tablespoon ground cumin—a palm-full

Several drops cayenne pepper sauce

½ teaspoon allspice

Salt and freshly ground black pepper

½ cup water

10 jumbo taco shells, warmed to package directions

TOPPINGS

1½ cups shredded Cheddar or smoked Cheddar, about ½ pound

1½ cups shredded Monterey pepper Jack, about ½ pound

Shredded romaine lettuce, 2 hearts

6 scallions, chopped

Diced red plum tomatoes

Yellow Pico De Gallo (see recipe, below)

Taco sauce, any brand

YELLOW PICO DE GALLO

3 yellow vine ripe tomatoes, seeded and diced

2 small jalapeño peppers, seeded and chopped

1 small white onion, chopped

3 tablespoons chopped fresh cilantro

Coarse salt

Yield: 10 tacos

1. Make Chipotle Turkey Filling: In a medium skillet preheated over medium-high heat, add the oil and turkey meat. Brown the meat for 2 or 3 minutes, breaking up any lumps, then add the onions and garlic. Cook for another 3 to 5 minutes. Stir in the chipotles in adobo, chili powder, and tomato sauce. Add water and season the filling with salt to taste. Reduce the heat to medium-low and simmer 10 to 15 minutes or until ready to serve.

2. Make Pork & Bell Pepper Filling: In a medium skillet preheated over medium-high heat add the oil and pork. Brown the meat for 2 or 3 minutes, breaking up any lumps. Strain off any excess oil. Add the peppers, cumin, cayenne sauce to taste, allspice, and salt and black pepper to taste and cook for another 5 minutes. Add water and reduce the heat to medium-low to keep the filling warm.

3. To assemble the bar, arrange the taco shells next to the stovetop. Serve the fillings from the skillets they were cooked in. Place toppings in small dishes on the opposite side of the stove top. Red beans and rice or store-bought refried beans make a great side dish.

YELLOW PICO DE GALLO
Combine all Pico de Gallo ingredients in a small bowl and serve.

KITCHEN TIP No time to make salsa? Store-bought works just fine in a pinch.

NOTE FROM THE KITCHENS

HOT FUDGE JUST TASTES SO MUCH BETTER WHEN IT'S HOMEMADE, AND YOU CAN USE YOUR FAVORITE BRAND OF CHOCOLATE. THIS MAKES A FANTASTIC GIFT FOR FRIENDS, TOO.

Hot Fudge Sundaes

8 ounces bittersweet chocolate, chopped (you can use morsels if you don't want to chop chocolate)

½ cup very strong black coffee

3 tablespoons salted butter, cut into pieces

4 tablespoons heavy cream

½ teaspoon ground cinnamon

1 pint chocolate ice cream

Suggested toppings: chopped peanuts, whipped cream, maraschino cherries

Yield: 4 servings

1. In a heavy saucepan over medium-low heat, melt the chocolate with the coffee. Once chocolate melts, remove the pan from the heat and stir in the butter, cream, and cinnamon.

2. Scoop the ice cream into serving dishes and top with the warm sauce and toppings of your choice.

KITCHEN TIP Use a serrated knife to chop the chocolate; it's the easiest way.

RACHAEL NEVER STOPS. The show tapes at a whirlwind pace; doing three to four shows a day means constant motion and a never-ending stream of information.

Quick Peaches & Golden Raisins Cobbler

5 to 6 cups frozen sliced peaches (1 large sack)

1 8-ounce package complete biscuit mix (recommended: Jiffy™ brand)

½ cup water

½ cup plus 2 tablespoons granulated sugar

2 teaspoons ground cinnamon

¼ teaspoon ground nutmeg—eyeball it

½ teaspoon allspice

⅛ teaspoon black pepper, a couple of pinches

Pinch salt

2 1-ounce boxes golden raisins, about ⅓ cup or a couple of handfuls

1 2-ounce package sliced almonds, about ¼ cup

Ice cream or whipped cream for serving (optional)

Yield: 4 servings

1. Preheat the oven to 425°F. Place the frozen peaches in an 8×8-inch glass baking dish and defrost in the microwave on high for about 3 minutes.

2. While the peaches are defrosting, make the cobbler topping: In a bowl, combine the biscuit mix with water. Stir until thoroughly combined but do not overwork. In another bowl, combine the ½ cup sugar, 1 teaspoon of the cinnamon, the nutmeg, allspice, black pepper, salt, and raisins.

3. Remove the peaches from the microwave and combine with the sugar mixture in the baking dish. Top the seasoned peaches with the wet biscuit mix, using your fingers to press it out until even. Top the biscuit mix with almonds. Mix the remaining 1 teaspoon cinnamon and 2 tablespoons sugar together and sprinkle over the top. Bake until the cobbler top is firm and lightly golden and peaches are bubbly and hot, about 20 to 25 minutes.

4. Serve warm as is or with ice cream and whipped cream if you have some on hand.

tyler FLORENCE

He's a passionate cook whose wide-eyed wonder for food and cooking never stops. He takes home-cooked classics to a whole new level, and he's happy to teach you how to do it too.

Q+A
WITH TYLER FLORENCE

WHY DID YOU BECOME A CHEF?
I had always loved to cook, and I just burned too much toast.

WHAT BROUGHT YOU TO NEW YORK CITY FROM THE SOUTH?
To be taken seriously as a chef, I thought I should have worked either in France or in New York. Since I didn't speak French, I decided to head to New York. New York really taught me how to cook, and it still continues to inspire me every day.

WHAT IS YOUR FAVORITE THING TO COOK AT HOME?
Ultimate Roast Chicken (page 198), and my son Miles' favorite meal, spaghetti with fresh tomatoes, extra-virgin olive oil, and Parmesan cheese.

ANY GUILTY FOOD PLEASURES?
French fries with mayonnaise.

WHAT ADVICE WOULD YOU GIVE AN ASPIRING TV COOK?
Don't skip the fundamental experience of working at a restaurant— it's crucial!

HOW DID YOU END UP ON TV?
Honestly, I was at the right place at the right time.

189

Fried Crab Wontons
with Sesame-Soy Dipping Sauce

WONTONS

- 1 2-inch piece fresh ginger, grated
- 2 shallots, chopped
- ½ carrot, chopped
- 1 green onion, chopped
- 2 tablespoons chopped fresh cilantro
- 1 tablespoon peanut oil
- Juice of ½ lemon
- 2 tablespoons mayonnaise
- 1 pound lump crabmeat (Dungeness, if you can get it), picked through for shells
- Salt and freshly ground black pepper
- 1 12-ounce package square wonton wrappers
- 1 egg white, for brushing
- Cornstarch, for dusting
- Vegetable oil, for deep-frying

DIPPING SAUCE

- ¾ cup soy sauce
- 3 tablespoons dark sesame oil
- 3 tablespoons rice wine vinegar
- 2 teaspoons minced fresh ginger

Yield: 60 wontons

1. Make the wontons: In a food processor, combine ginger, shallots, carrot, green onion, cilantro, peanut oil, and lemon juice. Pulse until fine. Put vegetable mixture in a mixing bowl, add the mayonnaise and the crabmeat, and season with salt and black pepper to taste. Be careful not to mash the crabmeat; you want texture when you bite into the wonton.

2. Lay a wonton wrapper on a flat surface and brush with the beaten egg white. Drop 1 tablespoon of the crab filling onto the center of the wrapper. Fold the wonton in half, corner to corner, to form a triangle. Press around the filling to knock out any air bubbles, then press the seam together to seal. You can leave them this shape or continue by brushing the 2 side points with beaten egg white. Then with your index finger in the center so you have something to press against, fold 2 sides into the center, slightly overlapping, and press the dough against your finger with your thumb to form a tight seal. (When these are folded they look like bishop's hats.) Lightly dust the filled wontons with cornstarch to keep them from sticking together and place on a cookie sheet.

3. Heat 2 to 3 inches of oil in a deep heavy saucepan to 370°F. Add a few of the wontons to the oil and cook, turning them 3 or 4 times to get them nicely browned all over, about 2 to 3 minutes. Carefully lift

FILLING THE WONTON

1. DIAGONALLY FOLD THE WRAPPER OVER THE FILLING WHILE GENTLY PRESSING OUT ANY EXCESS AIR. RUN YOUR FINGER ALONG THE EDGE TO BE SURE THE EGG WHITE SEAL IS SECURE.
2. THESE WONTONS CAN BE CONSTRUCTED AS TRIANGLES OR BISHOP'S HATS. USING THE EGG WHITE AS GLUE, BRUSH THE TWO POINTS OF THE TRIANGLE AND CONNECT THEM OVER YOUR INDEX FINGER AND SQUEEZE TO ADHERE.

them out of the pan with a slotted spoon and onto a paper towel-lined platter to drain. Cook all of the wontons this way.

4. Make the dipping sauce: Stir together the dipping sauce ingredients and serve with the wontons.

KITCHEN TIP Keep the rest of the wonton wrappers covered with a kitchen towel while you work to keep them from drying out and sticking to each other.

KITCHEN TIP These freeze really well and the recipe makes lots of wontons. Keep unfried extras in your freezer for impromptu guests.

"I ALWAYS CARRY A FLAVOR JOURNAL, so when the time comes to develop recipes, I can always look back at what I tasted recently."

Creamy Garlicky Mussels

4 pounds mussels

4 tablespoons unsalted butter

2 tablespoons extra-virgin olive oil

2 cloves garlic, peeled and smashed

4 sprigs fresh thyme

½ lemon, thinly sliced

¾ cup dry white wine*

½ cup low-sodium chicken broth

Salt and freshly ground black pepper

Serving suggestion: crusty French bread

Yield: 4 servings

1. Scrub the mussels with a vegetable brush under running water; discard any with broken shells or that remain opened when tapped. In a large pot over medium heat, melt 2 tablespoons butter with the olive oil. Add the garlic, thyme, and lemon slices and cook until everything has softened, about 5 minutes. Add the mussels and stir to coat them with all the flavorings. Add the wine, then the chicken broth; cover the pot and steam for 10 to 12 minutes, until the mussels open.

2. Remove the mussels from the pot. Discard any that didn't open. Take the meat out of 10 of the mussels and put it back into the pot along with the remaining 2 tablespoons butter. Using an immersion blender, buzz the liquid until the sauce thickens and becomes creamy. Season with salt and black pepper to taste.

3. Divide the remaining mussels among 4 serving bowls and spoon the sauce over them. Serve with plenty of crusty French bread to dip in the sauce.

KITCHEN TIP To clean mussels, pull off the "beards"—the little strands coming out from between the shells. If a shell it open, squeeze it shut—it should stay closed if the mussel is still alive. Here's a general rule: If they stay open, don't cook them. If any haven't opened by the time the rest are cooked, don't eat them.

*See Kitchen Tip on cooking with wine, page 114.

Scallop Ceviche with Melon, Chile & Mint

CEVICHE

2 pounds fresh bay or sea scallops, preferably with shells

Sea salt and freshly ground black pepper

Juice of 3 oranges

Juice of 3 lemons

Juice of 3 limes

Zest of 1 orange

Zest of 1 lemon

Zest of 1 lime

2 teaspoons granulated sugar

¼ cup extra-virgin olive oil

CANTALOUPE SALAD

1 small ripe cantaloupe, halved, seeded, peeled, and cut into small cubes

½ bunch fresh mint leaves, hand-torn, plus more for garnish

1 fresh red chile, cut in paper-thin circles

Yield: 12 appetizer servings

1. Make the ceviche: Start by assessing the scallops at the fish store. I usually inspect every one just to make sure that they're all in perfect shape, (i.e., not torn, and fresh with a sweet ocean smell). The next step is to remove the side muscle that connects the scallop to its shell; it's not hard to miss; just pull it off with your fingers. Keep the shells to serve the ceviche in. Using a sharp knife, slice the scallops in half lengthwise into disks; the thinner they are, the faster they'll "cook." Put the scallops in a glass bowl and season with a fair amount of salt and black pepper.

2. Put the citrus juices, zests, and sugar in a blender and give them a whirl to combine. Add the olive oil and blend again to emulsify. Pour the marinade over the scallops; there should be enough juice to allow the scallops to float freely. Cover and refrigerate for 2 to 3 hours, until the scallops are opaque.

3. Make the cantaloupe salad: In a separate bowl, combine the cantaloupe, mint, and chile; season with salt and black pepper to taste and toss gently to combine.

4. To serve: Spoon the scallop ceviche into the shells with a little bit of the citrus juice and top with a spoonful of the cantaloupe salad. Garnish each serving with some fresh mint.

KITCHEN TIP It's rare to find scallops still in the shell, so if you do, buy them; they don't get fresher than that. Many kitchen stores sell scallop shells that can be washed and reused.

WHEN WE TALK
ABOUT THE
PRESENTATION
SIDE, WE MEAN
THE SIDE
THAT'S GOING
TO FACE THE
DINER.
WE START
PRESENTATION
SIDE DOWN
SO THAT WE
CAN TAKE
ADVANTAGE
OF THE PAN'S
INITIAL HEAT
FOR A PERFECT,
EVENLY
GOLDEN-BROWN
CRUST.

Pan-Roasted Halibut with Prosciutto, Lemon, White Wine & Capers

½ cup all-purpose flour

Salt and freshly ground black pepper

2 6-ounce halibut fillets

2 tablespoons extra-virgin olive oil

3 tablespoons butter

2 slices prosciutto, cut into strips

½ cup white wine

Juice of ½ lemon

2 teaspoons capers

2 tablespoons chopped fresh flat-leaf parsley, plus whole sprigs, for garnish

Yield: 2 servings

1. Preheat the oven to 375°F. Put the flour on a deep plate or in a shallow bowl and season well with salt and black pepper. Dredge the fish in the flour. Put a medium oven-safe skillet over medium-high heat, add 1 tablespoon oil and 1 tablespoon butter, and get the skillet hot. Add the fillets, skin sides up, and cook until browned on 1 side, 2 to 3 minutes. At the same time, add the prosciutto and cook, stirring, to brown. Then flip the fish, put the skillet in the oven, and roast until the fish is just cooked through, about 10 minutes.

2. Remove the fish to 2 serving plates. Drain the prosciutto on paper towels. Put the skillet back over medium heat. Add the remaining oil and butter, white wine, lemon juice, capers, and parsley and bring to a boil; keep at a boil until reduced and thickened. Season with salt and black pepper to taste. Pour the sauce over the fish, top with the prosciutto, garnish with parsley sprigs, and serve immediately.

TYLER'S FAVORITE THING TO DO IS TO TAKE BASIC HOME-COOKED CLASSIC FOOD AND MAKE IT SUPERLATIVE—the best, the tastiest, the most flavorful, and most compelling that it can possibly be.

IT'S HARD NOT
TO ENJOY
ROAST CHICKEN,
AND THIS IS
ROAST CHICKEN
AT ITS BEST.
IT'S AN EASY,
IMPRESSIVE
DISH WITH
GREAT FLAVORS
AND A SAUCE
THAT DESERVES
THE NAME
ULTIMATE.

The Ultimate Roast Chicken

1   5½-pound free-range chicken

½   bunch each fresh oregano, thyme, and parsley

¼   pound unsalted butter, softened (½ cup)

    Kosher salt and freshly ground black pepper

1   orange, halved

½   head garlic

1   small white onion, peeled and halved, plus 1 onion

6   strips smoked bacon

2   tablespoons all-purpose flour

1½ cups chicken broth

¼   cup dry sherry

Yield: 4 to 6 servings

1. Preheat the oven to 425°F. Rinse the chicken with cool water, inside and out. Pat it dry with paper towels. Divide the herbs, keeping half of them whole. Finely chop the other half. In a small bowl, mash the softened butter with the chopped herbs until combined. Rub the herbed butter under the skin, as well as all over the outside of the chicken. Season the bird all over with salt and black pepper to taste.

2. Stuff the cavity with the orange, garlic, onion halves, and the remaining herbs. Tie the legs together with kitchen twine. Place the chicken, breast side up, in a roasting pan. Put the whole onion into the pan to help color and flavor the sauce. Lay the strips of bacon across the breast of the chicken and roast for 25 minutes.

3. Remove the bacon, baste the chicken with the drippings, and cook for another 25 minutes to brown the skin. The chicken is done when an instant-read thermometer registers 180°F when inserted into the thickest part of the thigh (the legs of the chicken should wiggle

easily from the sockets too). Remove the chicken to a platter and let stand for 10 minutes so the juices settle back into the meat before carving.

4. Meanwhile, remove the softened onion from the roasting pan. Tilt the pan so the drippings collect in one corner and skim off as much fat as possible, leaving the drippings. Place the roasting pan on top of the stove over medium heat and use a wooden spoon to scrape up the browned bits from the bottom of the pan. Stir the flour into the drippings to make a paste. Pour in the chicken broth in stages; continue to stir to prevent lumps. Stir in the sherry and bring to a boil. Cook for 5 minutes. Season with salt and black pepper to taste.

5. To serve, carve the chicken tableside and squeeze the oranges from the cavity over the meat.

Spicy Grilled Beef Tenderloin

4 pints cherry tomatoes

¼ cup extra-virgin olive oil, plus additional for drizzling and rubbing on meat

Sea salt and freshly ground black pepper

Juice of 2 limes

½ red onion, sliced thin

1 serrano chile, sliced thin

½ bunch chopped fresh cilantro, plus additional leaves for garnish

½ pound queso fresco or feta cheese, crumbled

1 4-pound beef tenderloin

Yield: 8 to 10 servings

1. Heat the broiler. Put the cherry tomatoes onto baking sheets, drizzle some olive oil over them, and season with salt and black pepper to taste. Broil until the tomatoes burst, about 4 to 5 minutes. Remove from the oven and allow them to cool a bit. In a large bowl add the ¼ cup olive oil, lime juice, onion, chile, chopped cilantro, cheese, and the tomatoes. Mix carefully to avoid breaking up the tomatoes too much. Adjust seasoning to taste with salt and black pepper; set aside.

2. Heat the grill or a grill pan to medium. Rub the meat with some olive oil and season it generously with salt and black pepper to taste. Grill the tenderloin, browning it on all sides, until an instant-read thermometer inserted into the center of the meat reads 130°F for medium-rare, about 20 minutes. Remove the meat to a cutting board, cover it with aluminum foil, and allow it to rest for 10 minutes before slicing.

3. Slice the meat thin, place it on a platter, and spoon on the cheesy tomato dressing. Garnish with a drizzle of olive oil and cilantro leaves.

KITCHEN TIP Rest meat after roasting it in order to give the juices, which cluster in the center of the meat during roasting, the chance to redistribute, making the meat uniformly juicy throughout. Meat continues to cook after it's removed from the oven.

Roast Leg of Lamb
with Dark Beer, Honey & Thyme

1   7- to 8-pound leg of lamb, thigh bone removed and shin bone in (have your butcher do this)

4   cloves garlic, chopped

3   tablespoons fresh thyme

3   tablespoons extra-virgin olive oil

    Kosher salt and freshly ground black pepper

2   cups stout beer or porter (recommended: Guinness™)

½   cup honey

1   teaspoon juniper berries, crushed

2   bay leaves

Yield: 6 to 8 servings

1. Preheat the oven to 375°F. Open the leg of lamb and season the inside with half the garlic, half the thyme, 1 tablespoon of the olive oil, and salt and black pepper to taste. Tie the lamb closed with butcher's twine. Place it in a roasting pan, brush with remaining 2 tablespoons olive oil, and season with salt and black pepper.

2. In a bowl, mix the beer, honey, remaining garlic and thyme, juniper berries, and bay leaves. Pour this over the lamb and put the roasting pan into the oven. Immediately turn the oven down to 325°F. Cook 12 to 15 minutes per pound for medium-rare, or until internal temperature reaches 130°F to 135°F, basting every 15 minutes.

3. Remove the roast from the oven, cover it loosely with foil, and allow it to rest for about 20 minutes before carving. Remove and discard bay leaves. Skim excess fat off the pan drippings. Serve with pan drippings alongside.

KITCHEN TIP Starting the oven high and then turning it down lets the lamb develop a crisp outside and a gently cooked interior.

KITCHEN TIP Stout and porter are dark, flavorful, and complex beers. The strong, assertive flavor of the lamb needs a robust beer to stand up to it; don't try this with a lager.

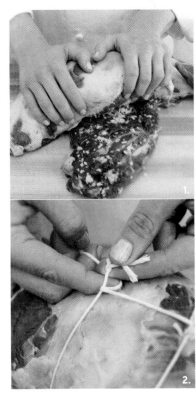

ROLLING THE LEG

1. AFTER SEASONING THE INTERIOR WITH HALF OF THE AROMATICS, ROLL UP THE BONED LEG INTO A UNIFORMLY THICK PACKAGE. 2. TIE THE LEG AT TWO-INCH INTERVALS WITH BUTCHER'S TWINE.

"ON MY DAYS OFF, I LIKE TO SPEND TIME catching up with friends, so I usually prepare a big family-style meal and make a big plate of something."

Spinach Salad with Honey-Brown Butter Dressing

4   tablespoons butter

1   shallot, chopped

1   tablespoon red wine vinegar

2   teaspoons honey

    Salt and freshly ground black pepper

6   loosely packed cups baby spinach

Yield: 4 servings

1. Melt the butter in a small skillet over medium heat. Add the shallot and cook until the shallot is tender and the butter turns a light brown color, 2 to 3 minutes. Remove from the heat and stir in the vinegar, honey, and salt and black pepper to taste.

2. Pour desired amount of dressing over the spinach in a bowl and toss. Serve immediately.

... RIGHT BEFORE YOU SERVE IT FOR OPTIMUM FLAVOR AND TEXTURE.

Chocolate Date Pudding Cake

    Nonstick cooking spray

6   ounces pitted dates (about 2 cups)

¾   cup water

1¼ cups granulated sugar

1   tablespoon pure vanilla extract

½   cup unsweetened cocoa powder

½   cup all-purpose flour

6   large egg whites

    Confectioners' sugar, for dusting

Yield: 8 servings

1. Preheat the oven to 375°F. Set a rack in the middle of the oven. Spray a 1½-quart soufflé dish with nonstick spray. Put the dates and water in a pot over medium-low heat. Cook and stir for 10 minutes, until the dates are very soft. Transfer the softened dates to a food processor and puree until smooth. Add the sugar and vanilla; puree again until well blended. Scoop out the puree into a mixing bowl. Sift together the cocoa powder and flour and add to the date mixture. Fold in using a rubber spatula; combine gently until well mixed.

2. In a mixing bowl, whip the egg whites until they form stiff peaks. Fold the egg whites into the date mixture.

3. Pour the batter into the soufflé dish, spreading it evenly with a spatula. Bake on the middle rack for 25 minutes, until the outside is just set. Cool to room temperature. Shake some confectioners' sugar on top and serve.

KITCHEN TIP Soft dates give this cake a rich moistness. To pit them, score lengthwise with paring knife, pull the meat apart, and remove the pit. You can also find pitted dates in some supermarkets.

...CAKE
...WATER
...TH ADDS
...OISTURE TO
...HE CAKE AND
SURROUNDS
THE PAN WITH
A UNIFORM
COOKING
TEMPERATURE
SO THE CAKE
COOKS EVENLY
AND DOESN'T
CRACK. THE
CHEESECAKE
SHOULD BE
WOBBLY IN THE
CENTER WHEN
YOU TAKE IT
OUT; IT'LL
CONTINUE TO
COOK FOR A
LITTLE WHILE
EVEN OUT OF
THE OVEN.

The Ultimate Cheesecake

CRUST

2 cups finely ground graham crackers (about 30 squares)

½ teaspoon ground cinnamon

1 stick unsalted butter, melted (½ cup)

Nonstick cooking spray

FILLING

1 pound cream cheese, softened (2, 8-ounce packages)

3 large eggs

1 cup granulated sugar

1 pint sour cream, beaten until smooth with a fork

Zest of 1 lemon

1 dash vanilla extract

LEMON BLUEBERRY TOPPING

1 pint blueberries

Zest and juice of 1 lemon

2 tablespoons granulated sugar

Yield: 6 to 8 servings

1. Preheat the oven to 325°F. For the crust: In a bowl, combine graham cracker crumbs, cinnamon, and butter with a fork until evenly moistened. Lightly coat the bottom and sides of an 8-inch springform pan with nonstick cooking spray. Pour the crumbs into the pan and, using the bottom of a measuring cup or the smooth bottom of a glass, press the crumbs down into the base and 1 inch up the sides. Refrigerate for 5 minutes.

2. For the filling: In the bowl of an electric mixer, beat the cream cheese on low speed for 1 minute until smooth and free of any lumps. Add the eggs, 1 at a time, and continue to beat slowly until combined. Gradually add sugar and beat until creamy, for 1 to 2 minutes. Add sour cream, lemon zest, and vanilla. Periodically scrape down the sides of the bowl and the beaters. The batter should be well mixed but not overbeaten. Pour the filling into the crust-lined pan and smooth the top with a spatula.

3. Set the cheesecake pan on a large piece of aluminum foil and fold up the sides around it. Place the cake pan in a large roasting pan. Pour boiling water into the roasting pan until the water is about halfway up the sides of the cheesecake pan; the foil will keep the water from seeping into the cheesecake. Bake for 45 minutes. Turn off the oven and let sit in the oven for 1 hour. The cheesecake should still jiggle (it will firm up after chilling), so be careful not to overbake. Remove from the water bath and let cool in pan for 30 minutes. Chill in the refrigerator, loosely covered, for at least 4 hours.

4. Loosen the cheesecake from the sides of the pan by running a thin metal spatula around the inside rim. Unmold and transfer to a cake plate. Using a spatula, spread a layer of Lemon Blueberry Topping (see recipe, below) over the surface. Slice the cheesecake with a thin, non-serrated knife that has been dipped in hot water and wiped dry. Repeat after each cut.

LEMON BLUEBERRY TOPPING

In a small saucepan, combine blueberries, lemon zest and juice, and sugar and simmer over medium heat until the fruit begins to break down slightly, 5 minutes or so. Let cool before spreading on cheesecake.

TYLER GETS INSPIRATION FOR HIS COOKING FROM EVERYTHING
AROUND HIM—whether it's a new ingredient, a building he saw on
his way to the studio, or a photograph he found in a magazine. His food is
spontaneous and creative, and he's always looking for a way to take it
one step closer to perfection.

wolfgang PUCK

He caters the glitziest
Hollywood awards
shows, runs several of
L.A.'s coolest restaurants,
and is always on the right
side of the velvet rope.
What else can we say?

Q+A WITH WOLFGANG PUCK

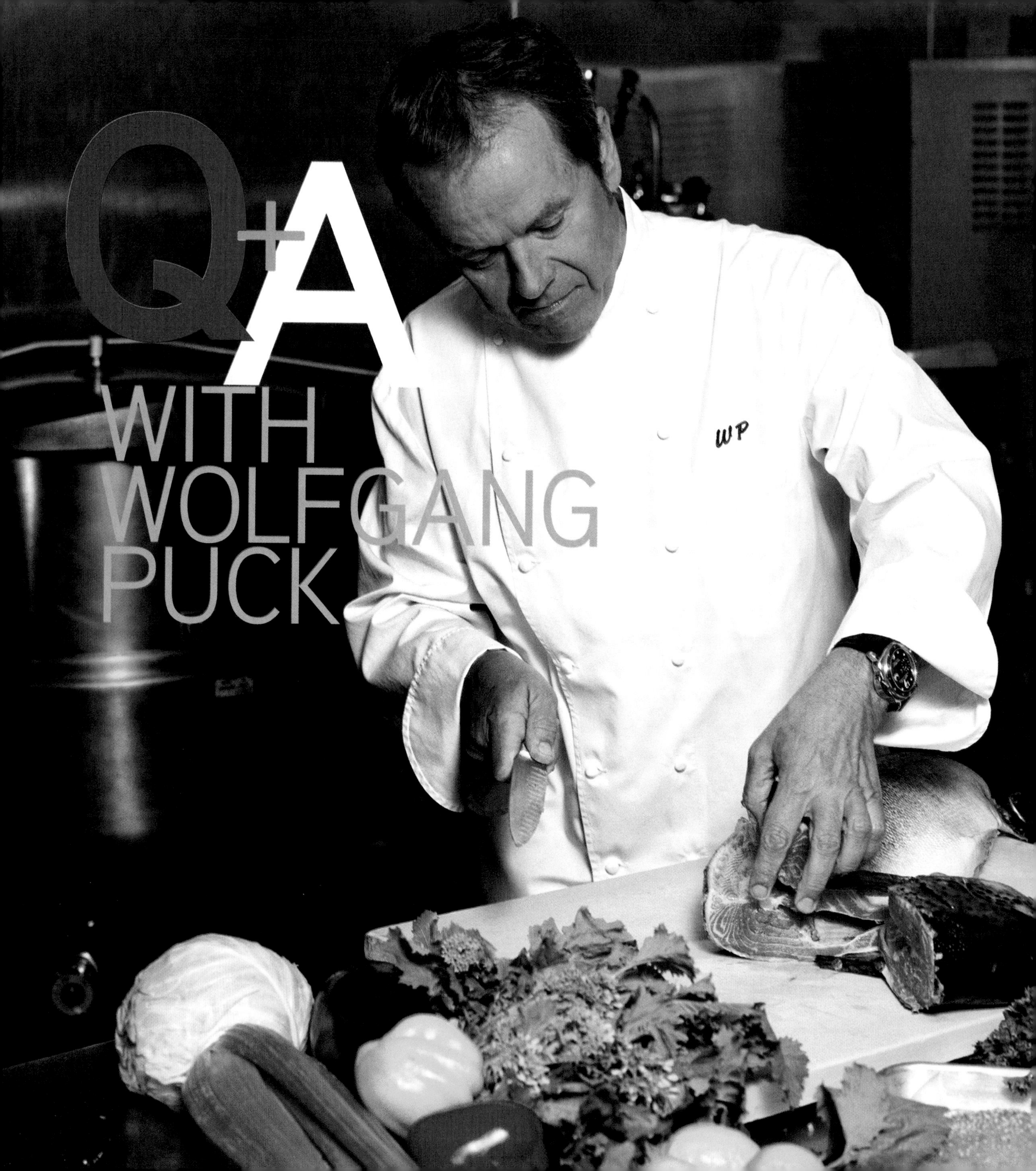

NAME THE THREE INGREDIENTS YOU MUST ALWAYS HAVE IN YOUR KITCHEN.
Salt, pepper, and love.

WHAT WAS YOUR BIGGEST HOLIDAY NIGHTMARE?
One year, my chef at Granita in Malibu made Thanksgiving dinner for us. I brought her beautiful turkey with all the trimmings home and put it in my oven to keep it warm. Unfortunately, I didn't have my glasses on, and instead of putting the oven on "bake," I put it on "broil." I was having Champagne in the dining room and started to smell something burning, but I never thought it was my turkey. So, after a while, the smell persisted, and I went to look. I opened the oven and out came a completely blackened turkey, with lots of billowing smoke. I covered it with a tablecloth so that no one would see it, ripped off the burnt skin, and sliced the turkey really nicely without skin. My friends said this is the best turkey they ever ate, because "it has such a wonderful smoky flavor."

HOW WOULD YOU DESCRIBE YOUR CUISINE?
I'm influenced by the different cultures that live in our city (Los Angeles). Above all, my cuisine is gutsy.

WHAT DON'T WE KNOW ABOUT YOU THAT MIGHT BE SURPRISING?
Even at my age, I still get excited about great food and ingredients. I'm still curious and always challenge myself to get better.

209

Chino Carrot & Ginger Soup

NOTE FROM THE KITCHENS

WOLFGANG'S A HUGE FAN OF GETTING FOOD STRAIGHT FROM THE SOURCE— THE CARROTS IN THIS SOUP COME FROM CHINO FARM NEAR SAN DIEGO, FAMOUS FOR ITS WIDE VARIETY OF ORGANIC PRODUCE. CHECK YOUR LOCAL FARMER'S MARKET FOR DIFFERENT COLORS OF CARROTS, BUT DON'T WORRY IF YOU CAN ONLY FIND THE ORANGE ONES; AS LONG AS YOU'RE USING FRESH, GOOD-QUALITY INGREDIENTS, THE SOUP WILL BE DELICIOUS.

¼ cup peanut oil

1 tablespoon minced garlic

1 tablespoon minced ginger

1 tablespoon minced green onion

Pinch crushed red pepper flakes

1 pound orange carrots, peeled and thinly sliced

1 pound yellow carrots, peeled and thinly sliced

1 pound white carrots, peeled and thinly sliced

1 tablespoon salt, plus additional for seasoning

½ teaspoon freshly ground white pepper, plus additional for seasoning

½ teaspoon ground turmeric

1 tablespoon honey, or to taste

8 cups vegetable stock, plus additional if necessary

1 cup heavy cream

4 ounces unsalted butter (8 tablespoons)

Oil, for deep-frying

½ cup julienned ginger (see Kitchen Tip, page 212)

Yield: 6 to 8 servings

1. In a stockpot, heat the oil and sauté the garlic, minced ginger, green onion, and crushed red pepper for 1 to 2 minutes, or just until glossy. Do not allow to develop color. Add the carrots, 1 tablespoon salt, ½ teaspoon white pepper, turmeric, and honey. Saute for 2 minutes, stirring constantly. Add the stock and bring to a boil. Lower to a simmer and add the cream. Cook, uncovered, for 40 minutes or until carrots are tender.

2. Transfer soup to a blender; add the butter and process to a puree. Strain soup into a new stockpot. If the soup is too thick, add extra stock. Taste and adjust seasoning with salt, white pepper, and honey. Keep warm.

3. Preheat the oil to 300°F. Deep-fry the julienned ginger until golden brown, about 1 minute, and drain on a plate lined with paper towels.

4. To serve: Ladle 6 to 8 ounces of soup into warm soup bowls. Garnish with fried ginger. Serve immediately.

"WE'RE LUCKY TO BE IN CALIFORNIA AND GET GREAT VEGETABLES AND FRUIT ALL YEAR LONG. Organic farmers like the Chinos make it even more interesting to cook with the seasons.**"** —WOLFGANG

Crab Cakes with Remoulade Sauce

2 cups heavy cream

3 cloves garlic, minced

2 sprigs fresh rosemary

1 tablespoon sweet paprika

2 tablespoons peanut oil

¾ cup brunoised red onion
  (see Kitchen Tip, right)

½ cup brunoised red bell pepper

½ cup brunoised yellow bell pepper

2 large eggs, lightly beaten

1 pound lump crabmeat

2 fresh jalapeños, brunoised

2 tablespoons minced fresh basil

2 tablespoons minced fresh parsley

1 tablespoon minced fresh tarragon

2 cups panko (Japanese bread crumbs),
  ground to a mealy consistency,
  divided

2 teaspoons salt

½ teaspoon freshly ground white pepper

½ cup all-purpose flour

½ cup clarified butter
  (see Kitchen Tip, right)

  Remoulade Sauce (see recipe, right)

Yield: 12 crab cakes (6 servings)

REMOULADE SAUCE

1 cup mayonnaise

1 tablespoon capers, minced

1 cornichon, minced

1 or 2 anchovies, minced

1 shallot, minced

1 teaspoon minced fresh chives

2 teaspoons minced fresh parsley

  Salt and freshly ground white pepper

Yield: 2 cups

1. In a saucepan, combine the heavy cream, garlic, rosemary, and paprika. Simmer over medium heat until reduced by half. Allow to cool to room temperature. In a sauté pan, heat the peanut oil. Sauté onion and bell peppers until glossy. Transfer to a plate and allow to cool to room temperature.

2. Preheat the oven to 350°F. In a mixing bowl, combine the eggs, crab, jalapeño, basil, parsley, tarragon, 1 cup of ground panko, salt, white pepper, reduced cream, and sautéed vegetables. Carefully mix until well blended. Divide the mixture into 12 portions. Shape into round, slightly flattened cakes, about 3-inch diameter by ½-inch thickness. On a baking sheet, combine the remaining 1 cup ground panko and flour. Coat the crab cakes generously.

3. In a sauté pan, heat ¼ cup of clarified butter. Pan-fry 6 crab cakes at a time, until golden on one side. Turn and transfer to preheated oven and bake for 5 minutes. Repeat the process with the remaining butter and crab cakes. Serve with Remoulade Sauce.

REMOULADE SAUCE

In a bowl, combine mayonnaise, capers, cornichon, anchovies, shallot, chives, and parsley until well blended. Season with salt and white pepper to taste.

KITCHEN TIP To brunoise means to cut into very small cubes, usually about ⅛ inch square. To make a brunoise, first make a julienne—that is, cut the vegetables into ⅛-inch-thick panels, then stack the panels together and cut them into ⅛-inch-wide "logs." To make a brunoise, dice the logs into cubes.

KITCHEN TIP Clarified butter contains no milk solids—which burn at high temperatures—so it's great for sautéeing. To make it, gently melt butter in a saucepan. Spoon off the foam that rises to the top, then pour off the clear yellow liquid, leaving the solids behind. It keeps, covered, in the fridge for several weeks.

"I WOULD TELL AN ASPIRING TV COOK THAT COOKING IN YOUR HOME IS QUITE DIFFERENT FROM COOKING ON TELEVISION. On television, you have to do many things at once, like being funny, being serious, being a true professional, and making people feel comfortable—but at home you can just relax and cook."

Pizza with Caramelized Onions & Crispy Bacon

- 2 teaspoons olive oil
- 6 slices bacon (about 4 ounces), cut into ½-inch pieces
- 2 small onions, peeled and thinly sliced
- 4 tablespoons mascarpone cheese
- ½ cup farmer's cheese
- Freshly grated nutmeg
- Freshly ground black pepper
- 2 6-ounce balls Pizza Dough (see recipe, below)
- 1 cup grated mozzarella
- 4 tablespoons grated Parmesan
- 4 tablespoons fresh thyme

Yield: 4 main-course servings or 8 appetizer servings

PIZZA DOUGH
- 1 package active dry or fresh yeast
- 1 teaspoon honey
- 1 cup warm (105°F to 115°F) water
- 3 cups all-purpose flour
- 1 teaspoon kosher salt
- 1 tablespoon extra-virgin olive oil, plus additional for brushing

Yield: enough dough for 2 medium pizzas or 4 small pizzas

1. Place a pizza stone on the middle rack of the oven and preheat the oven to 500°F. In a medium sauté pan, add the olive oil and heat over medium heat. When the oil is hot, add the bacon and cook until the bacon is very crispy and all of the fat is rendered. Remove the bacon with a slotted spoon and drain on a paper towel-lined plate. Remove all but 2 tablespoons bacon fat from the pan and discard. Place the pan over high heat. Add the onions to the hot bacon fat and cook until the onions are well browned, about 8 to 10 minutes, stirring often. Remove to a paper towel-lined plate.

2. In a small bowl, combine the mascarpone and farmer's cheeses. Season with nutmeg and black pepper to taste. Set aside.

3. On a lightly floured surface, stretch or roll each dough ball as thinly as possible into a 14- to 15-inch circle. Evenly spread the mascarpone mixture over each dough round. Sprinkle with the mozzarella and Parmesan cheeses, bacon, thyme, and sautéed onion. Bake until the pizza crust is nicely browned, about 8 to 10 minutes.

4. Remove pizza from the oven, transfer to a cutting board, cut into slices, and serve immediately.

PIZZA DOUGH
1. In a small bowl, dissolve the yeast and honey in ¼ cup of the warm water.

2. In a food processor, combine the flour and the salt. Add the 1 tablespoon oil, the yeast mixture, and the remaining ¾ cup water and process until the mixture forms a ball. (The pizza dough can also be made in a mixer fitted with a dough hook. Mix on low speed until the mixture comes cleanly away from the sides of the bowl and starts to climb up the dough hook.)

3. Turn the dough out onto a clean work surface and knead by hand 2 or 3 minutes. The dough should be smooth and firm. Cover the dough with a clean, damp towel and let it rise in a cool spot for about 2 hours. (When ready, the dough will stretch as it is lightly pulled.)

4. Divide the dough into 4 balls, about 6 ounces each. Work each ball by pulling down the sides and tucking under the bottom of the ball. Repeat 4 or 5 times. Then on a smooth, unfloured surface, roll the ball under the palm of your hand until the top of the dough is smooth and firm, about 1 minute. Cover the dough with a damp towel and let rest 1 hour. At this point, the balls can be rolled out and covered with toppings or wrapped in plastic and refrigerated for up to 2 days, until ready to use.

KITCHEN TIP To move the dough to the stone, either work the dough on top of a layer of parchment paper and transport it on that, or —if you have one—try a pizza paddle (or the back of a cookie sheet) that's been dusted liberally with cornmeal to prevent sticking.

KITCHEN TIP This recipe makes double the amount of dough you will need for the toppings, so you can either refrigerate the extra or top as desired—cook's choice!

Crispy Calamari with Chinese Noodles & Spicy Garlic Sauce

Peanut oil, for deep-frying

2 tablespoons peanut oil

¾ cup sliced Double-Blanched Garlic (see recipe, below)

2 tablespoons granulated sugar

1 cup rice wine

¼ cup rice wine vinegar

2 tablespoons plus 1 teaspoon dark soy sauce

4 ounces carrots, peeled, trimmed, and cut into julienne, about 1 cup

4 ounces haricots verts, trimmed, blanched, and refreshed, about 1 cup

4 ounces green onions, trimmed and cut into strips, about 1 cup

2 teaspoons Vietnamese chili sauce

Kosher salt

12 ounces fresh Chinese egg noodles or thin spaghetti

1 pound calamari, cleaned and cut into ¼-inch rings

Freshly ground black pepper

½ cup all-purpose flour

¼ teaspoon sesame oil

Yield: 4 servings

DOUBLE-BLANCHED GARLIC

3 heads garlic

Kosher salt

Yield: ¾ to 1 cup

1. Bring a large stockpot of water to a boil. In a wok or deep, heavy saucepan, heat about 3 inches of peanut oil to 375°F.

2. Make the sauce: In a large skillet or sauté pan, heat the 2 tablespoons peanut oil over medium-high heat and sauté the garlic just until golden, 2 to 3 minutes. Stir in the sugar and continue to sauté until the garlic begins to caramelize, 1 or 2 minutes longer. Add the rice wine, rice wine vinegar, and soy sauce. Add the carrots, haricots verts, and 3 ounces of the green onions, reserving 1 ounce as garnish. Stir in the chili sauce and continue to cook until the sauce is reduced by half. Meanwhile, add salt to the boiling water and cook the noodles until they are al dente. Drain the noodles well and stir them into the sauce until they are well coated.

3. Season the calamari with salt and black pepper to taste and toss with the flour to coat lightly. Deep-fry calamari in small batches in the hot peanut oil until golden, 1 or 2 minutes. (The easiest way to do this is to use a fine-mesh basket or strainer. Place calamari in the basket and gently ease the basket into the oil.) Drain on paper towels.

4. To serve, divide the noodles and vegetables among 4 large warm plates. Arrange the calamari over and around each portion and garnish with the remaining green onions. Drizzle a little sesame oil over the noodles and serve immediately.

DOUBLE-BLANCHED GARLIC

1. Prepare an ice bath. Separate the garlic into cloves and remove the ends of each clove. Fill a small saucepan with water. Salt lightly and bring to a boil. Carefully drop the whole cloves into the water and blanch for 30 seconds. Remove with a slotted spoon and immediately plunge into the ice water to stop the cooking process. Repeat the process.

2. Drain the garlic and dry it well. The peels should slip off easily. Cut the garlic into slices and use as needed.

KITCHEN TIP Blanching garlic mellows its bite while leaving the robust flavors intact.

KITCHEN TIP Vietnamese chili sauce, also called *nuoc cham*, is a spicy condiment indispensable on Vietnamese tables. It's made with sugar, hot peppers, garlic, lime juice, and fish sauce. Look for it in the Asian section of your grocery store. If you can't find it, search our website (www.foodnetwork.com) for a recipe.

Pork Chops with Cabbage & Sherry Vinegar Sauce

2 1-inch-thick center-cut pork chops

   Salt and freshly ground black pepper

2 tablespoons unsalted butter

1 tablespoon mild-flavored oil, such as almond or safflower

7 tablespoons balsamic vinegar

3 tablespoons sherry

1 cup brown veal stock

4 slices bacon, cut into ¼-inch pieces

6 ounces cabbage, cut into julienne

1 teaspoon Dijon mustard

2 tablespoons peeled, seeded, and chopped tomatoes

1 teaspoon minced chives

Yield: 2 servings

1. Season both sides of pork chops with salt and black pepper. Heat a heavy sauté pan over medium heat and add 1 tablespoon butter and the oil. Add the chops and saute for 5 minutes on each side, or until slightly pink on the inside. Remove the chops to a heated platter and pour off the excess fat.

2. Add 3 tablespoons of the vinegar and the sherry and cook, scraping the bottom of the pan with a wooden spoon, for 1 minute. Add the veal stock and, over moderate heat, reduce until slightly thickened. Set aside.

3. Sauté the bacon until crisp. Spoon off all but 2 tablespoons of the bacon fat, add the remaining 4 tablespoons vinegar, and cook for 1 minute, scraping the bottom of the pan with a wooden spoon. Add the cabbage and stir over high heat until heated through. Season with salt and black pepper to taste.

4. Heat the sauce and whisk in the Dijon mustard and remaining 1 tablespoon butter. Mound the cabbage onto heated plates. Place a pork chop on each bed of cabbage and top each chop with the sauce. Garnish with chopped tomatoes and sprinkle with chives.

KITCHEN TIP Always add mustard at the end of a cooked recipe. Cooking mustard too long can make it grainy.

KITCHEN TIP You can use store-bought veal stock here—just use a light hand with the seasoning, as store-bought stocks can be salty.

STAR POWER

WOLFGANG'S RESTAURANTS ARE ALWAYS PACKED with a glamorous see-and-be-seen scene, though he never lets that faze him. He's the consummate host and always seems to know everyone in the dining room, but he's happiest in the kitchen. When we're taping in Los Angeles, he'll be out visiting his restaurants and checking on the kitchens until 2 or 3 in the morning, then wide awake and ready to shoot the next morning at 6. We have no idea when he sleeps.

Pan-Roasted Chicken with Port & Whole-Grain Mustard

1 3- to 4-pound whole frying chicken, butterflied

Salt and freshly ground black pepper

3 tablespoons olive oil

½ cup port wine

½ cup chicken stock or 2 tablespoons barbecue sauce

⅓ cup heavy cream

1 tablespoon Dijon mustard

1 tablespoon Meaux (whole-grain) mustard

Salt and freshly ground black pepper

2 tablespoons finely chopped fresh parsley

2 tablespoons finely chopped fresh tarragon

Yield: 4 servings

1. Preheat the oven to 400°F. Season both sides of the chicken with salt and black pepper. Heat a very large oven-safe skillet, 14- or 16-inch diameter, over high heat. Add the olive oil and swirl it in the skillet. As soon as you begin to see slight wisps of smoke, carefully place the chicken, skin side down, in the skillet. Sear the chicken, undisturbed, while reducing the heat little by little to medium, until its skin has turned golden brown and crisp, 6 to 8 minutes. Carefully turn the chicken skin side up.

2. Put the skillet in the oven and cook until the chicken is deep golden brown, the juices run clear when pierced in the thickest part of the thigh, and an instant-read thermometer registers 180°F, about 10 to 20 minutes. When the chicken is done, transfer it to a plate and keep warm.

3. Pour off all but a thin layer of fat from the skillet. Add the port, put the skillet over high heat, and reduce by half. Add the chicken stock and reduce again. (If using barbeuce sauce, you don't have to reduce.) Add the cream, bring it to a boil, and cook for 3 minutes. Stir in the Dijon and Meaux mustards and season with salt and black pepper to taste. Return the chicken to the skillet and sprinkle with parsley and tarragon.

KITCHEN TIP Barbecue sauce is a great shortcut we learned from Wolfgang for a deep, rich sauce when you don't have a good stock handy.

KITCHEN TIP Butterflying a chicken makes it cook through much quicker than leaving it whole. Your butcher will happily butterfly a chicken for you, but it's quite easy to do it yourself.

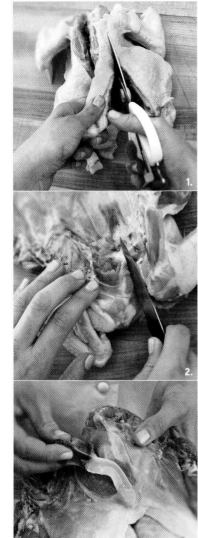

BUTTER-FLYING A CHICKEN

1. WITH THE CHICKEN BREAST DOWN ON A CUTTING BOARD, USE KITCHEN SHEARS TO SNIP ALONG BOTH SIDES OF THE BACKBONE. REMOVE THE BACKBONE AND FLATTEN OUT THE BIRD.
2. USE A PARING KNIFE TO MAKE A SMALL INCISION BETWEEN THE WINGS ALONGSIDE THE BREASTBONE TO FREE IT.
3. LIFT OUT THE BREASTBONE AND DISCARD.

221

Wolfgang's Beef Goulash

2 tablespoons extra-virgin olive oil

4 cups thinly sliced onions

1 tablespoon granulated sugar

3 cloves garlic, minced

1 tablespoon caraway seeds, toasted and ground

1½ tablespoons sweet paprika

1 teaspoon spicy paprika

2 tablespoons minced fresh marjoram leaves

1 teaspoon minced fresh thyme

1 bay leaf

3 tablespoons tomato paste

2 tablespoons balsamic vinegar

4 cups chicken stock

2½ pounds beef shoulder, cut into 2-inch cubes

1 teaspoon kosher salt

¼ teaspoon freshly ground black pepper

Spaetzle (see recipe, below)

Yield: 4 servings

SPAETZLE

4 large egg yolks

1 large egg

1¾ cups milk

1 pound all-purpose flour

¼ teaspoon freshly grated nutmeg

1 teaspoon salt, plus extra for seasoning

¼ teaspoon freshly ground white pepper, plus extra for seasoning

½ cup peanut oil

2 ounces unsalted butter (¼ cup)

1 tablespoon minced fresh parsley

1. In a large Dutch oven, heat the olive oil over medium to medium-low heat and sauté the onions and sugar until caramelized, about 45 minutes.

2. Add the garlic and ground caraway seeds. Cook for 1 minute. Add the sweet and spicy paprikas, marjoram, thyme, and bay leaf. Sauté another minute, until fragrant. Add the tomato paste. Add the vinegar and the stock and cook, scraping the bottom of the pot with a wooden spoon, for 1 minute. Add the beef, salt, and black pepper and bring to a boil, then lower to a simmer and cook, uncovered, until very tender, about 1½ hours, stirring occasionally.

3. Taste and adjust seasoning with more salt and black pepper. Remove and discard bay leaf. Serve with Spaetzle.

SPAETZLE

1. In a small bowl, beat together the egg yolks, egg, and milk. In a medium bowl, combine the flour, nutmeg, 1 teaspoon salt, and ¼ teaspoon white pepper. Add the egg mixture to the flour mixture and mix by hand, until just well blended and smooth. Do not overmix. Cover the bowl and refrigerate for at least 1 hour.

2. Bring salted water to a boil. Place a colander on top of the pot. Place the batter in the colander and smear through the holes with a rubber spatula to form spaetzle. Cook 4 to 5 minutes, or until al dente. Transfer cooked spaetzle to a bowl of ice water. When cool to the touch, drain well. Stir in half the oil. (At this point you can cover and refrigerate up to 2 days.)

3. Place a large sauté pan over high heat until it gets very hot. Add the remaining ¼ cup of oil and the cooked spaetzle. Sauté until golden. Season with salt and white pepper to taste. Toss with butter and sprinkle with parsley.

KITCHEN TIP Spaetzle means "little sparrows" in Austrian dialect. They're a classic accompaniment to this dish, but they're great on their own too.

Chinois-Grilled Lamb Chops with Cilantro-Mint Vinaigrette

MARINADE & LAMB

- 1 cup soy sauce
- 1 cup mirin (sweet saké)
- 1 tablespoon chopped fresh ginger
- 2 tablespoons sesame oil
- 2 cups chopped scallions
- 1 tablespoon crushed red pepper flakes
- 2 to 3 cloves garlic, finely chopped
- 2 2-pound racks lamb, trimmed

  Salt and freshly ground black pepper

  Fresh cilantro or mint leaves, for garnish

CILANTRO-MINT VINAIGRETTE

- 1 tablespoon honey
- ½ tablespoon chopped ginger
- ¼ cup each coarsely chopped mint, cilantro, and parsley
- ½ cup rice wine vinegar
- 1 egg yolk*

  Dash chile oil
- 1 cup peanut oil

  Salt and freshly ground black pepper

Yield: 4 servings

1. Preheat a grill to high heat. Prepare the marinade: In a bowl, mix together all the marinade ingredients, including salt and black pepper to taste. Pour them over the lamb and let it marinate for 1 hour. Remove from the marinade and let stand until ready to cook.

2. While the lamb is marinating, prepare the vinaigrette: Combine all the ingredients except peanut oil in a blender and blend. With the machine running, slowly add peanut oil. Season with salt and black pepper to taste and strain into a bowl.

3. Season the lamb with salt and black pepper to taste and place it on the hot grill. Grill to medium-rare, about 15 to 20 minutes, turning occasionally. (Alternately, cut the rack into chops and sauté them in a pan over high heat for about 2 minutes on each side. Cook the chops in several batches, if necessary, but don't crowd the pan.)

4. To serve, make a pool of the vinaigrette on each plate. Cut the lamb racks into double or single chops and place in the center of the vinaigrette. Garnish with cilantro or mint sprigs.

KITCHEN TIP Mirin, sometimes also called rice wine, is a type of sweet sake common in Japanese cooking. It's made out of glutinous rice, is low in alcohol, and adds a delicate sweetness that's great with meat.

*For more information on cooking with raw eggs, turn to page 254.

Caramelized Lemon-Lime Tart

Pâte Sucré (see recipe, below)

4 large eggs

4 large egg yolks

1 cup plus 2 tablespoons granulated sugar

⅔ cup fresh lemon juice

⅔ cup fresh lime juice

Zest of 2 small lemons

Zest of 2 small limes

6 ounces butter, softened and cut into small pieces (¾ cup)

Fresh raspberries or strawberries, for serving

Confectioners' sugar (optional)

Yield: 8 to 10 servings

PÂTE SUCRÉ

1¼ cups cake or pastry flour

4 tablespoons granulated sugar

¼ pound unsalted butter, chilled and cut into small pieces (½ cup)

1 large egg yolk

2 tablespoons heavy cream

Yield: one 9-inch tart shell

1. Preheat the oven to 350°F. Roll out the Pâte Sucré to a circle about ¼ inch thick and large enough to slightly overlap a 9-inch metal tart pan. Fit the dough into the pan and trim the edges. Line the bottom and sides of the shell with parchment or coffee filter papers or aluminum foil. Fill the lining with dried beans, rice, or aluminum beans, and bake in the oven for 20 to 25 minutes. Cool and remove the beans and the lining. Return the shell to the oven and bake until golden, 5 to 10 minutes longer.

2. In a large metal bowl, whisk together the whole eggs, egg yolks, 1 cup sugar, lemon and lime juices, and zests. Set over simmering water and continue to whisk until the mixture is very thick, about 20 minutes.

3. Turn off the flame and whisk in the butter, a few pieces at a time. (You don't want the mixture to cool down before all the butter is incorporated.) Strain the filling into a bowl. Scrape into the baked tart shell and smooth with a metal spatula. Cool and then refrigerate until firm, 3 to 4 hours, up to overnight.

4. Sprinkle the remaining 2 tablespoons of sugar evenly over the top of the filling. With a propane blowtorch, caramelize the sugar. (This can also be done under the broiler. Place the tart on the broiler tray directly under the flame, watching carefully to prevent burning. Or, if desired, eliminate the 2 tablespoons of sugar and arrange circles of raspberries on top of the tart. Sift a little confectioners' sugar over the berries just before serving.) Refrigerate the tart for at least 30 minutes.

5. Cut into slices and serve. Serve the tart with fresh strawberries or raspberries.

PÂTE SUCRÉ

1. In a food processor fitted with the steel blade, combine the flour and sugar. Add the butter and process until the texture resembles fine meal.

2. In a small bowl, whisk together the egg yolk and 1 tablespoon of the cream. Scrape into the machine and process until a ball begins to form, using the additional tablespoon of cream, if necessary. Remove the dough from the machine and on a lightly floured surface, press down into a circle. Wrap in plastic wrap and refrigerate for at least 1 hour.

KITCHEN TIP When you're using a wet, uncooked tart filling like the one here, blind-baking—that is, prebaking the crust before adding the filling—is essential. Weight the dough in the beginning to ensure the crispest possible crust, and since it's not going back into the oven, get it as golden brown as possible.

KITCHEN TIP The tart filling is being made over an improvised double boiler; the eggs are being barely, imperceptibly cooked, and too much heat will scramble them. Double boilers diffuse gentle heat—just enough for a perfect filling but not enough for eggs over easy.

Wolfgang's Sachertorte

CAKE

6 ounces bittersweet chocolate, cut into small pieces

3 ounces unsalted butter (6 tablespoons)

5 large egg yolks

4 ounces granulated sugar (9 tablespoons, divided)

5 large egg whites

¼ teaspoon salt

⅓ cup all-purpose flour, sifted

Whipped cream, for serving

APRICOT FILLING

1 cup apricot preserves

1 tablespoon apricot brandy

GLAZE

6 ounces bittersweet chocolate, cut into small pieces

1 ounce unsalted butter (2 tablespoons)

2 ounces heavy cream (¼ cup)

Yield: 8 to 10 servings

1. Preheat oven to 350°F. Butter and flour an 8×2-inch round cake pan. In a large metal bowl, combine the chocolate and butter, set over a pot of simmering water, and melt, stirring occasionally. Set aside to cool. In a mixer, using a wire whisk, whip the egg yolks with 1 ounce (2¼ tablespoons) of the sugar until light and ribbony. Beat in the chocolate mixture.

2. In another bowl, beat the egg whites and salt until soft peaks form. Slowly add the remaining 3 ounces (6¾ tablespoons) of sugar and continue to beat until stiff peaks form. Fold in the flour and then fold one-third of the egg whites into the chocolate mixture to lighten it. Fold in the remaining egg whites, gently but thoroughly. Pour into prepared cake pan. Bake for 35 minutes or until done. To check for doneness, insert a paring knife in center of cake. It should come out dry. Remove from the oven and cool completely on a rack.

3. Make the apricot filling: Pulse the apricot preserves in a food processor. Stir in brandy.

4. Flip the cake over so that the bottom becomes the top. Slice the cake into 3 equal layers. Spread half of the apricot filling on the bottom layer. Top with a second layer of cake. Spread the remaining apricot filling and top with the last layer of cake. Chill for at least 30 minutes.

5. Make the glaze: In a bowl, combine the chocolate and butter. Melt over a double boiler. In a small saucepan, bring the cream to a boil. Stir into the melted chocolate. Cool until it reaches glazing consistency. Place the cake on a rack set over a cookie sheet. Pour and spread the glaze over and around the cake. Chill for another 30 minutes before serving. Serve each slice with whipped cream alongside.

KITCHEN TIP To cut a cake into layers, first measure the cake and decide where the cuts should go. At each cutting point, insert 4 toothpicks into the cake along the circumference. Balance a long, serrated knife on two of the toothpicks and cut, using a gentle sawing motion, while rotating the cake simultaneously.

" SINCE I WAS BORN IN AUSTRIA, I GREW UP EATING LOTS OF SWEETS. To this day, my first stop in the kitchen is always the pastry department to sample cookies, ice creams, and the day's sorbets. " —WOLFGANG

food network
KITCHENS

We're the bridge
between the home
cook and the TV chef.
We're the team of cooks,
stylists, editors, writers,
and researchers who
make the magic happen.

Q+A

WITH FOOD NETWORK KITCHENS

WHAT'S A TYPICAL DAY LIKE AT THE FOOD NETWORK KITCHENS?

There's actually no such thing as a typical day. On any given day, we prep and style food for cooking shows; develop, test, and taste new recipes; write food columns; eat our "family lunch"; cater a party; sample recipes for contests; style a photo shoot . . . and we talk about food all day long.

DO YOU EAT ALL DAY LONG TOO?

Yes, we do. Thankfully, we're in New York, so we can walk it off.

DO YOU TRAVEL WITH THE SHOWS?

Some of our cooking shows are done right here in New York City. But we tape on locations all around the country. Our shows have brought us to locations as far flung as Los Angeles, Bali, and Baltimore.

WHAT'S THE KITCHEN LIKE?

It's huge, bigger than all our home kitchens put together. It sits on top of Chelsea Market, home of some of the best wholesale and retail food shopping in New York.

WHAT HAPPENS TO ALL THE FOOD?

There isn't actually that much food left over; since most of our recipes serve four people, there's not lots of waste. We donate whatever we can to local food charities.

233

MORNING
BREAKFAST,
AND SERVING
THEM IN THE
SKILLET MEANS
FEWER DISHES
TO WASH.

Baked Eggs with Farmhouse Cheddar & Potatoes

3   tablespoons unsalted butter

1½ pounds red-skinned potatoes, diced

¼   cup chopped fresh flat-leaf parsley

2   large cloves garlic, minced

1   teaspoon kosher salt

    Freshly ground black pepper

8   large eggs

1   cup shredded extra-sharp farmhouse
    Cheddar (about 4 ounces)

Yield: 4 servings

1. Preheat the oven to 400°F. Melt the butter in a large, well-seasoned cast-iron skillet over medium heat. Add the potatoes and cook, stirring occasionally, until tender and brown, about 15 minutes. Stir in the parsley, garlic, salt, and black pepper to taste and remove from the heat.

2. Push the potatoes aside to make 4 evenly spaced shallow nests and break 2 eggs into each. Bake until the egg whites are cooked and the yolks are still runny, about 10 minutes. Sprinkle the cheese over the eggs and continue baking until it just melts, about 1 minute more. Serve immediately.

ALL DAY, EVERY DAY, WE GET TO DO WHAT WE LOVE—work with food (really, really good food). And we get so many talented chefs passing through our kitchen on a day-to-day basis that, no matter how long we've been in the business, we never stop learning. Do we have a dream job? We think we do.

Tortilla Soup

2 tablespoons extra-virgin olive oil

1 medium onion, chopped

2 cloves garlic, sliced

1 chipotle in adobo sauce, minced

1 tablespoon chili powder

2 teaspoons kosher salt

6 cups chicken broth, low-sodium canned

1 cup corn kernels, fresh or frozen and thawed

1 ripe tomato, chopped

1 cup shredded cooked chicken

½ cup fresh cilantro leaves

¼ cup freshly squeezed lime juice (about 2 limes)

About a dozen corn tortilla chips, broken a bit

Lime wedges (optional)

Yield: 4 servings

1. Heat the oil in a medium saucepan over medium heat. Add the onion, garlic, chipotle, chili powder, and salt and cook until the onion softens, about 5 minutes. Add the chicken broth, bring to a boil, reduce the heat slightly, and simmer, uncovered, for 10 minutes. Add the corn and cook for 5 minutes more.

2. Pull the saucepan from the heat and stir in the tomato, chicken, cilantro, and lime juice. Divide the tortilla chips among 4 warmed bowls, ladle the soup on top, and serve. Serve with lime wedges, if desired.

KITCHEN TIP To get every last drop of juice from the limes, microwave them for a few seconds and roll them under the palm of your hand before halving to release the juice from the pulp.

Pesto-Stuffed Salmon with Tomato-Corn Salad

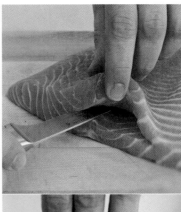

CUTTING A POCKET

LAY THE SALMON FILLET ON A WORK SURFACE. WITH A CUT SIDE FACING YOU, CUT A WIDE POCKET WITH A NARROW-BLADED KNIFE, TAKING CARE NOT TO CUT THROUGH THE TOP OR BOTTOM OF THE FISH.

SALMON

- ½ cup loosely packed fresh basil
- ½ cup loosely packed fresh parsley
- 2 tablespoons blanched whole almonds
- ¼ teaspoon minced garlic
- ¼ teaspoon kosher salt, plus additional for seasoning

  Freshly ground black pepper

- 3 tablespoons extra-virgin olive oil, plus additional for brushing
- 1 1½-pound center-cut skinless salmon fillet

  Vegetable oil for grilling

SALAD

- 1 pound ripe mixed small tomatoes, halved or diced
- 1 cup cooked fresh corn kernels (from 2 ears)
- 3 tablespoons extra-virgin olive oil
- 1 tablespoon white wine vinegar
- 2 teaspoons minced fresh marjoram or oregano

  Kosher salt and freshly ground black pepper

Yield: 4 servings

1. For the salmon: Pulse the basil, parsley, almonds, garlic, ¼ teaspoon salt, and black pepper to taste in a food processor to make a coarse paste. With the motor running, drizzle in the olive oil until incorporated. Next, cut the pocket (see photos at right). Hold the pocket open, season the inside with salt and black pepper to taste, and spread the pesto evenly inside the fish with a spoon. (The fish can be prepared up to this point a day ahead of grilling, then covered and refrigerated.)

2. Prepare an outdoor grill with a medium-high fire.

3. For the salad: Toss the tomatoes with corn. Add the olive oil, vinegar, marjoram, and salt and black pepper to taste. Toss again, taking care not to break up the tomatoes.

4. Lightly brush the grill grate with oil. Brush the fillet on both sides with olive oil and season the flesh side with salt and black pepper to taste. Lay the fish, flesh side down, on the grill and cook until there are distinct grill marks and you can lift the fish without it sticking, about 3 to 5 minutes. (Test it by gently lifting a corner—if it sticks, let it cook a bit longer.) When it lifts cleanly, carefully turn it about 45 degrees from its original position (don't turn it over). Cook for another 3 minutes, until marked. Season the skin side with salt and black pepper to taste, turn the fillet over, and cook about 3 to 5 minutes more, or until an instant-read thermometer inserted in the side registers about 125°F. Transfer the fish to a plate and let it rest for 5 minutes. Cut salmon into 4 equal pieces and transfer to serving plates. Serve salmon warm or at room temperature topped with the Tomato-Corn Salad. Drizzle with any extra juices from the salad.

WE'RE ALL ABOUT CLASSIC FOOD WITH A TWIST HERE; A SMALL UPDATE CAN MAKE YOU SEE A CLASSIC IN A WHOLE NEW LIGHT. These lamb burgers' Mediterranean flavors fit the bill perfectly.

Lamb Burgers with Feta

BURGERS

- 2 pounds ground lamb
- ½ cup plain whole-milk yogurt
- 1 tablespoon dried savory
- 3 cloves garlic, minced
- Finely grated zest of 1 lemon
- ¼ to ½ teaspoon crushed red pepper flakes
- 1½ teaspoons kosher salt, plus additional for seasoning
- Freshly ground black pepper
- 7 ounces feta cheese, crumbled into chunky pieces
- Extra-virgin olive oil, for brushing
- 6 small plain pita pocket breads (see Kitchen Tip, right)
- Sliced onions, tomatoes, and cucumbers, for garnish
- Arugula and fresh mint leaves, for garnish
- Tzatziki (see recipe, below) (optional)

Yield: 6 servings

TZATZIKI

- 2 cups plain whole-milk yogurt or 1 cup Middle Eastern-style plain yogurt
- 1 cucumber, peeled and seeded
- 2 teaspoons kosher salt, plus additional for seasoning
- ½ clove garlic, peeled
- 1 tablespoon extra-virgin olive oil
- 1 teaspoon freshly squeezed lemon juice
- ½ teaspoon dried mint, finely crumbled

Yield: about 1 cup

1. Prepare an outdoor grill with a medium-high fire.

2. Using your hands, mix the ground lamb, yogurt, savory, garlic, zest, red pepper, 1½ teaspoons salt, and black pepper to taste in a large bowl. Gently mix in the crumbled feta. Divide meat mixture into 6 equal portions, then into balls by gently tossing them from hand to hand. Shape into 1-inch-thick loosely packed oval patties. Press the center of each patty so it is slightly thinner than the edges.

3. Brush the burgers with olive oil and season with salt and black pepper to taste. Grill the burgers, turning once, until firm to the touch with a little bit of give, 8 to 10 minutes. Set aside while grilling pitas. Slit a burger-size opening in each pita, brush with olive oil, and season with salt and black pepper to taste. Grill until lightly toasted. Serve the burgers in the pitas with the garnishes of your choice and Tzatziki, if desired.

TZATZIKI

1. Stir yogurt and put in a coffee filter-lined strainer over a bowl. Let drain in refrigerator for at least 12 hours or overnight. (If using thick Greek or Middle Eastern yogurt, skip this step.) Discard watery liquid in bottom of bowl and put drained yogurt in a medium bowl.

2. Grate cucumber on wide-holed side of a box grater into another bowl. Sprinkle grated cucumber with 2 teaspoons salt and toss gently. Set aside 20 minutes, then squeeze cucumbers to express as much liquid as possible. Add the cucumber to the bowl of yogurt.

3. Smash garlic, sprinkle with a generous pinch of salt, and, with the flat side of a large knife, mash and smear to a coarse paste. Add garlic, oil, lemon juice, and mint to cucumber-yogurt mixture and stir to combine. Refrigerate for about an hour so flavors come together.

KITCHEN TIP Mini pitas are the perfect size here; the burgers fit snugly in the pocket without a lot of excess bread.

KITCHEN TIP Savory's great. It tastes like a blend of thyme, oregano, and a bit of rosemary, and it's totally food-friendly.

Chicken with Leeks, Watercress & Radish

3 tablespoons vegetable oil

4 bone-in chicken breast halves, with skin (about 2½ to 3 pounds)

½ teaspoon kosher salt, plus additional for seasoning

Freshly ground black pepper

4 tablespoons unsalted butter

2 leeks (white and light green parts), halved lengthwise, sliced crosswise, and rinsed

4 radishes, thinly sliced into rounds

¼ cup dry white vermouth

⅓ cup heavy cream

1 bunch watercress, stems trimmed (reserve a few sprigs for garnish), roughly chopped

Yield: 4 servings

1. Preheat the oven to 350°F. Heat a large skillet over medium-high heat; add the oil. Pat the chicken dry and season with some salt and black pepper to taste. Lay the chicken, skin sides down, in the skillet and cook undisturbed until the skin is golden and crispy, about 4 minutes. Add a nut-size bit of the butter to the skillet, and when the butter smells fragrant, turn the chicken and cook until opaque, about 4 minutes more. Put the chicken in a baking dish or roasting pan and bake just until firm to the touch, 10 to 12 minutes.

2. Pour all but 1 tablespoon fat from the skillet and return pan to the heat. Add the leeks and radishes and cook, tossing, until wilted, about 4 minutes. Season with the ½ teaspoon salt and black pepper to taste. Add the vermouth, bring to a boil, and reduce until syrupy. Stir in the cream and bring to a boil. Remove the skillet from the heat, add the watercress, and toss just until it is wilted. Add the remaining butter and swirl the skillet until it melts. Stir in any chicken juices that have collected in the roasting pan. Spoon the leek mixture onto 4 plates and arrange the chicken breasts on top. Garnish with the reserved watercress sprigs and serve.

KITCHEN TIP Clean leeks quickly by slicing them in half first lengthwise, then crosswise. Put them in a colander set into a big bowl of cool water, swish any sand or dirt free, and lift out.

THOUGH THE RECIPE TAKES A LOT OF WHAT WE LIKE TO CALL "INACTIVE PREP TIME" (WHICH ONE COULD ALSO CALL "WAITING"), IT'S WORTH IT. THOUGH YOU CAN GRILL THE TURKEY AS SOON AS IT'S RUBBED WITH THE SPICE PASTE, AND IT'LL BE GREAT, IF YOU HAVE THE PATIENCE, LET IT MARINATE FOR FULL-ON FLAVOR.

Butterflied Turkey with Yucatan Rub

TURKEY

- 1 gallon water
- 2 cups kosher salt
- 1 cup firmly packed light brown sugar
- 1 8- to 10-pound turkey, butterflied (back and breastbone removed by your butcher)

RUB

- ½ cup annatto paste (see Kitchen Tip, below)
- 8 cloves garlic, peeled and smashed
- 3 tablespoons dried oregano, preferably Mexican
- 1½ teaspoons ground coriander
- 1½ teaspoons freshly ground black pepper
- ¾ teaspoon kosher salt
- ¼ teaspoon ground allspice
- Juice of 3 limes (a scant ½ cup)
- Juice of 1 orange (about ⅓ cup)
- 3 tablespoons extra-virgin olive oil

Yield: 6 to 8 servings

1. For the turkey: The day before serving, heat 3 quarts of the water with salt and sugar in a large pan, stirring to dissolve salt and sugar. Remove from heat, add remaining 1 quart cold water, and stir. Set brine aside to cool to room temperature.

2. Put turkey in a large container and cover with the brine. Cover and refrigerate for 4 to 5 hours. (If you want to brine the turkey overnight, use half the amount of salt and sugar.)

3. For rub: Crumble annatto paste into a food processor and blend with the garlic, oregano, coriander, black pepper, salt, and allspice. Add the fruit juices and the olive oil and process to make a pasty sauce. Drain and pat the turkey very dry. Smear the rub all over the bird. Cover and refrigerate overnight.

4. Prepare an outdoor grill with a large medium-heat fire for direct and indirect grilling. Position a drip pan under the grate on indirect side of the grill.

5. Place turkey, breast side up, over the drip pan and grill, covered, until meat is cooked about halfway through, about 50 minutes. Turn and cook until an instant-read thermometer inserted in the thigh registers 170°F, about 50 minutes more. Move turkey to direct heat and rotate to evenly brown the skin in the last 10 minutes of cooking. Transfer to a carving board, cover, and let rest 10 minutes before carving.

KITCHEN TIP Annatto paste is a Mexican flavoring composed of ground annatto, or achiote, seeds mixed with herbs—usually oregano—and spices. The rust-colored paste is then pressed into a compact brick. Look for it in the Hispanic section of your grocery.

Butternut Squash, Apple & Onion Galette with Stilton

DOUGH

- 1¼ cups all-purpose flour

- Pinch salt

- 8 tablespoons cold unsalted butter, diced

- 1 large egg, lightly beaten

FILLING

- 1 large baking apple, such as Rome Beauty or Cortland

- 1 small or ½ medium butternut squash (about ¾ pound), halved, seeded, and skin on

- 1 small yellow onion, peeled, root end trimmed but intact

- 3 tablespoons unsalted butter, melted

- 2 teaspoons chopped fresh rosemary

- 2 teaspoons chopped fresh thyme

- Kosher salt and freshly ground black pepper

- 2 tablespoons whole-grain mustard

- ⅓ cup crumbled Stilton or other blue cheese (about 1½ ounces)

Yield: 6 servings

1. For the dough: Pulse the flour and salt together in a food processor. Add the butter and pulse about 10 times, until the mixture resembles coarse cornmeal with a few bean-size bits of butter in it. Add the egg and pulse 1 to 2 times more; don't let the dough form a mass around the blade. If the dough seems very dry, add up to 1 tablespoon of cold water, 1 teaspoon at a time, pulsing briefly. Remove the blade and bring the dough together by hand. Shape the dough into a disk, wrap it in plastic wrap, and refrigerate at least 1 hour.

2. For the filling: Halve and core the apple. Cut each half into 8 wedges and put them in a large bowl. Slice the squash and cut the onion into wedges so that both are as thick as the apple wedges and add them to the apples. Add the butter, rosemary, and thyme and toss gently to combine. Season with salt and black pepper to taste and toss again.

3. Preheat the oven to 400°F. Roll the dough on a lightly floured surface into a 12-inch disk. Transfer the dough to a baking sheet and brush with mustard. Starting 2 inches from the edge, casually alternate pieces of apple, squash, and onion in overlapping circles—if you have extra pieces of one or another, tuck them in where you can or double them up to use all the filling. Fold and pleat the dough over the edge of the filling. Bake until the crust is brown and the apple, squash, and onion are tender and caramelized, about 55 minutes. Scatter the cheese over the filling and bake until melted, about 5 minutes more. Cool the galette briefly on a wire rack. Cut into wedges and serve.

KITCHEN TIP Don't be afraid to cook this galette—or any of your pies or tarts, for that matter—until the crust is a rich golden brown. A pastry's buttery taste and flaky crispness really come through when it's fully cooked.

Parmesan, Pepper & Lemon Biscuits

2 cups all-purpose flour

1 tablespoon granulated sugar

1 tablespoon baking powder

1 tablespoon finely grated lemon zest

1 teaspoon cracked black pepper

½ teaspoon fine salt

6 tablespoons cold unsalted butter

½ cup diced plus ¼ cup finely grated Parmigiano-Reggiano cheese

¾ cup milk

Yield: 8 biscuits

1. Position a rack in the center of the oven and preheat to 450°F. Line a baking sheet with parchment paper.

2. Whisk the flour with the sugar, baking powder, lemon zest, black pepper, and salt in a large bowl. Cut butter into tablespoon-size pieces. Rub in 2 tablespoons of the butter with your fingertips until no visible pieces remain. Rub in the remaining 4 tablespoons butter just until it is in even, pea-size pieces. Scatter grated and diced cheese over the top and toss with a rubber spatula. Using a wooden spoon, stir the milk in to make a loose dough.

3. Turn dough onto a lightly floured work surface and pat into a rectangle about ½ inch thick (don't worry if dough doesn't all come together). Fold dough in thirds, like a business letter, and pat lightly into an 8×5-inch rectangle—about ¾ inch thick. Using a 2- to 3-inch round biscuit cutter, cut 6 biscuits and place on baking sheet. Press dough scraps together and cut 2 more biscuits. Bake until tops are lightly browned, about 15 minutes. Cool slightly on a rack; serve warm.

CHEESE BISCUITS FROM THE AMERICAN SOUTH get a southern Italian spin when you split 'em and fill them with prosciutto, arugula, and onion jam.

NOTE FROM THE KITCHENS

WE JUDGE A LOT OF RECIPE CONTESTS HERE. WHEN WE HAD ONE FOR CHOCOLATE, WE GOT A HUGE NUMBER OF VARIATIONS ON PEANUT BUTTER PIE FROM VIEWERS, SO WE FIGURED IT WAS TIME FOR US TO GET IN ON THE PB-PIE ACTION AND CREATE ONE OF OUR OWN.

Chocolate-Peanut Butter Pie

CRUST

1¼ cups dry-roasted, salted peanuts

½ cup granulated sugar

Pinch ground cloves

¼ cup unsalted butter, melted

6 ounces bittersweet chocolate

¼ cup heavy cream

FILLING

1½ cups milk

2 large eggs

1 cup confectioners' sugar

2 tablespoons cornstarch

Pinch fine salt

4 ounces cream cheese, cut into pieces

½ cup creamy peanut butter

1 teaspoon pure vanilla extract

TOPPING

2 ounces bittersweet chocolate

1¼ cups heavy cream, chilled

1 tablespoon confectioners' sugar

Yield: 8 servings

1. For the crust: Preheat the oven to 350°F. Pulse the peanuts, granulated sugar, and cloves in a food processor until the mixture resembles coarse sand. Pulse in the butter. Press the nut mixture evenly into the bottom of a 10-inch springform pan and bake until set, about 15 minutes. Set aside to cool slightly.

2. Melt the chocolate with the cream in a microwave, stirring every 30 seconds, until smooth and then spread the chocolate over the crust. Freeze the crust while making the filling.

3. For the filling: Whisk the milk, eggs, confectioners' sugar, cornstarch, and salt in a medium saucepan. Cook over medium heat, whisking constantly, until boiling. Continue to cook until the consistency of mayonnaise, about 2 minutes more. Transfer to a bowl. Whisk in the cream cheese, peanut butter, and vanilla. Spread evenly over the chocolate and refrigerate overnight, or until cold.

4. For the topping: Melt the chocolate in a microwave, stirring every 30 seconds, until smooth; cool slightly. Whip the cream with the confectioners' sugar until it holds slightly stiff peaks. Stir a large spoonful of the cream into the chocolate and then fold all the chocolate into the cream. Remove the pie from the pan. Spread the cream topping onto the pie with an offset spatula. Refrigerate for at least 30 minutes before serving.

ANY EXCUSE
WE GET TO MAKE
COOKIES,
WE DO IT.
NEW BABY?
WEDDING?
HOLIDAY?
THURSDAY
AFTERNOON?
WE MAKE COOKIES.
SNICKERDOODLES
ARE AMONG
OUR ALL-TIME
FAVORITES.
PARTIALLY
BECAUSE THEY'RE
DELICIOUS
AND PARTIALLY
BECAUSE WE
GET TO SAY
"SNICKERDOODLES."

Snickerdoodles

2¾ cups all-purpose flour

1 teaspoon baking soda

½ teaspoon fine salt

½ cup shortening

½ cup unsalted butter, softened

1½ cups plus 3 tablespoons granulated sugar

2 large eggs

1 tablespoon ground cinnamon

Yield: about 20 cookies

1. Preheat the oven to 350°F. Sift the flour, baking soda, and salt into a bowl.

2. With a handheld or standing mixer beat together the shortening and butter. Add the 1½ cups sugar and continue beating until light and fluffy, about 5 minutes. Add the eggs, one at a time, beating well after each addition. Add the flour mixture and blend until smooth.

3. Mix the 3 tablespoons sugar with the cinnamon in a small bowl. Roll the dough, by hand, into 1½-inch balls. Roll the balls in the cinnamon sugar. Flatten the balls into ½-inch-thick disks, spacing them evenly on unlined cookie sheets. Bake until light brown but still moist in the center, about 12 minutes. Cool on a rack.

KITCHEN TIP Everyone's oven is a little different. To make sure that cookies and cakes cook evenly, rotate the pans about halfway through cooking from right to left and top to bottom.

INDEX

INDEX

FOOD PHOTOGRAPHS ARE NOTED IN COLORED NUMERALS.

A

Almonds
 Chocolate Amaretti Cake, 104, 105
 Nonna's Lemon Ricotta Biscuits, 102, 103
Ancho chiles
 about, 39
 Ancho Chile-Mustard Sauce, 39
 Red Chile Horseradish, 33
Andouille Corn Bread Stuffing, 80–81
Andouille Cream, 80–81
Angry Shrimp with Citrus-Spinach
 Salad, 140, 141
Annatto paste, about, 241
Appetizers and snacks
 Bruschetta with White Bean Puree, 132
 Buffalo Popcorn Chicken Bites, 168
 Charred Corn Guacamole with Chips, 30
 Chili Dog Nachos, 170, 171
 Corn Dogs, 12, 13
 Crab Cakes with Remoulade Sauce, 212
 Crispy Olives Stuffed with Sausage, 130, 131
 Duck Pastrami, 72
 Fried Crab Wontons with Sesame-Soy
  Dipping Sauce, 190, 191
 Grilled Oysters with Mango Pico de
  Gallo & Red Chile Horseradish, 32, 33
 Grilled Shrimp in Lettuce Leaves with
  Serrano-Mint Sauce, 34, 35
 Mosaic Chicken Terrine, 154, 155
 Pizza with Caramelized Onions &
  Crispy Bacon, 215
 Scallop Ceviche with Melon, Chile
  & Mint, 194, 195
 Shrimp Dean Martinis, 172
 Spicy Chinese Five-Spice-Rubbed
  Chicken Wings with Creamy
  Cilantro Dipping Sauce, 50, 51
Apples
 Apple Tarte Tatin, 87
 Butternut Squash, Apple & Onion
  Galette with Stilton, 242, 243
 Piggy Pudding, 158
 removing cores from, 87
Apricots
 Apricot-Glazed Chicken with Dried
  Plums & Sage, 64
 Sicilian Harvest Salad, 136
 Wolfgang's Sachertorte, 229
Arancine with Ragu, 112
Artichokes
 Lemon-Braised Artichokes over Pasta, 134
 Mosaic Chicken Terrine, 154, 155
 Red Snapper en Papillote, 18, 19
 trimming, 134
Arugula
 Baby Arugula with Country Ham, Goat
  Cheese, Dried Cherries & Walnut
  Vinaigrette, 74, 75
 Pan-Grilled Veggie Sandwiches with
  Ricotta, Arugula & Balsamic, 54, 55
Asian-Style Braised Short Ribs, 82, 83

Asparagus
 blanching, 92
 Spaghetti with Asparagus, Smoked
  Mozzarella & Prosciutto, 92
Avocados
 Charred Corn Guacamole with Chips, 30

B

Baby Arugula with Country Ham, Goat
 Cheese, Dried Cherries & Walnut
 Vinaigrette, 74, 75
Baby Back Ribs with Espresso Barbecue
 Sauce, 138, 139
Bacon
 about, 95
 BLT-Smashed Potatoes, 178, 179
 Cinnamon-Pancetta Carbonara, 93
 Pizza with Caramelized Onions &
  Crispy Bacon, 215
 The Ultimate Roast Chicken, 198
Baked Eggs with Farmhouse Cheddar &
 Potatoes, 234
Banana-Black Walnut Cake, Tennessee, with
 Caramel Frosting, 160, 161
Barbecue sauce
 Espresso Barbecue Sauce, 139
 used as stock substitute, 221
Basil
 Angry Shrimp with Citrus-Spinach
  Salad, 140, 141
 Basil Cream Sauce, 150
 Mango-Basil Salsa, 58
 Pesto, 57, 150
 Pesto-Stuffed Salmon with Tomato-
  Corn Salad, 236, 237
Batali, Mario, 106–125
 Arancine with Ragu, 112
 Brown Chicken Stock, 123
 Clam Sauté, 114
 Lamb with Olives, 123
 Linguine with Crab, Radicchio &
  Garlic, 116, 117
 Mario's Basic Tomato Sauce, 111
 Osso Buco with Toasted Pine Nut
  Gremolata, 118, 119
 Penne with Cauliflower, 115
 Pork with Sweet Garlic & Fennel, 122
 Ragu, 112
 Rum and Ricotta Fritters, 124, 125
 Saffron Risotto, 112
 Stuffed Meatballs, 120
 Toasted Pine Nut Gremolata, 118, 119
 2-Minute Calamari, Sicilian
  Lifeguard-Style, 110, 111
Batidas, about, 43
Batidos, Fresh Fruit, 42, 43
Beans
 Black Bean Soup, 52
 Bruschetta with White Bean Puree, 132
 Red Wine Beef Stew with Potatoes &
  Green Beans, 62
 Tilapia with Lemon Vinaigrette, 98, 99

Beef
    Asian-Style Braised Short Ribs, 82, 83
    best cuts, for stews, 62
    Bubba's Country-Fried Steak & Gravy, 156
    Chili Dog Nachos, 170, 171
    Corn Dogs, 12, 13
    flank steak, cooking, 179
    flank steak, slicing, 179
    Grilled Steak & Papaya Salad, 40, 41
    Marinated Grilled Flank Steak with
      BLT-Smashed Potatoes, 178, 179
    Pressure Cooker Chili, 14
    Red Wine Beef Stew with Potatoes &
      Green Beans, 62
    roasted, resting before carving, 199
    round steaks, tenderizing, 156
    Spicy Grilled Beef Tenderloin, 199
    Stuffed Meatballs, 120
    tenderloin, about, 199
    Wolfgang's Beef Goulash, 223
Berries
    Blueberry-Pecan Crumble, 65
    Lemon Blueberry Cheesecake
      Topping, 204
Biscuits, Parmesan, Pepper &
    Lemon, 244, 245
Black Bean Soup, 52
Blenders, 133
Blind-baking, about, 101, 226
Blueberries
    Blueberry-Pecan Crumble, 65
    Lemon Blueberry Cheesecake
      Topping, 204
Blue cheese
    Butternut Squash, Apple & Onion
      Galette with Stilton, 242, 243
    Cabrales, about, 31
    Grilled Potato Salad with Watercress,
      Green Onions & Blue Cheese
      Vinaigrette, 31
Bourbon-Mashed Sweet Potatoes, 84, 85
Bow Ties with Pesto, Feta & Cherry
    Tomatoes, 56, 57
Breads
    Bruschetta with White Bean Puree, 132
    English Muffins, 20, 21
    Parmesan, Pepper & Lemon
      Biscuits, 244, 245
Broth, Parsley-Mint Pesto, 175
Brown, Alton, 8–25
    City Ham, 17
    Corn Dogs, 12, 13
    Eggplant Pasta, 16
    English Muffins, 20, 21
    French Onion Soup, 14
    Lemon-Ginger Frozen Yogurt, 23
    Moo-Less Chocolate Pie, 23
    Pineapple Upside-Down Cornmeal
      Cake, 24, 25
    Pressure Cooker Chili, 14
    Red Snapper en Papillote, 18, 19
Brown Chicken Stock, 123

Brunoise, 212
Bruschetta with White Bean Puree, 132
Bubba's Country-Fried Steak & Gravy, 156
Buffalo Popcorn Chicken Bites, 168
Burgers
    Lamb Burgers with Feta, 239
    Pork & Chorizo Burgers with Green
      Chile Mayonnaise, 73
    Tuna Burgers with Pineapple-Mustard
      Glaze & Green Chile-Pickle Relish, 36
Butter, clarifying, 212
Butterflied Turkey with Yucatan Rub, 241
Buttermilk Dressing, 76
Butternut Squash, Apple & Onion Galette
    with Stilton, 242, 243

C

Cabbage & Sherry Vinegar Sauce,
    Pork Chops with, 218
Cabrales cheese, about, 31
Caciocavallo cheese
    about, 115
    Penne with Cauliflower, 115
    Stuffed Meatballs, 120
Cakes
    baking, tips for, 248
    Chocolate Amaretti Cake, 104, 105
    Chocolate Date Pudding Cake, 203
    cutting into layers, 229
    Is It Really Better Than Sex? Cake, 163
    Mango Dos Leches, 142, 143
    Pineapple Upside-Down Cornmeal
      Cake, 24, 25
    Tennessee Banana-Black Walnut
      Cake with Caramel Frosting, 160, 161
    The Ultimate Cheesecake, 204
    Wolfgang's Sachertorte, 229
Calamari
    Crispy Calamari with Chinese Noodles
      & Spicy Garlic Sauce, 216, 217
    2-Minute Calamari, Sicilian
      Lifeguard-Style, 110, 111
Caramel Frosting, 160, 161
Caramelized Lemon-Lime Tart, 226
Caramelized Onions, 85
Carrots
    Chino Carrot & Ginger Soup, 210, 211
    white and yellow, buying, 211
Cauliflower, Penne with, 115
Ceviche, Scallop, with Melon, Chile
    & Mint, 194, 195
Charred Corn Guacamole with Chips, 30
Cheddar cheese
    Baked Eggs with Farmhouse Cheddar
      & Potatoes, 234
    Chili Dog Nachos, 170, 171
    Corn Casserole, 159
    Make-Your-Own-Tacos Bar, 180, 181
    Tomato Pie, 148, 149

INDEX

Cheese
Baby Arugula with Country Ham, Goat
Cheese, Dried Cherries & Walnut
Vinaigrette, 74, 75
Baked Eggs with Farmhouse Cheddar
& Potatoes, 234
Bow Ties with Pesto, Feta & Cherry
Tomatoes, 56, 57
Butternut Squash, Apple & Onion
Galette with Stilton, 242, 243
Cabrales, about, 31
caciocavallo, about, 115
Chili Dog Nachos, 170, 171
Cinnamon-Pancetta Carbonara, 93
Corn Casserole, 159
Cream of Mushroom Egg Noodle
Fake-Bake, Hold the Canned Soup, 176
Creamy Ricotta Tart with Pine Nuts, 101
Emmentaler, about, 176
French Onion Soup, 14
Grilled Mushroom Salad Subs, 173
Grilled Potato Salad with Watercress,
Green Onions & Blue Cheese
Vinaigrette, 31
Gruyère, about, 176
Lamb Burgers with Feta, 239
Make-Your-Own-Tacos Bar, 180, 181
mascarpone, about, 43
Mosaic Chicken Terrine, 154, 155
Nonna's Lemon Ricotta Biscuits, 102, 103
Pan-Grilled Veggie Sandwiches with
Ricotta, Arugula & Balsamic, 54, 55
Parmesan, Pepper & Lemon
Biscuits, 244, 245
Parmesan rinds, cooking with, 112
Penne with Cauliflower, 115
Pesto, 57, 150
Pizza with Caramelized Onions &
Crispy Bacon, 215
queso fresco, about, 38
ricotta, about, 103
Rum & Ricotta Fritters, 124, 125
Rum Buttered–Glazed Grilled Pineapple
with Vanilla-Scented Mascarpone, 43
Salami Salad with Tomatoes &
Mozzarella, 133
Shredded Chicken & Tomatillo Tacos with
Queso Fresco, 38
Spaghetti with Asparagus, Smoked
Mozzarella & Prosciutto, 92
Spicy Grilled Beef Tenderloin, 199
Stuffed Meatballs, 120
Stuffed Shells with Arrabbiata
Sauce, 94, 95
Swiss, types of, 176
Tomato Pie, 148, 149
The Ultimate Cheesecake, 204
Cheesecakes
baking in water bath, 204
The Ultimate Cheesecake, 204

Chiarello, Michael, 126–143
Angry Shrimp with Citrus-
Spinach Salad, 140, 141
Baby Back Ribs with Espresso Barbecue
Sauce, 138, 139
Bruschetta with White Bean Puree, 132
Crispy Olives Stuffed with Sausage, 130, 131
Homemade Tomato Soup, 133
Lemon-Braised Artichokes over Pasta, 134
Mango Dos Leches, 142, 143
Salami Salad with Tomatoes &
Mozzarella, 133
Seared Pork Tenderloin with Cocoa-Spice
Rub, 137
Sicilian Harvest Salad, 136
Chicken
Apricot-Glazed Chicken with Dried Plums
& Sage, 64
broilers, about, 64
Brown Chicken Stock, 123
Buffalo Popcorn Chicken Bites, 168
butterflying, 221
Chicken with Leeks, Watercress
& Radish, 240
Curried Chicken Salad in Lettuce Cups, 53
fryers, about, 64
legs, boned, buying, 81
Mosaic Chicken Terrine, 154, 155
Pan-Roasted Chicken with Port &
Whole-Grain Mustard, 220, 221
roasters, about, 64
Shredded Chicken & Tomatillo Tacos with
Queso Fresco, 38
Spicy Chinese Five-Spice-Rubbed
Chicken Wings with Creamy Cilantro
Dipping Sauce, 50, 51
stewing, about, 64
Stuffed Chicken Legs in Puff Pastry with
Andouille Cream, 80
Tortilla Soup, 235
The Ultimate Roast Chicken, 198
Chiffonade, 16
Chile oil, buying, 34
Chile powder, buying, 39
Chiles
ancho, about, 39
Ancho Chile–Mustard Sauce, 39
Angry Shrimp with Citrus-Spinach Salad,
140, 141
Corn-Jalapeño Relish, 76
de arbol, about, 39
Green Chile Mayonnaise, 73
Green Chile-Pickle Relish, 36
guajillo, about, 39
pasilla, about, 39
puree, preparing, 39
Red Chile Horseradish, 33
Scallop Ceviche with Melon, Chile & Mint,
194, 195
Serrano-Mint Sauce, 34, 35
Thai bird, about, 41
working with, 34

Chili, Pressure Cooker, 14
Chili Dog Nachos, 170, 171
Chinese five-spice powder, about, 51
Chino Carrot & Ginger Soup, 210, 211
Chinois-Grilled Lamb Chops with Cilantro-
    Mint Vinaigrette, 224, 225
Chocolate
    Chocolate Amaretti Cake, 104, 105
    Chocolate Date Pudding Cake, 203
    Chocolate-Peanut Butter Pie, 246, 247
    chopping, 183
    Hot Fudge Sundaes, 183
    melting in microwave, 104
    Moo-Less Chocolate Pie, 23
    Wolfgang's Sachertorte, 229
Chorizo & Pork Burgers with Green Chile
    Mayonnaise, 73
Cilantro
    Cilantro-Mint Vinaigrette, 224, 225
    Creamy Cilantro Dipping Sauce, 51
Cinnamon-Pancetta Carbonara, 93
Cinzano, about, 122
City Ham, 17
Clams
    Clam Sauté, 114
    cleaning, 114
    Emeril's Memory Stovetop Clam Boil, 78, 79
Cobbler, Quick Peaches & Golden
    Raisins, 184, 185
Cocoa-Spice Rub, Seared Pork Tenderloin
    with, 137
Coconut
    Is It Really Better Than Sex? Cake, 163
    toasting, 163
Cod with Burst Grape Tomatoes, Parsley-Mint
    Pesto Broth & Roast Fingerling Potato
    Crisps with Herbs, 175
Cookies
    baking, tips for, 248
    Snickerdoodles, 248
Corn
    Charred Corn Guacamole with Chips, 30
    Corn Casserole, 159
    Corn Dogs, 12, 13
    Corn-Jalapeño Relish, 76
    Emeril's Memory Stovetop Clam Boil, 78, 79
    Pesto-Stuffed Salmon with Tomato-Corn
        Salad, 236, 237
    preparing for grilling, 30
    removing from cob, 76
    Tortilla Soup, 235
Corn Bread Stuffing, Andouille, 80-81
Corn Dogs, 12, 13
Cornmeal
    Corn Dogs, 12, 13
    Pineapple Upside-Down Cornmeal
        Cake, 24, 25
Couscous
    Israeli, about, 111
    Red Snapper en Papillote, 18, 19
    2-Minute Calamari, Sicilian
        Lifeguard-Style, 110, 111

Crabmeat
    Crab Cakes with Remoulade Sauce, 212
    Fried Crab Wontons with Sesame-Soy
        Dipping Sauce, 190, 191
    Lady & Sons Crab-Stuffed Shrimp, 150
    Linguine with Crab, Radicchio
        & Garlic, 116, 117
Cream of Mushroom Egg Noodle Fake-Bake,
    Hold the Canned Soup, 176
Creamy Cilantro Dipping Sauce, 51
Creamy Garlicky Mussels, 193
Creamy Ricotta Tart with Pine Nuts, 101
Crème Fraîche-Mashed Potatoes, 152, 153
Creole Seasoning, Emeril's Essence, 81
Crispy Calamari with Chinese Noodles &
    Spicy Garlic Sauce, 216, 217
Crispy Olives Stuffed with Sausage, 130, 131
Curried Chicken Salad in Lettuce Cups, 53

D
Dates
    Chocolate Date Pudding Cake, 203
    pitted, buying, 203
    removing pits from, 203
Deen, Paula, 144–163
    Bubba's Country-Fried Steak & Gravy, 156
    Corn Casserole, 159
    Is It Really Better Than Sex? Cake, 163
    Lady & Sons Crab-Stuffed Shrimp, 150
    Mosaic Chicken Terrine, 154, 155
    Paula's House Seasoning, 153
    Piggy Pudding, 158
    Seared Diver Scallops with Bacon &
        Whole-Grain Mustard Rub & Crème
        Fraîche-Mashed Potatoes, 152, 153
    Stuffed Pork Chops with Grits, 157
    Tennessee Banana-Black Walnut Cake
        with Caramel Frosting, 160, 161
    Tomato Pie, 148, 149
Demitasse cups, 139
Desserts
    Apple Tarte Tatin, 87
    Blueberry-Pecan Crumble, 65
    Caramelized Lemon-Lime Tart, 226
    Chocolate Amaretti Cake, 104, 105
    Chocolate Date Pudding Cake, 203
    Chocolate-Peanut Butter Pie, 246, 247
    Creamy Ricotta Tart with Pine Nuts, 101
    Fresh Fruit Batidos, 42, 43
    Hot Fudge Sundaes, 183
    Is It Really Better Than Sex? Cake, 163
    Lemon-Ginger Frozen Yogurt, 23
    Mango Dos Leches, 142, 143
    Moo-Less Chocolate Pie, 23
    Nonna's Lemon Ricotta Biscuits, 102, 103
    Pineapple Upside-Down Cornmeal
        Cake, 24, 25
    Quick Peaches & Golden Raisins
        Cobbler, 184, 185
    Rum & Ricotta Fritters, 124, 125
    Rum Buttered-Glazed Grilled Pineapple
        with Vanilla-Scented Mascarpone, 43

INDEX

FOOD
PHOTOGRAPHS
ARE NOTED IN
COLORED
NUMERALS.

***Cooking with raw eggs
carries with it a slight risk
of salmonella, the bacteria
responsible for some food-borne
illnesses. When using raw eggs
in recipes, be sure to use clean,
fresh, grade A or AA eggs
without cracks that you know
have been refrigerated and
handled properly.*

Snickerdoodles, 248
Tennessee Banana-Black Walnut Cake
 with Caramel Frosting, 160, 161
The Ultimate Cheesecake, 204
Wolfgang's Sachertorte, 229
Dips
 Charred Corn Guacamole with Chips, 30
 Creamy Cilantro Dipping Sauce, 51
 Mango-Basil Salsa, 58
 Mango Pico de Gallo, 32, 33
 Pesto, 57, 150
 Yellow Pico de Gallo, 181
Dirty Risotto, 96
Double boilers, improvising, 236
Drinks
 batidas, about, 43
 Fresh Fruit Batidos, 42, 43
Duck Pastrami, 72

E
Eggplant Pasta, 16
Eggs**
 Baked Eggs with Farmhouse Cheddar &
  Potatoes, 234
 Cinnamon-Pancetta Carbonara, 93
 cooking, for tart filling, 226
Electric skillets, 14
Emeril's Essence Creole Seasoning, 81
Emeril's Memory Stovetop Clam Boil, 78, 79
English Muffins, 20, 21
Espresso Barbecue Sauce, 139

F
Fennel
 buying, 122
 Pork with Sweet Garlic & Fennel, 122
Feta cheese
 Bow Ties with Pesto, Feta & Cherry
  Tomatoes, 56, 57
 Lamb Burgers with Feta, 239
 Spicy Grilled Beef Tenderloin, 199
Fish. *See also* Shellfish
 Cod with Burst Grape Tomatoes, Parsley-
  Mint Pesto Broth & Roast Fingerling
  Potato Crisps with Herbs, 175
 overfished varieties of, 98
 Pan-Roasted Halibut with Prosciutto,
  Lemon, White Wine & Capers, 196, 197
 Pesto-Stuffed Salmon with Tomato-Corn
  Salad, 236, 237
 red snapper, buying, 19
 Red Snapper en Papillote, 18, 19
 Roasted Salmon with Roasted Plum
  Tomatoes & Caramelized Lemons, 60, 61
 salmon, cutting pocket in, 237
 salmon, health benefits from, 61
 Tilapia with Lemon Vinaigrette, 98, 99
 tuna, chopping fine, 36
 Tuna Burgers with Pineapple-Mustard
  Glaze & Green Chile-Pickle Relish, 36
Flay, Bobby, 26–45
 Charred Corn Guacamole with Chips, 30

Fresh Fruit Batidos, 42, 43
Grilled Oysters with Mango Pico de Gallo
 & Red Chile Horseradish, 32, 33
Grilled Potato Salad with Watercress,
 Green Onions & Blue Cheese
 Vinaigrette, 31
Grilled Shrimp in Lettuce Leaves with
 Serrano-Mint Sauce, 34, 35
Grilled Steak & Papaya Salad, 40, 41
Rum Buttered-Glazed Grilled Pineapple
 with Vanilla-Scented Mascarpone, 43
Shredded Chicken & Tomatillo Tacos with
 Queso Fresco, 38
Spice-Rubbed Pork Tenderloin with
 Ancho Chile-Mustard Sauce, 39
Tuna Burgers with Pineapple-Mustard
 Glaze & Green Chile-Pickle Relish, 36
Florence, Tyler, 186–205
 Chocolate Date Pudding Cake, 203
 Creamy Garlicky Mussels, 193
 Fried Crab Wontons with Sesame-Soy
  Dipping Sauce, 190, 191
 Pan-Roasted Halibut with Prosciutto,
  Lemon, White Wine & Capers, 196, 197
 Roast Leg of Lamb with Dark Beer,
  Honey & Thyme, 200, 201
 Scallop Ceviche with Melon, Chile &
  Mint, 194, 195
 Spicy Grilled Beef Tenderloin, 199
 Spinach Salad with Honey-Brown Butter
  Dressing, 203
 The Ultimate Cheesecake, 204
 The Ultimate Roast Chicken, 198
Food Network Kitchens, 230-248
 Baked Eggs with Farmhouse Cheddar &
  Potatoes, 234
 Butterflied Turkey with Yucatan Rub, 241
 Butternut Squash, Apple & Onion Galette
  with Stilton, 242, 243
 Chicken with Leeks, Watercress & Radish, 240
 Chocolate-Peanut Butter Pie, 246, 247
 Lamb Burgers with Feta, 239
 Parmesan, Pepper & Lemon
  Biscuits, 244, 245
 Pesto-Stuffed Salmon with Tomato-Corn
  Salad, 236, 237
 Snickerdoodles, 248
 Tortilla Soup, 235
French Onion Soup, 14
Fresh Fruit Batidos, 42, 43
Fried Crab Wontons with Sesame-Soy
 Dipping Sauce, 190, 191
Fried Oyster Salad with Buttermilk Dressing
 & Corn-Jalapeño Relish, 76
Fried Rosemary, 136
Fritters, Rum & Ricotta, 124, 125
Frosting, Caramel, 160, 161
Fruit. *See also specific fruits*
 citrus, grating, 103
 citrus, juicing, 235
 citrus, segmenting, 141
 citrus, zesting, 58

G

Galette, Butternut Squash, Apple & Onion, with Stilton, 242, 243
Garlic
    blanched, flavor of, 217
    Crispy Calamari with Chinese Noodles & Spicy Garlic Sauce, 216, 217
    crushing, 52, 139
    Double-Blanched Garlic, 217
    mashing, 139
    mincing, 139
    presses, about, 52
    roasting, 153
    Sweet Garlic, 122
Ginger
    Chino Carrot & Ginger Soup, 210, 211
    Lemon-Ginger Frozen Yogurt, 23
Goat Cheese, Country Ham, Dried Cherries & Walnut Vinaigrette, Baby Arugula with, 74, 75
Goulash, Wolfgang's Beef, 223
Grapes
    Curried Chicken Salad in Lettuce Cups, 53
    Sicilian Harvest Salad, 136
Green Chile Mayonnaise, 73
Green Chile-Pickle Relish, 36
Greens. *See also* Spinach
    Baby Arugula with Country Ham, Goat Cheese, Dried Cherries & Walnut Vinaigrette, 74, 75
    Chicken with Leeks, Watercress & Radish, 240
    Curried Chicken Salad in Lettuce Cups, 53
    Grilled Potato Salad with Watercress, Green Onions & Blue Cheese Vinaigrette, 31
    Grilled Shrimp in Lettuce Leaves with Serrano-Mint Sauce, 34, 35
    lettuce leaves, separating, 34
    Pan-Grilled Veggie Sandwiches with Ricotta, Arugula & Balsamic, 54, 55
Gremolata, Toasted Pine Nut, 118, 119
Grilled dishes
    Baby Back Ribs with Espresso Barbecue Sauce, 138, 139
    Butterflied Turkey with Yucatan Rub, 241
    Charred Corn Guacamole with Chips, 30
    Chinois-Grilled Lamb Chops with Cilantro-Mint Vinaigrette, 224, 225
    Grilled Mushroom Salad Subs, 173
    Grilled Oysters with Mango Pico de Gallo & Red Chile Horseradish, 32, 33
    Grilled Potato Salad with Watercress, Green Onions & Blue Cheese Vinaigrette, 31
    Grilled Shrimp in Lettuce Leaves with Serrano-Mint Sauce, 34, 35
    Grilled Steak & Papaya Salad, 40, 41
    Lamburgers with Feta, 239
    Marinated Grilled Flank Ssteak with BLT-Smashed Potatoes, 178, 179

Pan-Grilled Veggie Sandwiches with Ricotta, Arugula & Balsamic, 54, 55
Pesto-Stuffed Salmon with Tomato-Corn Salad, 236, 237
Pork & Chorizo Burgers with Green Chile Mayonnaise, 73
Root Beer-Glazed Pork Chops with Bourbon-Mashed Sweet Potatoes & Caramelized Onions, 84, 85
Rum Buttered-Glazed Grilled Pineapple with Vanilla-Scented Mascarpone, 43
Shredded Chicken & Tomatillo Tacos with Queso Fresco, 38
Spicy Grilled Beef Tenderloin, 199
Tuna Burgers with Pineapple-Mustard Glaze & Green Chile-Pickle Relish, 36
Grits, 157
Guacamole, Charred Corn, with Chips, 30
Guajillo chiles, about, 39

H

Halibut, Pan-Roasted, with Prosciutto, Lemon, White Wine & Capers, 196, 197
Ham
    Baby Arugula with Country Ham, Goat Cheese, Dried Cherries & Walnut Vinaigrette, 74, 75
    city, about, 17
    City Ham, 17
    country, about, 75
    prosciutto, about, 92
    scoring, 17
    Spaghetti with Asparagus, Smoked Mozzarella & Prosciutto, 92
Herbs. *See also* Basil
    to chiffonade, 16
    Cilantro-Mint Vinaigrette, 224, 225
    Creamy Cilantro Dipping Sauce, 51
    fresh, in salads, 61
    fresh, storing, 61
    Fried Rosemary, 136
    herbes de Provence, about, 100
    Parsley-Mint Pesto Broth, 175
    recao, about, 33
    savory, about, 239
    Scallop Ceviche with Melon, Chile & Mint, 194, 195
    Serrano-Mint Sauce, 34, 35
    Toasted Pine Nut Gremolata, 118, 119
Homemade Tomato Soup, 133
Honey-Brown Butter Dressing, 203
Horseradish, Red Chile, 33
Hot dogs
    Chili Dog Nachos, 170, 171
    Corn Dogs, 12, 13
Hot Fudge Sundaes, 183

I

Ice cream
    Fresh Fruit Batidos, 42, 43
    Hot Fudge Sundaes, 183
    scoops, sizes of, 20

INDEX

Is It Really Better Than Sex? Cake, 163

J
Jalapeño-Corn Relish, 76
Julienne, defined, 212

L
Lady & Sons Crab-Stuffed Shrimp, 150
Lagasse, Emeril, 66–87
  Apple Tarte Tatin, 87
  Asian-Style Braised Short Ribs, 82, 83
  Baby Arugula with Country Ham, Goat Cheese, Dried Cherries & Walnut Vinaigrette, 74, 75
  Duck Pastrami, 72
  Emeril's Essence Creole Seasoning, 81
  Emeril's Memory Stovetop Clam Boil, 78, 79
  Fried Oyster Salad with Buttermilk Dressing & Corn-Jalapeño Relish, 76
  Mushroom Confit with Pasta Rags & Truffle Oil, 70
  Pork & Chorizo Burgers with Green Chile Mayonnaise, 73
  Root Beer-Glazed Pork Chops with Bourbon-Mashed Sweet Potatoes & Caramelized Onions, 84, 85
  Stuffed Chicken Legs in Puff Pastry with Andouille Cream, 80
Lamb
  boned leg, rolling up, 201
  Chinois-Grilled Lamb Chops with Cilantro-Mint Vinaigrette, 224, 225
  Lamb Burgers with Feta, 239
  Lamb with Olives, 123
  Pressure Cooker Chili, 14
  roasting, 201
  Roast Leg of Lamb with Dark Beer, Honey & Thyme, 200, 201
de Laurentiis, Giada, 88–105
  Chocolate Amaretti Cake, 104, 105
  Cinnamon-Pancetta Carbonara, 93
  Creamy Ricotta Tart with Pine Nuts, 101
  Dirty Risotto, 96
  Nonna's Lemon Ricotta Biscuits, 102, 103
  Pork Chops alla Pizzaiola, 100
  Shrimp Fra Diavolo, 96
  Spaghetti with Asparagus, Smoked Mozzarella & Prosciutto, 92
  Stuffed Shells with Arrabbiata Sauce, 94, 95
  Tilapia with Lemon Vinaigrette, 98, 99
Leeks
  BLT-Smashed Potatoes, 178, 179
  Chicken with Leeks, Watercress & Radish, 240
  cleaning, 240
Lemons
  Caramelized Lemon-Lime Tart, 226
  Lemon Blueberry Cheesecake Topping, 204
  Lemon-Braised Artichokes over Pasta, 134
  Lemon-Ginger Frozen Yogurt, 23
  Lemon Vinaigrette, 98
  Nonna's Lemon Ricotta Biscuits, 102, 103
  Roasted Salmon with Roasted Plum Tomatoes & Caramelized Lemons, 60, 61
  zest of, grating, 103
Lettuce
  Curried Chicken Salad in Lettuce Cups, 53
  Grilled Shrimp in Lettuce Leaves with Serrano-Mint Sauce, 34, 35
  leaves, separating, 34
Lieberman, Dave, 46–65
  Apricot-Glazed Chicken with Dried Plums & Sage, 64
  Black Bean Soup, 52
  Blueberry-Pecan Crumble, 65
  Bow Ties with Pesto, Feta & Cherry Tomatoes, 56, 57
  Curried Chicken Salad in Lettuce Cups, 53
  Pan-Grilled Veggie Sandwiches with Ricotta, Arugula & Balsamic, 54, 55
  Red Wine Beef Stew with Potatoes & Green Beans, 62
  Roasted Salmon with Roasted Plum Tomatoes & Caramelized Lemons, 60, 61
  Spicy Chinese Five-Spice Rubbed Chicken Wings with Creamy Cilantro Dipping Sauce, 50, 51
  Spicy Coconut Shrimp with Mango-Basil Salsa & Lime Jasmine Rice, 58
Limes
  Caramelized Lemon-Lime Tart, 226
  juicing, 235
  Lime Jasmine Rice, 58
  Yucatan Rub, 241
Linguine with Crab, Radicchio & Garlic, 116, 117

M
Main dishes—meat
  Asian-Style Braised Short Ribs, 82, 83
  Baby Back Ribs with Espresso Barbecue Sauce, 138, 139
  Bubba's Country-Fried Steak & Gravy, 156
  Chinois-Grilled Lamb Chops with Cilantro-Mint Vinaigrette, 224, 225
  City Ham, 17
  Grilled Steak & Papaya Salad, 40, 41
  Lamb Burgers with Feta, 239
  Lamb with Olives, 123
  Make-Your-Own-Tacos Bar, 180, 181
  Marinated Grilled Flank Steak with BLT-Smashed Potatoes, 178, 179
  Osso Buco with Toasted Pine Nut Gremolata, 118, 119
  Piggy Pudding, 158
  Pork & Chorizo Burgers with Green Chile Mayonnaise, 73
  Pork Chops alla Pizzaiola, 100
  Pork Chops with Cabbage & Sherry Vinegar Sauce, 218
  Pork with Sweet Garlic & Fennel, 122
  Pressure Cooker Chili, 14
  Red Wine Beef Stew with Potatoes & Green Beans, 62

Roast Leg of Lamb with Dark Beer,
Honey & Thyme, 200, 201
Root Beer-Glazed Pork Chops with
Bourbon-Mashed Sweet Potatoes &
Caramelized Onions, 84, 85
Seared Pork Tenderloin with Cocoa-Spice
Rub, 137
Spice-Rubbed Pork Tenderloin with
Ancho Chile-Mustard Sauce, 39
Spicy Grilled Beef Tenderloin, 199
Stuffed Meatballs, 120
Stuffed Pork Chops with Grits, 157
Wolfgang's Beef Goulash, 223
Main dishes—pasta & grains
Arancine with Ragu, 112
Bow Ties with Pesto, Feta & Cherry
Tomatoes, 56, 57
Cinnamon-Pancetta Carbonara, 93
Cream of Mushroom Egg Noodle Fake-
Bake, Hold the Canned Soup, 176
Crispy Calamari with Chinese Noodles
& Spicy Garlic Sauce, 216, 217
Dirty Risotto, 96
Linguine with Crab, Radicchio
& Garlic, 116, 117
Penne with Cauliflower, 115
Spaghetti with Asparagus, Smoked
Mozzarella & Prosciutto, 92
Stuffed Shells with Arrabbiata Sauce, 94, 95
Main dishes—pizza & sandwiches
Grilled Mushroom Salad Subs, 173
Pan-Grilled Veggie Sandwiches with
Ricotta, Arugula & Balsamic, 54, 55
Pizza with Caramelized Onions &
Crispy Bacon, 215
Main dishes—poultry
Apricot-Glazed Chicken with Dried
Plums & Sage, 64
Butterflied Turkey with Yucatan Rub, 241
Chicken with Leeks, Watercress &
Radish, 240
Pan-Roasted Chicken with Port and
Whole Grain Mustard, 220, 221
Shredded Chicken & Tomatillo Tacos with
Queso Fresco, 38
Stuffed Chicken Legs in Puff Pastry with
Andouille Cream, 80
The Ultimate Roast Chicken, 198
Main dishes—seafood
Angry Shrimp with Citrus-Spinach
Salad, 140, 141
Clam Sauté, 114
Cod with Burst Grape Tomatoes, Parsley-
Mint Pesto Broth & Roast Fingerling
Potato Crisps with Herbs, 175
Creamy Garlicky Mussels, 193
Crispy Calamari with Chinese Noodles
& Spicy Garlic Sauce, 216, 217
Emeril's Memory Stovetop Clam Boil, 78, 79
Lady & Sons Crab-Stuffed Shrimp, 150
Pan-Roasted Halibut with Prosciutto,
Lemon, White Wine & Capers, 196, 197

Pesto-Stuffed Salmon with Tomato-Corn
Salad, 236, 237
Red Snapper en Papillote, 18, 19
Roasted Salmon with Roasted Plum
Tomatoes & Caramelized Lemons, 60, 61
Seared Diver Scallops with Bacon &
Whole-Grain Mustard Rub & Crème
Fraîche-Mashed Potatoes, 152, 153
Shrimp Fra Diavolo, 96
Spicy Coconut Shrimp with Mango-Basil
Salsa & Lime Jasmine Rice, 58
Tilapia with Lemon Vinaigrette, 98, 99
Tuna Burgers with Pineapple-Mustard
Glaze & Green Chile-Pickle Relish, 36
2-Minute Calamari, Sicilian
Lifeguard-Style, 110, 111
Make-Your-Own-Tacos Bar, 180, 181
Mangoes
Fresh Fruit Batidos, 42, 43
Mango-Basil Salsa, 58
Mango Dos Leches, 142, 143
Mango Pico de Gallo, 32, 33
preparing, 33
Marinated Grilled Flank Steak with
BLT-Smashed Potatoes, 178, 179
Mario's Basic Tomato Sauce, 111
Mascarpone cheese
about, 43
Rum Buttered-Glazed Grilled Pineapple
with Vanilla-Scented Mascarpone, 43
Mayonnaise
Green Chile Mayonnaise, 73
Remoulade Sauce, 212
Meat. See also Beef; Lamb; Pork; Veal
roasted, resting before carving, 199
Meatballs, Stuffed, 120
Melon, Chile & Mint, Scallop Ceviche
with, 194, 195
Milk, scalding, 143
Mint
Cilantro-Mint Vinaigrette, 224, 225
Parsley-Mint Pesto Broth, 175
Scallop Ceviche with Melon, Chile
& Mint, 194, 195
Serrano-Mint Sauce, 34, 35
Mirin, about, 225
Moo-Less Chocolate Pie, 23
Mosaic Chicken Terrine, 154, 155
Mozzarella cheese
Pizza with Caramelized Onions &
Crispy Bacon, 215
Salami Salad with Tomatoes &
Mozzarella, 133
Spaghetti with Asparagus, Smoked
Mozzarella & Prosciutto, 92
Stuffed Shells with Arrabbiata Sauce, 94, 95
Tomato Pie, 148, 149
Muffins
English Muffins, 20, 21
Nonna's Lemon Ricotta Biscuits, 102, 103
Mushrooms
buying and storing, 176

INDEX

cleaning, 176
Cream of Mushroom Egg Noodle Fake-Bake, Hold the Canned Soup, 176
Dirty Risotto, 96
Grilled Mushroom Salad Subs, 173
Mushroom Confit with Pasta Rags & Truffle Oil, 70

Mussels
Creamy Garlicky Mussels, 193
debearding, 193

Mustard
adding to recipes, 218
Ancho Chile-Mustard Sauce, 39

N
Nachos, Chili Dog, 170, 171
Nonna's Lemon Ricotta Biscuits, 102, 103

Noodles
Cream of Mushroom Egg Noodle Fake-Bake, Hold the Canned Soup, 176
Crispy Calamari with Chinese Noodles & Spicy Garlic Sauce, 216, 217
Spaetzle, 223

Nuts
black walnuts, about, 161
Blueberry-Pecan Crumble, 65
Chocolate Amaretti Cake, 104, 105
Creamy Ricotta Tart with Pine Nuts, 101
Nonna's Lemon Ricotta Biscuits, 102, 103
Pesto, 57, 150
pine nuts, about, 101
pine nuts, toasting, 101
Tennessee Banana-Black Walnut Cake with Caramel Frosting, 160, 161
Toasted Pine Nut Gremolata, 118, 119
Walnut Vinaigrette, 74, 75

O

Olives
Crispy Olives Stuffed with Sausage, 130, 131
jarred olive paste, about, 132
Lamb with Olives, 123
pitting, 123

Onions
browning, 14
Caramelized Onions, 85
French Onion Soup, 14
Pizza with Caramelized Onions & Crispy Bacon, 215

Oranges
Angry Shrimp with Citrus-Spinach Salad, 140, 141
Yucatan Rub, 241
Osso Buco with Toasted Pine Nut Gremolata, 118, 119

Oysters
Fried Oyster Salad with Buttermilk Dressing & Corn-Jalapeño Relish, 76
Grilled Oysters with Mango Pico de Gallo & Red Chile Horseradish, 32, 33

P

Pancetta
about, 95
Cinnamon-Pancetta Carbonara, 93
Stuffed Shells with Arrabbiata Sauce, 95
Pan-Grilled Veggie Sandwiches with Ricotta, Arugula & Balsamic, 54, 55
Pan-Roasted Chicken with Port & Whole-Grain Mustard, 220, 221
Pan-Roasted Halibut with Prosciutto, Lemon, White Wine & Capers, 196, 197

Papayas
green, about, 41
Grilled Steak & Papaya Salad, 40, 41
shredding, tools for, 41

Parmesan cheese
Arancine with Ragu, 112
Cinnamon-Pancetta Carbonara, 93
Mosaic Chicken Terrine, 154, 155
Parmesan, Pepper & Lemon Biscuits, 244, 245
Pesto, 57, 150
rinds, cooking with, 112
Stuffed Shells with Arrabbiata Sauce, 94, 95

Parsley
Parsley-Mint Pesto Broth, 175
Toasted Pine Nut Gremolata, 118, 119
Pasilla chiles, about, 39

Pasta
Bow Ties with Pesto, Feta & Cherry Tomatoes, 56, 57
Cinnamon-Pancetta Carbonara, 93
Cream of Mushroom Egg Noodle Fake-Bake, Hold the Canned Soup, 176
Crispy Calamari with Chinese Noodles & Spicy Garlic Sauce, 216, 217
dry, in recipes, 116
fresh, in recipes, 116
Israeli couscous, about, 111
Lemon-Braised Artichokes over Pasta, 134
Linguine with Crab, Radicchio & Garlic, 116, 117
Mushroom Confit with Pasta Rags & Truffle Oil, 70
Penne with Cauliflower, 115
Red Snapper en Papillote, 18, 19
Spaetzle, 223
Spaghetti with Asparagus, Smoked Mozzarella & Prosciutto, 92
Stuffed Shells with Arrabbiata Sauce, 94, 95
2-Minute Calamari, Sicilian Lifeguard-Style, 110, 111

Pastry dough
baking, tips for, 243
blind-baking, 101, 226
Paté Sucre, 226
Paté Sucre, 226
Paula's House Seasoning, 153
Peaches & Golden Raisins Cobbler, Quick, 184, 185
Peanut Butter-Chocolate Pie, 246, 247

Pecan-Blueberry Crumble, 65
Penne with Cauliflower, 115
Peppers. *See also* Chiles
  Grilled Mushroom Salad Subs, 173
  Make-Your-Own-Tacos Bar, 180, 181
  Pan-Grilled Veggie Sandwiches with
    Ricotta, Arugula & Balsamic, 54, 55
  piquillo, about, 173
Pesto
  leftover, ideas for, 57
  leftover, storing, 57
  Pesto, 57, 150
Pesto-Stuffed Salmon with Tomato-Corn
  Salad, 236, 237
Pickle-Green Chile Relish, 36
Pico de Gallo, Mango, 32, 33
Pico de Gallo, Yellow, 181
Pies. *See also* Tarts
  baking tips, 243
  blind-baking crusts, 101, 226
  Butternut Squash, Apple & Onion Galette
    with Stilton, 242, 243
  Chocolate-Peanut Butter Pie, 246, 247
  Moo-Less Chocolate Pie, 23
  Tomato Pie, 148, 149
Piggy Pudding, 158
Pineapple
  Is It Really Better Than Sex? Cake, 163
  Pineapple Upside-Down Cornmeal
    Cake, 24, 25
  Rum Buttered-Glazed Grilled Pineapple
    with Vanilla-Scented Mascarpone, 43
  Tuna Burgers with Pineapple-Mustard
    Glaze & Green Chile-Pickle Relish, 36
Pine nuts
  about, 101
  Creamy Ricotta Tart with Pine Nuts, 101
  Pesto, 57
  Toasted Pine Nut Gremolata, 118, 119
  toasting, 101
Piquillo peppers, about, 173
Pizza
  Pizza Dough, 215
  Pizza with Caramelized Onions &
    Crispy Bacon, 215
  transferring to pizza stone, 215
Plums, Dried, & Sage, Apricot-Glazed Chicken
  with, 64
Pork. *See also* Bacon; Ham; Pork sausages
  Baby Back Ribs with Espresso Barbecue
    Sauce, 138, 139
  chops, cutting pocket in, 157
  Make-Your-Own-Tacos Bar, 180, 181
  Pork & Chorizo Burgers with Green Chile
    Mayonnaise, 73
  Pork Chops alla Pizzaiola, 100
  Pork Chops with Cabbage & Sherry
    Vinegar Sauce, 218
  Pork with Sweet Garlic & Fennel, 122
  Pressure Cooker Chili, 14

Root Beer–Glazed Pork Chops with
    Bourbon-Mashed Sweet Potatoes &
    Caramelized Onions, 84, 85
  Salami Salad with Tomatoes &
    Mozzarella, 133
  Seared Pork Tenderloin with Cocoa-Spice
    Rub, 137
  Spice-Rubbed Pork Tenderloin with
    Ancho Chile-Mustard Sauce, 39
  Stuffed Pork Chops with Grits, 157
Pork sausages
  Andouille Corn Bread Stuffing, 80–81
  Andouille Cream, 80–81
  Crispy Olives Stuffed with Sausage, 130, 131
  Dirty Risotto, 96
  Emeril's Memory Stovetop Clam Boil, 78, 79
  Piggy Pudding, 158
  Pork & Chorizo Burgers with Green Chile
    Mayonnaise, 73
  Stuffed Pork Chops with Grits, 157
Potatoes
  Baked Eggs with Farmhouse Cheddar &
    Potatoes, 234
  BLT-Smashed Potatoes, 178, 179
  Bourbon-Mashed Sweet Potatoes, 84, 85
  Crème Fraîche-Mashed Potatoes, 152, 153
  Emeril's Memory Stovetop Clam Boil, 78, 79
  fingerling, about, 175
  Grilled Potato Salad with Watercress,
    Green Onions & Blue Cheese
    Vinaigrette, 31
  parboiling, 31
  Red Wine Beef Stew with Potatoes &
    Green Beans, 62
  Roast Fingerling Potato Crisps with
    Herbs, 175
Poultry. *See also* Chicken
  Butterflied Turkey with Yucatan Rub, 241
  Duck Pastrami, 72
  Make-Your-Own-Tacos Bar, 180, 181
Pressure Cooker Chili, 14
Prosciutto
  Pan-Roasted Halibut with Prosciutto,
    White Wine & Capers, 197
  about, 92
  Spaghetti with Asparagus, Smoked
    Mozzarella & Prosciutto, 92
  Stuffed Meatballs, 120
Puck, Wolfgang, 206–229
  Caramelized Lemon-Lime Tart, 226
  Chino Carrot & Ginger Soup, 210, 211
  Chinois-Grilled Lamb Chops with Cilantro-
    Mint Vinaigrette, 224, 225
  Crab Cakes with Remoulade Sauce, 212
  Crispy Calamari with Chinese Noodles
    & Spicy Garlic Sauce, 216, 217
  Pan-Roasted Chicken with Port &
    Whole-Grain Mustard, 220, 221
  Pizza with Caramelized Onions &
    Crispy Bacon, 215
  Pork Chops with Cabbage & Sherry
    Vinegar Sauce, 218

INDEX

FOOD
PHOTOGRAPHS
ARE NOTED IN
COLORED
NUMERALS.

Spaetzle, 223
Wolfgang's Beef Goulash, 223
Wolfgang's Sachertorte, 229
Pudding, Piggy, 158

Q

Queso fresco
about, 38
Shredded Chicken & Tomatillo Tacos with
Queso Fresco, 38
Quick Peaches & Golden Raisins
Cobbler, 184, 185

R

Radicchio
Linguine with Crab, Radicchio
& Garlic, 116, 117
Sicilian Harvest Salad, 136
Tilapia with Lemon Vinaigrette, 98, 99
Ragu, 112
Raisins
Quick Peaches & Golden Raisins
Cobbler, 184, 185
Sicilian Harvest Salad, 136
Ray, Rachael, 164–185
Buffalo Popcorn Chicken Bites, 168
Chili Dog Nachos, 170, 171
Cod with Burst Grape Tomatoes, Parsley-
Mint Pesto Broth & Roast Fingerling
Potato Crisps with Herbs, 175
Cream of Mushroom Egg Noodle Fake-
Bake, Hold the Canned Soup, 176
Grilled Mushroom Salad Subs, 173
Hot Fudge Sundaes, 183
Make-Your-Own-Tacos Bar, 180, 181
Marinated Grilled Flank Steak with BLT-
Smashed Potatoes, 178, 179
Quick Peaches & Golden Raisins
Cobbler, 184, 185
Shrimp Dean Martinis, 172
Recao, about, 33
Red Chile Horseradish, 33
Red snapper
buying, 19
Red Snapper en Papillote, 18, 19
Red Wine Beef Stew with Potatoes & Green
Beans, 62
Relishes
Corn-Jalapeño Relish, 76
Green Chile-Pickle Relish, 36
Remoulade Sauce, 212
Rice
Arancine with Ragu, 112
Dirty Risotto, 96
Lime Jasmine Rice, 58
Saffron Risotto, 112
Rice wine, about, 225
Ricotta cheese
about, 103
Creamy Ricotta Tart with Pine Nuts, 101
Nonna's Lemon Ricotta Biscuits, 102, 103

Pan-grilled Veggie Sandwiches with
Ricotta, Arugula & Balsamic, 54, 55
Rum & Ricotta Fritters, 124, 125
Stuffed Shells with Arrabbiata Sauce, 94, 95
Risotto
Dirty Risotto, 96
Saffron Risotto, 112
Roasted Salmon with Roasted Plum Tomatoes
& Caramelized Lemons, 60, 61
Roast Fingerling Potato Crisps with Herbs, 175
Roast Leg of Lamb with Dark Beer, Honey &
Thyme, 200, 201
Root Beer-Glazed Pork Chops with Bourbon-
Mashed Sweet Potatoes & Caramelized
Onions, 84, 85
Rosemary, Fried, 136
Rum & Ricotta Fritters, 124, 125
Rum Buttered-Glazed Grilled Pineapple with
Vanilla-Scented Mascarpone, 43

S

Sachertorte, Wolfgang's, 229
Saffron Risotto, 112
Salad dressings. See also specific salads
Blue Cheese Vinaigrette, 31
Buttermilk Dressing, 76
Cilantro-Mint Vinaigrette, 224, 225
Honey-Brown Butter Dressing, 203
Lemon Vinaigrette, 98
Walnut Vinaigrette, 75
warm, pouring over greens, 203
Salads
Angry Shrimp with Citrus-Spinach
Salad, 140, 141
Baby Arugula with Country Ham, Goat
Cheese, Dried Cherries & Walnut
Vinaigrette, 74, 75
Curried Chicken Salad in Lettuce Cups, 53
Fried Oyster Salad with Buttermilk
Dressing & Corn-Jalapeño Relish, 76
Grilled Potato Salad with Watercress,
Green Onions & Blue Cheese
Vinaigrette, 31
Grilled Steak & Papaya Salad, 40, 41
Salami Salad with Tomatoes &
Mozzarella, 133
Sicilian Harvest Salad, 136
Spinach Salad with Honey-Brown Butter
Dressing, 203
Salami Salad with Tomatoes
& Mozzarella, 133
Salmon
cutting pocket in, 237
health benefits from, 61
Pesto-Stuffed Salmon with Tomato-Corn
Salad, 236, 237
Roasted Salmon with Roasted Plum
Tomatoes & Caramelized Lemons, 60, 61
Salsa
Mango-Basil Salsa, 58
Mango Pico de Gallo, 32, 33
Yellow Pico de Gallo, 181

Salt, gray, about, 132
Sandwiches and burgers
    Grilled Mushroom Salad Subs, 173
    Lamb Burgers with Feta, 239
    Pan-Grilled Veggie Sandwiches with
        Ricotta, Arugula & Balsamic, 54, 55
    Pork & Chorizo Burgers with Green Chile
        Mayonnaise, 73
    Tuna Burgers with Pineapple-Mustard
        Glaze & Green Chile-Pickle Relish, 36
Sauces
    Ancho Chile-Mustard Sauce, 39
    Andouille Cream, 80-81
    Basil Cream Sauce, 150
    Creamy Cilantro Dipping Sauce, 51
    Espresso Barbecue Sauce, 139
    Hot Fudge Sauce, 183
    Mario's Basic Tomato Sauce, 111
    Pesto, 57, 150
    Ragu, 112
    Remoulade Sauce, 212
    Serrano-Mint Sauce, 34, 35
    Sesame-Soy Dipping Sauce, 190, 191
    tomato, freezing, 111
    Tzatziki, 239
Sausages. See Pork sausages
Savory, about, 239
Scallops
    buying and preparing, 153
    Scallop Ceviche with Melon, Chile &
        Mint, 194, 195
    Seared Diver Scallops with Bacon &
        Whole-Grain Mustard Rub & Crème
        Fraîche-Mashed Potatoes, 152, 153
    shells, buying, 194
Seafood. See Fish; Shellfish
Seared Diver Scallops with Bacon &
    Whole-Grain Mustard Rub & Crème
    Fraîche-Mashed Potatoes, 152, 153
Seared Pork Tenderloin with Cocoa-Spice
    Rub, 137
Serrano-Mint Sauce, 34, 35
Sesame-Soy Dipping Sauce, 190, 191
Shellfish
    Angry Shrimp with Citrus-Spinach
        Salad, 140, 141
    Clam Sauté, 114
    clams, cleaning, 114
    Crab Cakes with Remoulade Sauce, 212
    Creamy Garlicky Mussels, 193
    Crispy Calamari with Chinese Noodles
        & Spicy Garlic Sauce, 216, 217
    Emeril's Memory Stovetop Clam Boil, 78, 79
    Fried Crab Wontons with Sesame-Soy
        Dipping Sauce, 190, 191
    Fried Oyster Salad with Buttermilk
        Dressing & Corn-Jalapeño Relish, 76
    Grilled Oysters with Mango Pico de Gallo
        & Red Chile Horseradish, 32, 33
    Grilled Shrimp in Lettuce Leaves with
        Serrano-Mint Sauce, 34, 35
    Lady & Sons Crab-Stuffed Shrimp, 150

Linguine with Crab, Radicchio
    & Garlic, 116, 117
mussels, debearding, 193
Scallop Ceviche with Melon, Chile &
    Mint, 194, 195
scallops, buying and preparing, 153
scallop shells, buying, 194
Seared Diver Scallops with Bacon &
    Whole-Grain Mustard Rub & Crème
    Fraîche-Mashed Potatoes, 152, 153
shrimp, cooking tip, 58
Shrimp Dean Martinis, 172
Shrimp Fra Diavolo, 96
shrimp, peeling and deveining, 96
shrimp, stuffing, tips for, 150
Spicy Coconut Shrimp with Mango-Basil
    Salsa & Lime Jasmine Rice, 58
2-Minute Calamari, Sicilian
    Lifeguard-Style, 110, 111
Sherry vinegar, about, 173
Shredded Chicken & Tomatillo Tacos with
    Queso Fresco, 38
Shrimp
    Angry Shrimp with Citrus-Spinach
        Salad, 140, 141
    cooking, 58
    Grilled Shrimp in Lettuce Leaves with
        Serrano-Mint Sauce, 34, 35
    Lady & Sons Crab-Stuffed Shrimp, 150
    peeling and deveining, 96
    Shrimp Dean Martinis, 172
    Shrimp Fra Diavolo, 96
    Spicy Coconut Shrimp with Mango-Basil
        Salsa & Lime Jasmine Rice, 58
    stuffing with filling, 150
Sicilian Harvest Salad, 136
Side dishes
    BLT-Smashed Potatoes, 178, 179
    Bourbon-Mashed Sweet Potatoes, 84, 85
    Butternut Squash, Apple & Onion Galette
        with Stilton, 242, 243
    Caramelized Onions, 85
    Corn Casserole, 159
    Crème Fraîche-Mashed Potatoes, 152, 153
    Eggplant Pasta, 16
    Grits, 157
    Lemon-Braised Artichokes over Pasta, 134
    Lime Jasmine Rice, 58
    Mushroom Confit with Pasta Rags &
        Truffle Oil, 70
    Roast Fingerling Potato Crisps with
        Herbs, 175
    Spaetzle, 223
    Spaghetti with Asparagus, Smoked
        Mozzarella & Prosciutto, 92
    Tomato Pie, 148, 149
Skillets, electric, 14
Snickerdoodles, 248
Soups. See also Stews
    Black Bean Soup, 52
    Chino Carrot & Ginger Soup, 210, 211
    French Onion Soup, 14

261

INDEX

FOOD
PHOTOGRAPHS
ARE NOTED IN
COLORED
NUMERALS.

Homemade Tomato Soup, 133
pureeing, 133
Tortilla Soup, 235
Spaetzle, 223
Spaghetti with Asparagus, Smoked
Mozzarella & Prosciutto, 92
Spice-Rubbed Pork Tenderloin with Ancho
Chile-Mustard Sauce, 39
Spices
chile powder, buying, 39
Chinese five-spice powder, about, 51
Emeril's Essence Creole Seasoning, 81
grinding, 137
Paula's House Seasoning, 153
Spice Rub, 39
Yucatan Rub, 241
Spicy Chinese Five-Spice-Rubbed Chicken
Wings with Creamy Cilantro Dipping
Sauce, 50, 51
Spicy Coconut Shrimp with Mango-Basil
Salsa & Lime Jasmine Rice, 58
Spicy Grilled Beef Tenderloin, 199
Spinach
Angry Shrimp with Citrus-Spinach
Salad, 140, 141
Grilled Mushroom Salad Subs, 173
Lemon-Braised Artichokes over Pasta, 134
Sicilian Harvest Salad, 136
Spinach Salad with Honey-Brown Butter
Dressing, 203
Stuffed Meatballs, 120
Squash
Butternut Squash, Apple & Onion Galette
with Stilton, 242, 243
Pan-Grilled Veggie Sandwiches with
Ricotta, Arugula & Balsamic, 54, 55
Stews
best beef cuts for, 62
browning meat for, 62
Pressure Cooker Chili, 14
Red Wine Beef Stew with Potatoes &
Green Beans, 62
Wolfgang's Beef Goulash, 223
Stocks
Brown Chicken Stock, 123
freeezing, 123
store-bought, about, 218
veal, substitute for, 221
Stuffed Chicken Legs in Puff Pastry with
Andouille Cream, 80
Stuffed Meatballs, 120
Stuffed Pork Chops with Grits, 157
Stuffed Shells with Arrabbiata Sauce, 94, 95
Stuffing, Andouille Corn Bread, 80–81
Sweet Garlic, 122
Sweet Potatoes, Bourbon-Mashed, 84, 85
Swiss cheese
Cream of Mushroom Egg Noodle Fake-
Bake, Hold the Canned Soup, 176
types of, 176

T

Tacos
Make-Your-Own-Tacos Bar, 180, 181
Shredded Chicken & Tomatillo Tacos with
Queso Fresco, 38
Tarts
Apple Tarte Tatin, 87
baking tips, 243
blind-baking crusts, 101, 226
Butternut Squash, Apple & Onion Galette
with Stilton, 242, 243
Caramelized Lemon-Lime Tart, 226
Creamy Ricotta Tart with Pine Nuts, 101
Techniques
apples, coring, 87
artichokes, trimming, 134
barbecue sauce, for pan sauces, 221
beef flank steak, cooking, 179
beef flank steak, slicing, 179
beef roast, resting before carving, 199
beef round steaks, tenderizing, 156
blind-baking, 101, 226
brunoise, making a, 212
butter, clarifying, 212
cake, cutting into layers, 229
cakes, baking, 248
cheesecake, baking, 204
chicken, butterflying, 221
chiffonade, making a, 16
chile puree, preparing, 39
chiles, working with, 34
chocolate, chopping, 183
chocolate, melting in microwave, 104
citrus fruits, segmenting, 141
citrus fruits, zesting, 58
clams, cleaning, 114
coconut, toasting, 163
cookies, baking, 248
corn, preparing for grilling, 30
corn, removing kernels from, 76
dates, pitting, 203
eggs, cooking for tart fillings, 226
galettes, baking, 243
garlic, blanching, 217
garlic, crushing, 52, 139
garlic, mashing and mincing, 139
garlic, roasting, 153
ham, scoring, 17
herbs, storing, 61
julienne, making a, 212
lamb leg, boned, rollling, 201
lamb, roasting, 201
leeks, cleaning, 240
lemon zest, grating, 103
lettuce leaves, preparing for wrapping, 34
limes, juicing, 235
mangoes, preparing, 33
meat, resting after roasting, 199
milk, scalding, 143
mushrooms, storing and cleaning, 176
mussels, debearding, 193

mustard, adding to recipes, 218
olives, pitting, 123
onions, browning, 14
pancake mix, for breading, 168
papaya, shredding, 41
parboiling foods, 31
Parmesan rinds, cooking with, 112
pesto, storing, 57
pies, baking, 243
pine nuts, toasting, 101
pizza, transferring to stone, 215
pork chops, creating pocket in, 157
root beer, for meat glaze, 85
rosemary, frying, 136
salads, warm, preparing, 203
salmon, creating pocket in, 237
scallops, preparing for cooking, 153
shrimp, cooking, 58
shrimp, peeling and deveining, 96
shrimp, stuffing with filling, 150
soups, pureeing, 133
spices, grinding, 137
stew meat, browning, 62
stocks, freeezing, 123
tarts, baking, 243
terrines, using bricks for weights, 155
tomatillos, preparing, 38
tomatoes, peeling, 115
tomatoes, salting and draining, 149
tomato sauce, freezing, 111
tuna cans, for metal ring molds, 20
tuna, chopping fine, 36
vanilla beans, seeding, 43
vegetables, blanching, 92
wine, cooking with, 114
wontons, unfried, freezing, 191
wonton wrappers, filling, 191
wonton wrappers, working with, 191
yogurt, draining, 23
Tennessee Banana-Black Walnut Cake with
    Caramel Frosting, 160, 161
Terrine, Mosaic Chicken, 154, 155
Thai bird chiles, about, 41
Tilapia with Lemon Vinaigrette, 98, 99
Toasted Pine Nut Gremolata, 118, 119
Tofu
    Moo-Less Chocolate Pie, 23
    silken, about, 23
Tomatillos
    Shredded Chicken & Tomatillo Tacos with
        Queso Fresco, 38
    storing and preparing, 38
Tomatoes
    BLT-Smashed Potatoes, 178, 179
    Bow Ties with Pesto, Feta & Cherry
        Tomatoes, 56, 57
    Cod with Burst Grape Tomatoes, Parsley-
        Mint Pesto Broth & Roast Fingerling
        Potato Crisps with Herbs, 175
    Eggplant Pasta, 16
    Homemade Tomato Soup, 133

Mario's Basic Tomato Sauce, 111
    peeling, 115
    Penne with Cauliflower, 115
    Pesto-Stuffed Salmon with Tomato-Corn
        Salad, 236, 237
    plum, roasting, 61
    Pork Chops alla Pizzaiola, 100
    Red Snapper en Papillote, 18, 19
    Roasted Salmon with Roasted Plum
        Tomatoes & Caramelized Lemons, 60, 61
    Salami Salad with Tomatoes &
        Mozzarella, 133
    salting and draining, 149
    sauces, freezing, 111
    Shrimp Fra Diavolo, 96
    Spicy Grilled Beef Tenderloin, 199
    Stuffed Shells with Arrabbiata Sauce, 94, 95
    Tomato Pie, 148, 149
    Yellow Pico de Gallo, 181
Tortillas
    Make-Your-Own-Tacos Bar, 180, 181
    Shredded Chicken & Tomatillo Tacos with
        Queso Fresco, 38
    Tortilla Soup, 235
Tuna
    cans, creating metal rings from, 20
    chopping, for burgers, 36
    Tuna Burgers with Pineapple-Mustard
        Glaze & Green Chile-Pickle Relish, 36
Turkey
    Butterflied Turkey with Yucatan Rub, 241
    Make-Your-Own-Tacos Bar, 180, 181
2-Minute Calamari, Sicilian
    Lifeguard-Style, 110, 111
Tzatziki, 239

U
The Ultimate Cheesecake, 204
The Ultimate Roast Chicken, 198

V
Vanilla beans, seeding, 43
Veal
    Arancine with Ragu, 112
    Osso Buco with Toasted Pine Nut
        Gremolata, 118, 119
    Ragu, 112
    Stuffed Meatballs, 120
Vegetables. See also specific vegetables
    blanching, 92
    to brunoise, 212
    to julienne, 212
    leafy, to chiffonade, 16
Vietnamese chili sauce, about, 217
Vinaigrettes
    Blue Cheese Vinaigrette, 31
    Cilantro-Mint Vinaigrette, 224, 225
    Lemon Vinaigrette, 98
    Walnut Vinaigrette, 75
Vinegar, sherry, about, 173

W
Walnuts
    Baby Arugula with Country Ham, Goat
        Cheese, Dried Cherries & Walnut
        Vinaigrette, 74, 75
    black, about, 161
    Pesto, 57, 150
    Tennessee Banana-Black Walnut Cake
        with Caramel Frosting, 160, 161
Watercress
    Chicken with Leeks, Watercress &
        Radish, 240
    Grilled Potato Salad with Watercress,
        Green Onions & Blue Cheese
        Vinaigrette, 31
Wolfgang's Beef Goulash, 223
Wolfgang's Sachertorte, 229
Wontons
    filling, tips for, 191
    freezing, 191
    Fried Crab Wontons with Sesame-Soy
        Dipping Sauce, 190, 191
    working with, 191

Y
Yellow Pico de Gallo, 181
Yogurt
    draining, 23
    Lemon-Ginger Frozen Yogurt, 23
    Tzatziki, 239
Yucatan Rub, 241

ENJOY!